From Washington and Adams to Trump and Biden

The Stories Behind the Story of Every Presidential Election

With Special Focus on the *Volatile* Presidential Election of 2020

Everett E. Murdock PhD

H.O.T. Press

H.O.T. Press
Los Angeles, California
www.hotpresspublishing.com

Publishing fine books since 1983

Copyright 2020 by Dr. Everett E. Murdock
All rights reserved

ISBN: 0-923178-39-2
ISBN-13: 978-0-923178-39-0

Acknowledgments

I had planned to acknowledge all of the books on U.S. history that provided me with background information, but I soon realized that would be an impossible task because of the extensive research I did while writing this book. In fact, I've been reading books on U.S. history for much of my life. Let me just say I am truly indebted to anybody who has written anything about U.S. history. I assume they did it simply because they are, like me, interested in the history of our country.

I am also indebted to those who took the time to put information about U.S. history on the internet. Once again, I started to list them, but I soon found the list growing into the hundreds (and even then I knew I was leaving a lot of them out). So I will just say this: if you've ever put anything about the history of presidential elections on the internet, I probably read it while researching this book, and I am therefore, indebted to you.

And as always, my endless thanks to Zoe for her masterful editing, rewriting, rethinking, and . . . well actually, for making this book happen.

Books by Everett "Doc" Murdock (Partial List)

Textbooks

• **From Washington and Adams to Hillary and Trump**: Stories behind the Story of Every Presidential Election

• **Obama Won but Romney Almost was President**: How the Democrats Targeted Electoral College Votes to Win the 2012 Election

• **How to Write Fiction: Tools and Techniques** (with original stories as examples)

Novels

• **Death as Concept**

• **The Storyteller of Cottage H**

• **The Robots of Cottage H**

• **God's Messenger – God's Victim**: A *Bildungsroman* Stockholm Syndrome Novel

• **The Pain Artist**: An American Hikikomori

• **My Vietnam War:** A Novel

• **A Psalm for Cock Robin**: A Harp and His (Dead) Mother Mystery

• **Crueltown**: A Drew Steele Los Angeles-Las Vegas Mystery

• **The End of the Civil War**: A Drew Steele Civil War Mystery

• **Who Owns Arizona**: A Drew Steele Civil War Mystery

Contents

Introduction..7

Chapter One - The "Rules" of Presidential Elections are Created........8

Chapter Two - Presidents Elected Without Popular Elections...........19

Chapter Three - Political Parties Evolve..23

Chapter Four - Flaws in the Electoral College System........................29

Chapter Five - Evolving Presidential Politics......................................33

Chapter Six - The Politics of Slavery..41

Chapter Seven - A Country Divided Against Itself............................75

Chapter Eight - Democrats Versus Republicans.................................82

Chapter Nine - The Politics of War...110

Chapter Ten - Postwar and Cold War Politics...................................126

Chapter Eleven - The Politics of War and Antiwar...........................232

Chapter Twelve - Secret Presidential Power.....................................156

Chapter Thirteen - Foreign Wars and Presidential Scandal............167

Chapter Fourteen - The Electoral College System Fails Again........174

Chapter Fifteen - Presidential Politics and the War on Terrorism....179

Chapter Sixteen - TV Celebrity Versus Experienced Politician 201

Chapter Seventeen - Impeachment, Racial Strife, and Pandemic 256

Index..306

Introduction

They say, if you want to know what the future will bring, study the past. You might think studying the history of past presidential elections would do little to prepare you for what happens in modern elections, because in the past, much of the drama took place behind closed doors. But in the twenty-first century, in the age of 24-hour cable TV news and the internet, there is no such thing as closed doors. In today's elections, every aspect of the presidential election plays out in plain view, either on America's TV screens or on the internet. Every statement by every candidate is analyzed and discussed, often in dismay, but sometimes in outrage and even unrestrained anger.

In this book, I will demonstrate a different way to understand presidential elections, by analyzing them in the context of the past.

A Book of Stories

If you looked at my list of published books in the front matter of this book, you will have noticed that although I published two prior books on presidential elections, I am also a novelist.

Basically, **I'm a storyteller, and that's how I look at presidential elections,** There is always a story underlying each presidential election, a story that made the voters vote for one candidate and not the other. Therefore, this book is a book of stories—not fictional stories, but stories about what happened behind the scenes, stories that, in the end, **determined which candidate ended up being elected president** and which candidate was relegated to the lonely halls of history.

Often the story that determined the winner was related to war or some other national crisis, but sometimes it was simply a story about what one candidate did (or didn't do).

In each chapter, watch for "**story boxes**" that tell those stories, in detail.

Presidential election outcomes are often dictated by the "rules" of the **Electoral College system** of electing a President. Watch for "**comment boxes**" that describe in detail how the decidedly odd rules that govern how we elect our presidents can sometimes end up determining which candidate wins.

Chapter One
The "Rules" of Presidential Elections are Created

Let's begin with an analysis of how and why our "founding fathers" came up with the concept of an "Electoral College," a very strange way of choosing a national leader. Why didn't they just let the people vote for their president?

To better understand what the Electoral College is and how it came to be, we need to go back and look at the initial meetings of representatives from the original thirteen states.

The Constitutional Convention

In 1787, a **Constitutional Convention** was convened to lay out a governing structure for the newly formed group of united states. The document that eventually came out of that convention was the **United States Constitution**. Getting agreement as to how the new government should be organized was not an easy task. **There was considerable controversy regarding the issue of slavery, and it ended up being a significant determinant of how our government was formed**. Even after the delegates to the Constitutional Convention had agreed to maintain the British concept of a two-house legislature, there was **much disagreement about how the two houses should be structured**. Eventually, it was decided that the **House of Representatives** would be apportioned according to the *total* population of a state. That meant the states with larger populations would have more representation in the House. Of course, the states with smaller populations were not happy about that, and they argued against it. Eventually, the smaller states were able to force **a compromise, the creation of a Senate wherein each state would have two senators, no matter how large or small the population of the state**. Of course, the big states didn't like that one bit, because it meant states with much smaller populations would have equal clout in the government. But no other solution could be agreed upon, so that method was eventually agreed upon. To better understand how compromises like that came about, we need to remember that the Constitutional Convention was made up of representatives from each of the states, **and each state was given one vote**. That meant **the least populated states had as much decision-making power as the more populous states**. The delegates from the smaller states felt the larger states would dominate the new government; therefore, at the convention, they often stuck together when voting.

One major area of contention that arose regarding the apportioning of seats in the House of Representatives had to do with slaves. The Southern **slave-holding states wanted to count their millions of slaves as part of their apportionment** (even though the slaves were not considered to be citizens of the United States). There was also the issue of taxes. Because **slaves were legally the property of the slave owner**, the Northern states said they **should be taxed as property**. The Southern states disagreed, saying they were not property, but living beings. In other words, **the Southern states wanted to have it both ways**.

Neither side was willing to budge, and **it looked as if the convention would be bogged down in the slavery issue forever**. Yet another strange compromise with the Southern slave states was agreed upon in order to get the government-making process moving again: it was decided, for purposes of representation in the House of Representatives, **slaves would count as three-fifths of a person**. It was a decision that would have long lasting effects. It is estimated that before the Civil War, there were about nine million free whites living in the South, compared to about four million slaves. Based on the Three-Fifths Compromise, that meant **the South was given credit for an extra 2,400,000 people** when assigning the number of seats in the House of Representatives. If the apportionment had been based on free population, the slave states should have been apportioned 33 seats in the House of Representatives, but **by including their slaves and counting them as three-fifth of a person, they got 47 seats**.

Originally, the only national office that was elected by public vote was for members of the House of Representatives. Even **the**

members of the U.S. Senate were selected by state political leaders. At that time, only males were allowed to vote, and in many states, only men who owned property could vote.

> **COMMENT**
>
> The original method of **appointing senators, rather than electing them, continued to be in force until 1913** when a constitutional amendment was proposed to require direct election of senators. Many political leaders fought against the proposed amendment, and it took a year before it was finally ratified by 37 states (one more state, Delaware, ratified it in 2010). Alabama, Florida, Georgia, Kentucky, Maryland, Mississippi, Rhode Island, South Carolina, and Virginia *did not* ratify it, and **Utah made a point of explicitly rejecting it** (even today, some members of the legislature in Utah are still trying to overturn that amendment).
>
> However, once it was made the law of the land, even the states that didn't ratify the new constitutional amendment had to allow **public election of senators**.
>
> The difficulty of getting three-fourths of the states to ratify such a common-sense concept as the public election of senators *by the citizens of their state* tells us how difficult it would be to get three-fourths of the states to go along with the idea of getting rid of the Electoral College system of electing presidents and vice presidents and allow a normal voting process.

Dispute over How the President Should Be Chosen

How the president was to be elected turned out to be one of the most contentious dispute at the **Constitutional Convention**. As a result, it was one of the last issues to be resolved. Some of the delegates thought Congress should choose the president. Others felt there should be **a presiding committee**. Even though **most of the delegates felt the people ought to be allowed to elect their president**, a dissenting minority did not agree. The dissenting delegates had two reasons for being against a popular vote: first, **the delegates from the smaller states, especially the slave states, knew the more populous anti-slave states would control the presidential elections**, and second, many of the delegates didn't trust the people to make *the right* decision.

The first point, that the smaller states would get outvoted by the states with larger populations, was true then and is still true today—if the president was elected by popular vote, the larger-population states would have more say in who got to be president.

Because **the delegates from the Southern slave states often voted together to stymie the wishes of the larger Northern anti-slave states,** a compromise had to be found that would give the smaller Southern slave states more voting power.

The second point, that they didn't trust the voters, is less defensible in a democracy. There were a lot of reasons put forward as to why the president should not be directly elected by the people, but they all came down to the same point: **the delegates at the Constitutional Convention did not believe the people were informed enough to make such an important decision**.

After much contentious debate, in order to come to *some* agreement, **the majority had to give up on the idea of a normal popular vote for president**. The people *would not* be allowed to vote for their president; instead, the political leaders in each of the states would decide who they wanted to be president and vice president. They would appoint **electors** who would get together to hash out who the president and vice president should be.

After even more haggling, the delegates decided each state would be assigned **one electoral vote for each of the states' representatives in Congress**. The gathering of those state representatives to vote for a president has come to be known as **the "Electoral College."** It is still how presidents are elected today.

The Electoral College method of choosing a president meant the Southern states were given many extra electors in the Electoral College. **As a result, for many years, Southerners, especially slave owners, dominated the Presidency, the House of Representatives, and the Supreme Court.**

STORY

Ten of the first twelve presidents were slave holders.

George Washington, the first president, was a wealthy Virginia plantation owner who owned more than 200 slaves before, during, and after he was president. The selection of Philadelphia to be the nation's capital presented a problem for Washington: he brought some of his slaves with him, and Pennsylvania had passed a law that said slaves that lived in the state for six months automatically became free. Washington got around the law by transporting his slaves across the state border and back again every six months.

The second president, **John Adams**, was from Massachusetts which was not a slave state. However, some years before he became president, he was given a slave as a gift. He used her as the family cook.

Thomas Jefferson, the third president, owned a 5,000 acre plantation in Virginia and owned more than 100 slaves. One of his slaves, a light-skinned woman known as **Sally Hemings**, was rumored to have been his mistress after his wife died. It was said she bore several of his children while he was president, all of whom, by law, remained slaves. Modern DNA evidence and analysis of the timing of his visits to his estate at Monticello seem to have proved the truth of that rumor.

James Madison, the fourth president, owned a large tobacco plantation in Virginia. He inherited hundreds of slaves and continued to hold them throughout his life.

James Monroe, the fifth president, was a Virginia plantation owner and owned many slaves.

John Quincy Adams, the sixth president, being from Massachusetts, was barred by state law from owning slaves.

Andrew Jackson, the seventh president, bought his first slave, a young woman, when he was only 21 years old. He later became a businessman, and for a while, he was in the business of buying and selling slaves. At one time, he owned more than 300 slaves.

Martin Van Buren, the eighth president, was from a slave-holding family, but he personally owned only one slave.

William Henry Harrison, the ninth president, was from a Virginia plantation family that owned many slaves. Harrison was said to have illegally taken several of them with him when he traveled to states where slavery was against the law.

John Tyler, the tenth president, was also a Virginia tobacco plantation owner who owned many slaves.

James K. Polk, the eleventh president, was a slave holder from North Carolina.

Zachary Taylor, the twelfth president, was born into a slave-holding family in Virginia. Although he chose a military career, he held onto his slaves. While he was president, he held about 100 slaves.

After 1850, the rapidly increasing populations of the Northern states began to break the stranglehold Southern states had on electing presidents. At the same time, owning slaves became much more controversial in the North. As a result, political candidates for national office, even those from Southern states, tended to transfer their slaves to a relative before running for office.

The fact that small states get proportionally more electors in the Electoral College violates one of the most basic principles that guided the framers of the constitution, that all voters should be equal. Today, legal scholars say the Electoral College could be ruled unconstitutional if it wasn't specifically laid out in the constitution. The method of selecting electors was left vague. It simply said "the states" would choose their electors and those electors would get together to choose the president and vice president. There was no provision for assessing the people's wishes and **none of them envisioned public presidential elections**.

> **COMMENT**
> There are several aspects of the Electoral College system that are relatively unknown. For example, many do not know that **according to the Constitution, the electors do not have to vote for the candidate that won their state** in the election (and over the years, many electors have refused to do so). **In fact, there is nothing in the Constitution about elections.**
>
> Today, most people expect the outcome of the Electoral College vote to be the same as the voting in the general election. However, several times in U.S. history, that has not been true.
>
> Most Americans can't understand why we need an Electoral College. They ask why they can't just vote for president like they vote for every other political office. Public opinion polls repeatedly show **most Americans favor abolishing the Electoral College**, and there have been hundreds of proposals introduced in Congress to reform or eliminate the Electoral College. **In fact, more constitutional amendments have been introduced to abolish the Electoral College than on any other subject.** But they all failed, and as a result, Americans still do not get to directly vote for their president.

In 1789, **6 of the 13 original states decided to hold a popular vote** for president, even though they knew their votes wouldn't count. They still wanted their opinions to be heard, and eventually all the states began to hold general presidential elections, forcing the political leaders of the states to pay attention to which candidate the people wanted. Eventually, the states adopted the modern system in which electors *represent* the winner of the popular vote.

To make sure the electors didn't just vote for their state's local candidate, it was written into the Constitution that the electors had to vote for at least one candidate from outside their state.

The votes of all the electors from the states would be tallied and added together, and the candidate that got the most votes would be named president. The candidate that came in second would be named vice president.

> **COMMENT**
>
> As stated in the Constitution, if a candidate does not win an absolute majority of the electors, the decision gets sent to the House of Representatives where **each state delegation gets one vote**. They have to choose from among the three candidates who received the most electoral votes. Some have speculated that the framers of the Constitution assumed that such an approach would result in a variety of candidates being put forward by the electors and no one candidate would ever get the required majority; therefore, the decision would always come back to the House. In other words, they assumed the votes of the state electors in the Electoral College would be considered *nominations* from which the House of Representatives would choose a president and vice president. But it didn't turn out that way. The Electoral College (the term "Electoral College" does not appear in the Constitution but began to appear in newspapers sometime in the early 1800s) was created at a time when political parties did not exist. In the late 1700s, two political parties emerged—the **Federalists** and the **Democratic-Republicans**—they immediately got involved in the selection of electors. It became crucial for both political parties to *try* to make sure the electors they chose were loyal **to the party** and would vote the way the party wanted them to.
>
> Today, the two main political parties in the United States, the **Democrats** and the **Republicans**, pretty much control the elections. As a result, the presidential election now almost always comes down to a face-off between the candidates nominated by those two parties. For that reason, one of the two major party candidates almost always wins the required absolute majority of the Electoral College votes, and therefore the decision never gets sent to the House of Representatives.

Despite its flaws, the Electoral College system can't be changed without changing the U.S. Constitution. That would require a constitutional amendment to pass both houses of congress and get the approval of three-fourths of the states. The states with fewer voters would have to give up their proportional voting advantage, which makes it unlikely to happen.

Another Electoral College rule was written into the Constitution to keep electors from voting for their own locals. It says **electors cannot vote for a president and vice president from the same state**. (Although that requirement is still in the Constitution, it has been all but forgotten. In 2000, the Republicans nominated two Texans, George Bush and Dick Cheney.)

Today the electors in 48 of the 50 states (all except Maine and Nebraska) are *supposed to* give 100% of the electoral votes to the candidate who wins a state's popular vote. A candidate who wins the popular vote **by even a single vote margin, gets *all* of that state's electoral votes**. That means **the votes for the less popular candidate are thrown out**.

This **"winner-take-all"** method is not written into the Constitution, and originally only three states used it. But in the mid 1800s, with the emergence of political parties, there was pressure to adopt the winner-take-all method. That self-serving decision was to shape all presidential elections to come and has caused much of the controversy surrounding elections.

Much later, *some* states passed laws that stated an elector could be fined if he or she did not vote for the candidate that won their state's popular vote. Nevertheless, in past presidential elections, there have been more than 150 instances in which an elector *did not* vote for the popular vote winner. These electors are referred to as "faithless electors."

As more states were added to the Union, the number of members in the Electoral College increased, and in 1961, a constitutional amendment (the Twenty-Third Amendment) allotted three Electoral College votes to the District of Columbia. As a result, the total number of members of the Electoral College has been permanently set at 538, meaning a presidential candidate must win 270 Electoral College votes. The number of electors each state gets is rebalanced every ten years, based on the census. The rebalancing is based on the number of people living in a state, not on the number of registered voters or even on the number of legal residents. As a result, states that have had an influx of illegal immigrants have been gaining electoral votes, and the states whose populations have not been growing in population have been losing electoral votes.

How Well Has the Electoral College System Worked?

In the nation's past presidential elections, the Electoral College method of selecting the president has concurred with the popular vote 93% of the time. You might ask, only 93%? Shouldn't the winner of the popular vote *always* get to be president?

Yes, but then there would be no need for the Electoral College. The truth is, as we shall see, **the Electoral College system is so archaic and so flawed, it's kind of surprising it only fails seven percent of the time**.

The chapters that follow describe each of the U.S. presidential elections, what influenced them, and the role the Electoral College system played in the outcome.

Chapter Two
Presidents Elected Without Popular Elections

The Presidential Election of 1789

The first presidential election took place in January of 1789. Most citizens of the new country felt **George Washington**, a Virginia plantation owner and slave holder, should be the president because he had been the commander of the **Continental Army.**

When the members of the Electoral College cast their ballots in the spring of 1789, **Washington got 69 electoral votes and John Adams got 34 electoral votes**. Based on the Electoral College rules at that time, it meant Washington became president, and Adams, the person who came in second, became vice president.

> **STORY**
>
> George Washington was not all that eager to take on the role of being president of the new country. After years of war, some thought he might have been content to retreat to his comfortable home in Mount Vernon with its many slaves in servitude. But he eventually agreed to serve and made the seven day trip to New York City—then the nation's capital—to be sworn in.
>
> He was carried across the Hudson River in a boat with red, white, and blue decorations, and there were many celebratory cannon firings from the boats in the harbor as he passed. On April 30th, after the politicians had worked out how the formal inauguration should be conducted, Washington was escorted to Federal Hall on Wall Street where he was sworn into office by

a local judge. Washington took the oath of office wearing a brown suit (the only one he could find that was made in America), and as befitting a military general, he had a fancy sword hanging from his side.

The Presidential Election of 1792

In the second presidential election, held in 1792, **Washington** again received the most electoral votes and was reelected president. **John Adams** again got the second most votes, which meant he would continue to serve as vice president.

STORY

When the presidential election of 1792 was held, there were **15 states in the union**, the 13 original states plus Vermont and Kentucky, which had just been added to the union.

As before, every member of the Electoral College cast his vote for Washington. However, for the first time, there was some **discord among the Federalists** (the only political party at that time). **Treasury Secretary Alexander Hamilton** thought there should be a strong federal government, but **Secretary of State Thomas Jefferson** disagreed: he felt the main power should lie with the states.

The dispute was centered around Hamilton's creation of a national bank and his proposed stronger role of the federal government in the economy. In response, Jefferson, along with **James Madison**, a U.S. Congressman from Virginia who had participated in the development of the U.S. Constitution, put together a new political party known as the **Democratic-Republicans**. **George Clinton**, the governor of New York, allied with them and the new party put his name up as a vice presidential candidate against Adams. He got very few votes, and in fact,

> some of the electors that favored the Democratic-Republican position voted instead for Jefferson
>
> It was later learned that Washington had been thinking about retiring after his first term, but when the dissonance within the Federalist Party arose, he decided to run for another term in an attempt to bring the two sides together. He was unable to do that, and the argument over "states rights" versus a strong centralized government continued.

In 1792, only two states, Maryland and Pennsylvania allowed popular voting for president, but the concept of a general election was becoming popular. **Voters demanded the opportunity to cast a vote for their national leader, even if the Electoral College system made their vote meaningless.**

The Presidential Election of 1796

In the third presidential election, George Washington chose not to run for reelection. As a result, there *was* more contention for the office. As a result, political parties were to play a major role in this election. Vice President John Adams ran for the office as a representative of the **Federalist** Party. Former Secretary of State Thomas Jefferson and Senator Aaron Burr ran on the **Democratic-Republican** ticket.

> ### STORY
> The Federalist Party—originally the only American political party—believed the United States should maintain good relations with Britain. They had negotiated, in 1794, **a treaty with Britain that became known as the Jay Treaty.**

> The **Democratic-Republicans** were strongly opposed to the Jay Treaty as well as most of the other Federalist policies.
>
> **The Federalists found most of their support in New England and in the larger cities**, while **the Democratic-Republicans found support in the rural south**.
>
> In seven of the states, Connecticut, Delaware, New Jersey, New York, Rhode Island, South Carolina, and Vermont, the electors were chosen by the state legislatures. That meant **whichever party controlled a state's legislature controlled the selection of that state's electors**.
>
> In some states, public elections were held to vote for electors (after the electors said which candidate they were backing). In Kentucky, Maryland, North Carolina, and Virginia, the voters in each district **got to vote for one elector**. **Georgia and Pennsylvania held a statewide election to select electors**. Massachusetts, New Hampshire, and Tennessee used a combination of the two.
>
> **Under the Electoral College system, the political leaders of the states were not bound by the outcome of those popular votes, but they did tell them who the people wanted to be their president.**

In 1796, for the first time, the Electoral College vote was close, with 71 votes going to Adams and 68 going to Jefferson. By the rules in place at that time, it meant John Adams would be named president, and his opponent, Thomas Jefferson, would be vice president. It would be **the only time in U.S. history that the president and the vice president came from different parties.**

Chapter Three
Political Parties Evolve

The Presidential Election of 1800

Details of the 1800 presidential election read like a fictional novel of intrigue, and much of the intrigue was due to the structure of the Electoral College. With the advent of popular voting in some states, a few of the candidates actually campaigned. They got on their horses (literally as well as figuratively) and set out to meet the voters. Today, we are so used to national presidential campaigning it is hard to imagine that not much national campaigning took place in the early presidential elections. Politics was something that was usually done in Philadelphia (the Capital of the nation at that time).

The emergence of two opposing political parties set the stage for a new level of antagonism. **The Federalist party put up John Adams** for president and Charles Pickney for vice president; **the Democratic-Republican party put up Thomas Jefferson** for president and Aaron Burr for vice president. Most of the antagonism was over the Federalist's continuing alignment with Britain and their plan to build up a centralized federal government and create an army. There was concern that the Federalists wanted to create a military in order to help Britain in its ongoing war with France. Despite the Federalist's well-entrenched position in the seat of national power, **the Democratic-Republicans were better organized at the local level.**

STORY

In 1800, there was a long and bitter campaign for electoral votes. The campaign established many of the campaigning

---

methods we see in modern presidential elections, including the invention of **the smear campaign.** Jefferson was seen as a philosopher, so the Federalists tried to paint him as being against religion. They claimed God was on their side and that a vote for Adams was a vote for God and a religious presidency, while **a vote for Jefferson would be a vote against God**.

In return, the Democratic-Republicans tried to paint the Federalists as **against the common man** and in favor of the rich and powerful (sound familiar?). They also attacked the **Alien and Sedition acts** that had been passed by the Federalists in congress and signed by the Federalist President Adams. The acts, supposedly enacted because of a perceived threat from France, made it more difficult for immigrants to become U.S. citizens. It also gave the president the power to deport immigrants if they were deemed "dangerous to the peace and safety of the United States." The acts also gave the president the power to limit freedom of speech, again if in the president's opinion such speech was "dangerous to the peace and safety of the United States." The Democratic-Republican attack on the acts was fairly successful because many citizens felt the acts went too far, especially when most people felt the chance of an attack from France was unlikely. They said some aspects of the acts were clearly unconstitutional in that they violated the first amendment which states, "Congress shall make no law respecting an establishment of religion, or prohibiting the free exercise thereof; or abridging the freedom of speech press; or the right of the people to peaceably assemble and to petition the Government for a redress of grievances."

However, **all of the members of the Supreme Court had been appointed by Washington and were seen as Federalists**. Therefore, most people felt there was no chance of getting the Supreme Court to overturn the acts even if they were blatantly unconstitutional.

> Jefferson came right out and said **the acts had been created as a way to keep the Federalists in power** by quashing any criticism. In fact, the Federalists did use the acts and the threat of war to restrict what newspapers printed. They had some newspaper editors arrested and some newspapers were shut down. The newspapers that were shut down were almost always publications that leaned toward the Democratic-Republicans. That fact was especially important because newspapers were just beginning to play a more important role in elections than word of mouth.
>
> One result of the Democratic-Republican fight against the Alien and Sedition acts was that they had considerable success in getting the newly arrived immigrants on their side, especially those from France and Ireland. It was the first election in which candidates tried to appeal to **special interest groups**.

In 1800, there was a great deal of focus on the Electoral College. Both sides saw the **flaws in the Electoral College system** and so they tried to manipulate those flaws to their own advantage. Both political parties also promised significant political favors to states that could swing electoral votes their way.

One of the more notable manipulations of electoral votes occurred during the 1800 election. Virginia was one of the states in which the voters **in each congressional district** voted for one elector. Thomas Jefferson realized that if his home state of Virginia would have allocated **all** of its electoral votes to him in the 1796 election, he would have been elected president. Therefore, before the 1800 election, he convinced the Virginia state legislature to **change to a system in which the candidate that won the most electors, got all the electors**. It became known as the **winner-take-all** system of allocating electoral votes. Other states realized they would have to do the same to get more power in presidential elections. Over the next fifty years, the winner-take-all method gradually became the standard way of allocating electoral votes. At the time, nobody realized how profoundly that one simple change would affect the selection of presidents in the future.

Today, only Maine and Nebraska still allocate electoral votes proportionally, the system that was apparently intended by the original framers of the constitution.

STORY

In 1800, each state could choose its own election day. Therefore, the election that year went on for seven months. The last state to vote was South Carolina, and the word went out that Adams and Jefferson were tied in the Electoral College. The electors from South Carolina were solidly behind the Democratic-Republican party, meaning Jefferson and Burr were sure to win the national election. Therefore, a plan was hatched to have the South Carolina electors withhold one vote from Burr to make sure Jefferson would be president and Burr would come in second, making him the vice president (remember, at that time, members of the Electoral College had to vote for two candidates). No one knows what went wrong, but all of the South Carolina electors ended up voting for *both* Jefferson and Burr meaning the tie vote was maintained, and that meant neither candidate had a majority. As stipulated in the Electoral College section of the Constitution, the decision about who would be president was sent to the House of Representatives.

One simple solution would have been for Burr to withdraw from consideration, but he refused.

When the election of the president goes to the House of Representatives, **a candidate has to get an absolute majority of the states** (not a majority of the representatives). That meant, nine of the sixteen states would have to come to an agreement about who they wanted to be president.

The **lame duck** Federalists in the House of Representatives did not have enough power to swing the election their way, but they did have enough votes to keep the Democratic-Republicans from electing their preferred candidates.

Ballot after ballot was taken with no clear winner. Days went by with no movement by either side.

At some point, the Federalists began to vote for Burr, apparently taking on an **anybody-but-Jefferson** attitude. It was clear, if this went on, nobody was ever going to win. **It was quite possible that there would be no president in 1800.** That presented a dire situation because the Constitution had no contingency for such an outcome (and still doesn't today).

After 34 ballots with neither side budging, everybody in Congress realized **the Electoral Collage system was a complete failure**. But because the process was mandated by the U.S. Constitution, Congress couldn't do anything about it. To change the Electoral College system, they would have had to pass a bill to amend the Constitution and get three-fourths of the states to ratify it. They knew the South would not give up the advantage they had in the Electoral College, so that was not a viable option.

Meanwhile, word about the stalemate in the House of Representatives was leaking out to the public. **People were upset about the whole flawed Electoral College system** of electing a president which meant the people had no real say in the election, and now their representatives in Congress seemed to be engaged in partisan squabbling that was going nowhere. If the people had been allowed to simply vote for president, all the squabbling needn't to have happened.

In the halls of Congress, there were rumors of armed bands of citizens marching on the capital to take things into their own hands. It was said they were **coming to demand, by force of arms if need be, that Jefferson, the candidate most of them had voted for, be named president.**

> Finally, in response to what was clearly turning out to be dangerous situation, Jefferson approached the Federalist leaders and gave them assurances that he would not completely wipe out everything they had accomplished during the twelve years they had been in power. In response, in preparation for the 35th ballot, Federalist Party leader Alexander Hamilton (who strongly disliked Burr) allowed a few moderate Federalists to change their votes from Burr to Jefferson which meant, **finally, Jefferson would be the president**. Burr, having come in second, had to settle for the vice presidency.

It has been suggested that the framers of the Constitution anticipated that no one candidate would get the required number of electoral votes, meaning **the election of the president would usually be decided by the House of Representatives**. The problem was, they **hadn't considered the possibility that political parties would emerge**. They couldn't have realized that political parties would complicate the presidential election process by fighting with each other for advantage.

However, the framers of the Constitution did provide a mechanism for changing it through **an amendment process**. But they didn't want the Constitution they had so carefully crafted to be easy to change, so they stipulated that it would take agreement in Congress *and* agreement among three-fourths of the states to change it. They couldn't have realized how hard it would be to get that many states to agree on anything.

Chapter Four
Flaws in the Electoral College System

The decidedly messy **presidential election of 1800** initiated a debate in Congress about how to "fix" the Electoral College system. The debate was wide ranging and often contentious, but despite the obvious flaws in the system, **the politicians of that era still did not want the decision about who would be president to be in the hands of the people.** In the end, the only thing they changed was to stipulate that the electors should make separate choices for president and vice president.

It is still true today that whichever political party controls the smaller-population states has much to gain by keeping the Electoral College system.

COMMENT

When the first few presidents were chosen, **only a few states held general elections**. Therefore, with the Electoral College system in place, decision about who would be president was pretty much up to the political leaders in the states.

Although Americans now take the election of a president very seriously, voting for the president in an public election is not even mentioned in the Constitution.

Some states have passed laws that say the members of the state's slate of electors **have to** vote for the winner of that state's general presidential election. However, the most the state can do is levy a fine on an elector who disobeys that *suggestion*. Some legal scholars say **such laws are unconstitutional.** There is nothing in the U.S. Constitution that says an elector has to vote in any specified way.

> Although there is much ado about today's presidential elections, and untold amounts of money are spent on trying to get Americans to vote for one candidate or another, the results of that voting actually has no legal status. No matter who the citizens of the country vote for, members of the Electoral College can vote for anybody they want to. Despite periodic legal decisions restricting the electors, **many electors have ignored the popular vote** and done just that.

The most glaring problem with the Electoral College system is that sometimes the voting of the electors does not agree with the choice the voters made in the general election. This has happened several times over the years, and lately it is starting to happen more often. So why haven't the people risen up to demand an end to the Electoral College? Hard to say. It's probably because we tend to forget about things if they seem to be working "all right." Only when things go terribly wrong, do we get riled up and want to do something about it. Even then, those that benefit from keeping the Electoral College system just the way it is have always blocked any attempt to change it.

> **COMMENT**
>
> **The presidential elections of 1796 and 1800 revealed the flaws in the Electoral College system. They are:**
>
> **1. There is nothing in the Electoral College section of the Constitution about the electors being guided by the popular vote.** In fact, there is nothing about a popular vote. It simply says "the states" will select the electors. In practice, that means electors can, and sometimes do, vote for their own personal preference (see the later section on "faithless electors").

> **2. The current Electoral College winner-take-all system may influence how people vote.** Because of the winner-take-all system, if the pre-election polls show that most of the voters in a state are clearly planning to vote for one candidate, there is little point for the people in that state to vote for any presidential candidate.
>
> **3. A viable third-party candidate can change the outcome.** A third-party candidate could take enough votes away from one of the main party candidates to change the outcome. A viable third-party candidate could make it hard for any candidate to get an absolute majority, which would send the decision about who becomes president to the House of Representatives. Therefore, whichever party controls the House would actually get to decide who becomes president. In the past, third-party candidates *have* gained some Electoral College votes, but those elections were not close. It seems likely that sooner or later, a strong third-party candidate will throw the election to the House of Representatives.
>
> **4. States with smaller populations have proportionally more electors than states with larger populations.** Because even the smallest states are guaranteed under the Constitution to get at least three electoral votes, those states have a greater say in who will get to be president. As a result, a vote for president by a Wyoming resident counts about four times more than a vote by a California resident.

After the drawn-out battle in the House of Representatives with Burr refusing to cooperate, Aaron Burr was no longer looked on as favorably by the Democratic-Republicans.

The presidential campaign of 1800 saw, for the first time, **inflammatory, personal attacks** on the good names of the candidates. Personal attacks were not taken as lightly back then as they are now, and as a result, they **often resulted in duels**. After the 1800 election, a series of letters were circulated accusing Aaron Burr of various despicable acts. After the next election, Alexander Hamilton, the former Secretary of the Treasury, campaigned aggressively against Burr, and Burr was defeated in his quest to be the governor of New York. The insults continued even after the election until eventually, **Burr challenged Hamilton to a duel.** Hamilton accepted, and on the morning of July 11, 1804, while Burr was still finishing out his term as vice president, the dueling parties were taken by boat to New Jersey (to avoid the anti-duel laws of New York state). There is disagreement about exactly what happened because everyone present was instructed to turn away before shots were fired. The idea was that if they didn't directly see what happened, they couldn't be brought into court to testify about it.

What is known is that Burr killed Hamilton with a single shot from his pistol, but being the vice president of the United States, he was never prosecuted for killing Hamilton.

Chapter Five
Evolving Presidential Politics

The Presidential Election of 1804

Although there was trouble brewing in Europe at the time of the presidential election of 1804, it was a period of relative peace in the United States. The American shipping trade had been further developed under President Jefferson, which resulted in an improved economy, and his successful negotiation and completion of the Louisiana Purchase was widely seen as a great achievement.

Jefferson was strongly favored to win reelection. But he no longer looked favorably on his vice president, Burr, so he dumped Burr in favor of New York Governor **George Clinton**.

Jefferson and Clinton were elected over **Charles Cotesworth Pinckney**, a Federalist from South Carolina, and **Rufus King** from New York.

STORY

In 1803, President Jefferson was negotiating a deal with France to purchase a huge tract of land in and around New Orleans. He felt it was the best way to protect the port of New Orleans through which a great deal of the nation's farm produce passed. After Spain transferred *some* of the territory west of the Mississippi to France, Jefferson undertook to buy the land from France. Napoleon, the ruler of France, knew that his ongoing conflicts with Britain would eventually lead to war, so he needed all the money he could get. Therefore, he proposed to sell **all** of France's land west of the Mississippi to the United States for the total sum of 15 million dollars (about 3 cents an acre). The deal became known as **the Louisiana Purchase**.

There was resistance in Congress over the deal, but **the Southern states favored it as long as Jefferson, a slave holder, agreed to allow the institution of slavery to expand into the new territory**. The U.S. assumed the new land stretched from the Gulf of Mexico in the south and into Canada to the north and all the way from the Mississippi River to the Rocky Mountains in the West. However, Spain disputed that and continued to claim it owned some of that land. **Jefferson funded an expedition led by Lewis and Clark to map the new territory**. Following river routes and with the guidance of friendly Indians, Lewis and Clark eventually made it all the way to the West Coast near what is now Portland, Oregon. Spain sent troops to try to stop them, but they could never find the Lewis and Clark party. With the threat from Spain still looming, Jefferson established forts in several places along the route, and the new lands were to play a key role in three future conflicts, the Indian Wars, the War of 1812, and the Civil War.

The Presidential Election of 1808

By 1808, the nomination of presidential candidates was still in the hands of members of Congress. After President Jefferson decided to retire, a caucus of the Democratic-Republicans nominated Secretary of State **James Madison** of Virginia, with **George Clinton** as the vice presidential nominee.

A caucus of the Federalists again nominated **General Charles Cotesworth Pinckney** of South Carolina, with former U.S. Senator **Rufus King** of New York as the vice presidential nominee.

STORY
Although the nominations for president in 1808 featured the "usual suspects," men that had been involved in the founding of the new country, the election showed that the nation was

> evolving toward a desire for a broader selection of candidates. For the first time, there was more dissonance in the selection of the candidates, and in the end, a great deal of "localism" in the Electoral College.
>
> Virginia "insider," James Madison was the Democratic-Republican candidate, but the party selected a non-Virginian, New Yorker, **George Clinton**, to be his vice president. Clinton was not so sure he wanted to serve in a continuation of the Jeffersonian "Virginia dynasty." Nevertheless, he allowed them to put his name into nomination as the Democratic-Republican vice presidential nominee.
>
> There was also somewhat of a revolt in the Democratic-Republican caucus from the so-called "quids," men who supported Monroe rather than Madison and promoted a strict interpretation of the Constitution. They felt the Democratic-Republicans were moving away from the nation's founding principles.

Madison won in the Electoral College, 122 to Pinckney's 47. Clinton got the second most votes and was therefore to be Madison's vice president. That meant that the new president would have to work with the existing vice president.

The Presidential Election of 1812

During the early part of the 19th century, **the Democratic-Republican party was as dominant** in U.S. politics as the Federalist had been in the first few presidential elections. This was because **the South voted as a block to make sure every new president continued to favor the established system of slavery**. As a result, the Democratic-Republican presidential candidates were always **slave holders** from Virginia. With the support of *all* the Southern states, they won easily.

In the election of 1812, Virginia plantation owner, **James Madison,** was nominated for reelection. He chose **Elbridge Gerry**, the former governor of Massachusetts as his running mate.

The Federalists, desperate for a win, supported a dissident Democratic-Republican, **DeWitt Clinton**.

The election campaign was mostly about the issue of slavery, but there was also a war going on: early in the election campaign, the United States once again declared war on Britain, a war that became known as **the War of 1812**.

The war was popular, and as a result, the people overwhelmingly voted to give Madison a second term (**Americans have a long history of reelecting presidents when a war is under way**).

STORY

The war of 1812, like all wars, changed the political landscape and influenced several of the presidential elections that were to follow. The war started as an outgrowth (some said as a sideshow) of **ongoing battles between two great military powers of that era, Britain and France**. Much of their war was being fought on the high seas, and when Britain tried to blockade France, trade ships from the United States sometimes got caught up in the conflict.

In the early 1800s **Napoleon Bonaparte was running roughshod over Europe**, but **Britain ruled the seas**. Britain put together an alliance of countries against Bonaparte's France, and in the early months of 1812, they **began to capture American trade ships**. Britain claimed the trade ships were helping the French, if only to re-supply France with needed goods. The American trade ships were taken as the spoils of war, and **the captured sailors were forced to serve on British warships**.

In response, on the first day of June in 1812, **the United States shocked the world by declaring war on Britain**. It was a reaction not only to the taking of American ships, but also a reaction to a perceived violation of America's neutrality in the European conflict. President Madison declared Britain's actions were an affront to America's honor.

Although America's declaration of war on Britain surprised many people throughout the world, the U.S. had some ongoing unsettled issues with Britain that played a part in it. For one thing, Britain had been trying to thwart the American expansion into American western territories that the British wanted for themselves. They were arming the western Indian tribes, trying to get them to organize against the United States.

In addition, there were many in **the U.S. government that hoped not only to expand into the West, but also into Canada**. Toward that end, one of the first American acts in the war was to invade Canada. American forces under General Hull, the governor of Michigan territory, **invaded Canada** north of Detroit. However, the attack was not well coordinated and **the British not only easily repelled it, but in response attacked Detroit. Within a month, General Hull was forced to surrender Detroit to the British.**

Several sea battles ensued, with American ships faring surprisingly well, but the land battles did not go so well. **De Witt Clinton**, the governor of New York, **sent troops into Canada** near Niagara Falls. But they were soon forced back and became trapped at the edge of the Niagara River with no way to cross back into the United States. Three hundred Americans were killed and nearly a thousand were taken prisoner.

Although the war wasn't going so well for the Americans, the people were mostly behind Madison.

The Star-Spangled Banner, our current national anthem, was written during this war of 1812. The song's lyrics came from a poem titled "Defence of Fort McHenry" written by a 35-year-old lawyer named Francis Scott Key. He wrote the poem soon after he witnessed the British Navy's 25-hour bombardment of Fort McHenry, a large fort built in 1798 to defend Baltimore Harbor. At the time, the poem was sung to the tune of a British song written for a men's social club in London. With that tune more or less intact, **117 years later, in 1913, the**

song was declared to be the national anthem of the United States.

In the War of 1812, even pirates played a role. Realizing that the U.S. was outmatched in naval power, the U.S. government offered to commission any armed vessel that was willing to help, even pirate vessels.

The famous pirate, Jean Lafitte, had been operating several smuggling ships out of New Orleans and had only recently been forced to retreat to an out-of-the-way bay farther south.

A few months after the U.S. declared war on Britain, the British sent a delegation to try to recruit Lafitte to their side. They offered Lafitte and his men British citizenship and land in British areas of the western part of North America if they would fight against the Americans. Lafitte was a good enough tactician to see that the Americans held the land and therefore the advantage. He turned down the offer (surprisingly, he didn't kill the envoys).

When **the British mounted an offensive against New Orleans**, Andrew Jackson brought troops to repel them.

The city was in dire straits and Jackson was outnumbered. He had only two ships and a few thousand unseasoned troops. When he learned Lafitte had many ships and seasoned fighting men, Jackson approached him with a deal: **if the pirates would help defend the city, Jackson promised them full pardons**. After the pirate agreed, Jackson managed to convince the Louisiana legislature to make the pardons official.

It is said that Lafitte's trained fighting men, and the pirates' knowledge of the area, were instrumental in the defense of New Orleans. (However, he was still a pirate at heart, and he went back to pirating as soon as the war was over.)

Napoleon tried to invade and hold Russia, but he failed. He invaded Russia with 400,000 troops but came back with only 40,000. As a result, several countries united against France, and by 1814 Napoleon was completely defeated. After

Napoleon signed a peace treaty with Britain, that put an end to the issues that had led to the war with Britain. The United States and Britain decided to call it a stalemate, and the two countries signed **the Treaty of Ghent** on the day before Christmas, 1814.

The treaty was signed in Europe, which meant the news had to come by ship, the news that the war was over had to come by ship. And even after the news of the treaty had reached the East Coast, given the lack of rapid communications during that era in the West, it **took over two months to reach all the troops that were still fighting in the western territories.** The last major battle of the war, a British victory at the second Battle of Fort Bowyer at Mobile Bay, Alabama, took place on February 11, 1815.

Although the war was a stalemate with no territorial gains or losses, it did bring about **a feeling of national pride and unity.** It marked the beginning of the **"era of good feelings"** between the U.S. and Britain.

The Presidential Election of 1816

In **1816, James Monroe,** yet another member of the slaveholding "ruling class" of Virginia, won easily. He was to be the last U.S. President to have borne arms in the Revolutionary War.

STORY

At the beginning of 1815, there was a secret meeting of Federalist representatives from Connecticut, Rhode Island, Massachusetts, New Hampshire, and Vermont who were **tired of southern slave holders always being elected president** because of the built-in bias of the Electoral College. There was contention regarding about whether the electoral votes of the new state of Indiana should be counted. Representative John W. Taylor of New York objected to it, but he was voted down and the votes of Indiana *were* counted.

The Presidential Election of 1820

By **the election of 1820**, the Federalist party was no more. Democratic-Republican **James Monroe ran for reelection unopposed**. It would be the last time any candidate was to run for president unopposed.

After the War of 1812, politics in the early 1800s seemed relatively calm, except for the ongoing troubles with the Indian tribes.

STORY

In 1820, **the issue of slavery was dividing the people**: more and more people of the United States were saying slavery was not only inhuman, but it was also unconstitutional. America, they said, was supposed to be the land of the free, and yet slavery was still the law of the land in the United States when most other countries had outlawed it. **France had officially abolished slavery** (Napoleon did however enslave some of the citizens of countries he invaded.) Even **Russia and other eastern European countries had abolished slavery** many years before. **Denmark and Norway had abolished slavery**, and even declared the slave trade illegal. In 1807, **the British not only abolished slavery, their ships began stopping slave ships and arresting their captains**. It is estimated that **the British freed more than 150,000 captured Africans**. American's neighbors, **Canada and Mexico had either abolished slavery or were in the process of doing it district by district**. The divisive **issue of slavery continued as the nation expanded westward,** but the **Missouri Compromise** of 1821 maintained the balance of slave states and free states.

Chapter Six
The Politics of Slavery

Dissonance over the issue of slavery had been brewing in the United States ever since the country declared its independence from Britain. By the early 1800s, it became the predominant issue in presidential politics.

Many Northerners were outraged at the very idea of slavery, saying it was contrary to the United States Bill of Rights. Those in favor of slavery pointed out that there was no specific mention of slavery in the U.S. Constitution. Which was not surprising because **many of the framers of the Constitution, including George Washington, John Adams, Thomas Jefferson, and James Madison were slave owners**.

Whenever new states petitioned to join the United States, it brought the slavery issue into focus. The Southern slave states feared that if new states were allowed to join the Union as free states, the shift of power in Congress might lead to the eventual outlawing of slavery altogether. As a result, **the slave states used their disproportional power in the Senate to keep new states from joining the Union unless they agreed to allow slavery**.

The situation came to a head when Missouri wanted to join the United States. Missouri was the first state to be created out of lands of the Louisiana purchase. Most of the region's citizens had come from the South; therefore, there was an assumption that it would be a slave state. A House of Representatives committee approved Missouri's petition to become a state in 1819, but **James Tallmadge of New York added an amendment specifying Missouri had to be a free state**. Furthermore, his amendment stated that the new state would be prohibited from importing slaves and that all current slaves that had been born in the region would have to be freed when they reached the age of 25. The bill was passed by the House on February 17, 1819. Of course, **the Southern

slave states used their disproportionate power in the Senate to vote it down. After much contentious debate, as so often happens in politics, a compromise was reached. The compromise was that **the northern part of Massachusetts would break off to become a new state (Maine)**, and it would be admitted to the Union as a free state at the same time **Missouri would be admitted as a slave state**. That way, the balance would be maintained, **assuring that the free states couldn't pass any anti-slave legislation**. The law also included a stipulation that slavery would not be allowed in any territory north of latitude 36° 30' North (which marked the northern border of Missouri). The law became known as **the Missouri Compromise**. As is typical of such compromises, neither side was happy about it. **Thomas Jefferson said the compromise would eventually lead to the destruction of the Union**. John Randolph, a Virginia slave owner, denounced the compromise and called Henry Clay, the Speaker of the House, "the great compromiser" (not a complimentary term). He sent plenty of other insults Clay's way, and not surprisingly, soon thereafter, the two met to fight a duel. Although shots reportedly were fired, the word that came back from the dueling ground was that the only injury was to Randolph's clothes (in other words, Clay did fire at Randolph, but it was a near miss).

Regardless of Randolph's stand on slavery, he felt all governing power should be in the hands of the states. He thought states ought to be free to accept or reject federal laws.

STORY

It is interesting to note that despite being a slave owner all his life, Randolph wrote a will that decreed all of his slaves should be freed upon his death. Known as **manumission**, the practice of specifying the freeing of slaves in a will was becoming more common as the debate about slavery heated up.

Randolph's will not only freed his slaves, it also **provided money to be used to resettle his slaves in the free state of**

Ohio. After he died, three hundred and eighty three of Randolph's former slaves accepted the offer.

However, at that time, racism was as rampant in Ohio as it was most everywhere else in the country, so when the former slaves arrived, they were met by **mobs of angry white men with guns** who drove them farther on west. Sadly, the Ohio land that had been paid for with money from Randolph's will had already been sold off to white men, and **the sellers had run off with the money**. None of the Ohio law enforcement officials were willing to do anything about it, so all the former Randolph slaves could do was move on.

Eventually, many of them were employed by Quakers that were sympathetic to their plight. The rest of them either found employment doing odd jobs in the few Ohio places that would accept them, or they moved on farther west to an unknown fate.

Thomas Jefferson also specified in his will that some of his slaves be freed, but his was a very different story from that of Randolph. Even as he served as president, it was rumored that Jefferson had been using one of his slaves as a mistress (slave owners using female slaves sexually was not all that uncommon during the slave era). **Modern DNA evidence revealed that a light-skinned slave, Sally Hemings, bore six of Jefferson's children.** All of the Jefferson-Hemings children were light-skinned, and although they were legally still slaves, three of them left the Jefferson plantation and lived as white in Northern states. Jefferson did not attempt to retrieve them, and **in his will he freed all of the Hemings children**.

The Presidential Election of 1824

The presidential election of 1824 turned out to be quite contentious. It was the **first election in which the candidate that won the most votes--both popular and in the Electoral College--did not get to be president.**

As I noted earlier, after the demise of the Federalist Party, the Democratic-Republican Party, dominated by Southern slave holders, pretty much had things their own way, not only in presidential elections, but also in running the country. In all the presidential elections since 1796, the winner had been a member of the Democratic-Republican Party. But by 1824, the people of the country were becoming disillusioned with the brand of **"insider politics"** that had become the norm. That disillusionment was soon to loosen the Democratic-Republican party's grip on political power.

Following the established precedent of serving only two terms, in 1824, **President Monroe chose not to run for reelection**. He said he was ready to retire to his estate at Monroe Hill near Charlottesville, Virginia (his estate is now part of the campus of the University of Virginia).

As a result, **the 1824 election season** began, just as it had for all prior elections since the demise of the Federalist Party, with a **Democratic-Republican Congressional nominating caucus** (known then as the **"King Caucus"**) being held to decide who would be the next president and vice president. For president, they selected yet another Southern slave holder, **William Harris Crawford** of Georgia, but for vice president, they selected **Albert Gallatin** from the non-slave state of Pennsylvania.

STORY

The official **Democratic-Republican candidates, Crawford and Gallatin** were not well known at the time of their nomination. Nevertheless, both of them had been in and around politics for much of their adult lives.

In 1803, **Crawford was elected to the Georgia House of Representatives**, and in 1807 he was appointed to the U.S. Senate by the Georgia legislature (remember, **at that time, U.S. senators were not elected by the people but were appointed by state legislatures**). In 1813, President James Madison had appointed Crawford to serve as minister to France. He served in that post until the end of the War of 1812, and when he returned from France, Madison appointed him Secretary of War. Later, he was named Secretary of the Treasury. He remained in that position until, despite serious health problems, he was nominated to be a candidate for president.

Albert Gallatin's story is a more complex and interesting one. Born into a wealthy and influential family in Switzerland, he studied at the elite Academy of Geneva where he discovered the philosophy of Jean-Jacques Rousseau and Physiocracy (the belief that the wealth of nations is based on land and agriculture).

In 1880, at age 19, he began hearing about the type of democracy that was being undertaken in the United States. Like many other young Europeans, he was fascinated with this new experiment in democratic government and soon set out to see it for himself.

In America, he tried various business ventures without much success, so he had to make his living teaching French. Eventually, he was able to use his family's influence to get a position at Harvard College. That didn't last long. He again set out to make his fortune in various businesses from farming to retailing to glass making. At one point, in response to the perceived threat from France, the Commonwealth of Pennsylvania called out to its militia and Gallatin signed a contract to make muskets for them. That didn't turn out to be very profitable either.

But **Gallatin had always had an interest in politics, and in 1793, he lobbied for an appointment to the U.S. Senate**, aligning himself with the Democratic-Republicans and against the Federalists. He was appointed to the Senate, but the Federalists protested his appointment, saying he had not been a citizen of the United States for a long enough period to be a senator. It went to a vote, and **the Federalists used their voting power to remove him from the Senate**. But he did not go without at fight, and when the proceedings of the Senate were made public, it brought him some attention, especially from the anti-Federalist forces. Back home in Pennsylvania, he played a role in **the Whiskey Rebellion**, a protest against a new tax on whiskey that grew violent. When **the government sent in the Army to put down the protest**, Gallatin used his notoriety and his skillful oratory to calm the situation. As a result, **he was elected to the House of Representatives in 1795 where he became an anti-Federalist leader of the Democratic-Republicans**. From then on, he held various positions in the government until 1824 when he was nominated to be a candidate for vice president by the Democratic-Republican caucus.

With the people crying out for more open politics, some politicians in the Democratic-Republican party saw opportunity, and many decided against participating in the "king making" party caucus. To the great surprise of the party leaders, **only 66 of the party's 231 members showed up**. The caucus went ahead and nominated Crawford and Gallatin, but the lack of party participation was a sign of things to come. Soon after the "official" Democratic-Republican caucus had nominated Crawford and Gallatin, three other Democratic-Republicans, **John Quincy Adams, Henry Clay**, and **Andrew Jackson,** defied the party leaders. *They wanted to be president.*

STORY

The unofficial Democratic-Republican candidates, John Quincy Adams, Henry Clay, and Andrew Jackson were better known than Crawford and Gallatin. Adams was the son of the former president. Reportedly, he suffered from depression and was unsure of himself and not all that interested in politics. Nevertheless, he followed in his father's footsteps by serving as a foreign minister in several European countries.

Upon his return, he was still not sure he wanted to get involved in politics, but friends of his father pushed him in that direction. In 1802, he was elected to the Massachusetts State Senate. That same year, he ran as the Federalist candidate for the United States House of Representatives, but he lost. Nevertheless, the Federalists soon got him appointed to the U.S. Senate where he served until 1808. As a senator, **he angered the Federalists who had appointed him by supporting the Louisiana Purchase which they were against**. The Federalists, who controlled the Massachusetts legislature, decided to replace him. In response, **Adams became a Democratic-Republican**. When James Madison, a Democratic-Republican, was elected president, he appointed Adams as foreign minister to Russia. His wife Louisa went with him, and it was said she made up for his lack of charm in social situations. In fact, she soon became a favorite invitee at the tsar's parties.

By 1818, Adams was back in the U.S. serving as Secretary of State in the cabinet of Democratic-Republican President James Monroe. With the election of 1824 drawing near, and it looking more and more like the election was going to be wide open, the New England Democratic-Republican party went looking for a "favorite son" candidate. Their choice fell to Adams, and eventually he accepted their nomination.

Henry Clay was from a Virginian family who owned a large number of slaves. But Henry was not interested in the life of the plantation owner and instead decided to become a lawyer even though he had no formal education in the law. To learn about the law, he secured an appointment as an assistant to the Virginia State Attorney where he learned about courtroom proceedings and politics. In 1797, he moved to Kentucky to practice law on his own. In Kentucky, everyone agreed he had a knack for politics and oratory, and in 1803, he was elected to the Kentucky General Assembly. It wasn't long before he was appointed by the Kentucky legislature to the U.S. Senate even though he was only 29 years old (the Constitution requires U.S. senators to be over the age of thirty). No one seemed to notice, or if they did, they didn't care.

In 1807, Clay returned to Kentucky where he was soon elected Speaker of the Kentucky House of Representatives.

However, his aggressive approach to lawmaking angered several members of the legislature, and he was involved in some scuffles on the floor of the House. One such scuffle resulted in **Clay challenging a legislator named Humphrey Marshall to a duel**. The rules of the duel were that each man would get three shots. One of Clay's shots grazed Marshall's chest, and one of Marshall's shots hit Clay in the thigh. Both men survived and honor was served.

In 1810, the Kentucky state legislature again appointed Clay to the U.S. Senate. But one year later, he was elected to the U.S. House of Representatives. Because of his reputation, he was elected Speaker of the House on the first day in office. Thereafter, he was re-elected five times to the House, and each time, he was also reelected as Speaker of the House. **It is important to note that Clay completely changed the role of the Speaker of the House from parliamentarian (merely a keeper of the rules) to political leader**. He was the first U.S. Speaker of the House to appoint his allies to key committee chairmanships as a way of controlling what became law and what did not. He also used his position to support hostilities against Britain, which, in time, evolved into the War of 1812.

By 1812, **Clay was becoming quite prosperous. He owned a 600-acre tobacco and hemp plantation and 60 slaves of his own**. In 1816, he became president of the **American Colonization Society, a group that wanted to send free blacks back to Africa**. Under Clay's leadership, the group founded a colony in Africa called Monrovia. **Clay said the god of nature

had decreed against the amalgamation of the black and white races as proven by the obvious differences of skin color and physical constitution. The main purpose of the group was to deport free blacks because they posed a threat to the practice of slavery, but some abolitionists from the North also got behind the effort. As the election of 1824 loomed, it became clear that the Democratic-Republican caucus's nomination of Crawford and Gallatin was not receiving wide support. Clay then made his bid for the presidency.

Andrew Jackson was the first candidate for president that could be described as an outsider. Although he was, like Clay, a Southerner who owned slaves, he was not part of the Southeast coast group of political insiders. He was from Tennessee. Little is known about Jackson's childhood except that his father had died in the Revolutionary War before he was born. His two brothers had also died in the Revolutionary War.

When Jackson was thirteen, he joined up with a local militia so he too could fight in the Revolutionary War. They made him a courier, but he was soon **captured by the British and held as a prisoner of war**. He was mistreated, almost starved to death, and contracted smallpox. It left him with a lifelong hatred of the British. Soon after his release, his mother died, leaving him **an orphan at the age of fourteen**. After that, he was bounced around between relatives, worked at various odd jobs, and got little education. Eventually, he went to North Carolina to study law. Not all that much is known about his studies, or about his early law career, but he was said to have practiced law in the western part of North Carolina, the area that was to become the state of Tennessee. When Tennessee became a state in 1796, Jackson was **elected as its first representative in Congress**. Meanwhile, he was growing wealthy from investments and from his law practice. He bought up huge tracks of land in Tennessee, and **eventually accrued 150 slaves.** He also became an active member of the Tennessee militia. During the

War of 1812, several Indian tribes banded together, and with the aid of the British, they attacked western towns. Jackson took his Tennessee militia into battle against them, and the Indians were repelled. Jackson's rank was raised to major general, and he started to get a national reputation as a capable military leader. **In 1814, when New Orleans came under British attack, Jackson took over command of the region's defense.** Many others came to join the defense effort, including **Davy Crockett** and **Sam Houston**, and by the beginning of 1815, the British were routed. During that conflict, Jackson became widely known as a tough and very strict officer. The word got out that his men called him **"Old Hickory"** (tough as old hickory wood), and the nickname stuck. **By the end of the War of 1812, Jackson was being seen as a national hero.** He received an official gold medal of thanks from the U.S. Congress, and more than a few political leaders began thinking of him as a potential political candidate. In 1823, the Tennessee legislature appointed him U.S. senator and encouraged him to run for president in the presidential election of 1824.

As the 1824 presidential election campaign progressed, it started to become clear that William Crawford, the Democratic-Republican party's official choice for president, was not fairing well.

The campaigning had hardly begun when Crawford suffered a stroke that was said to have been brought on by an overdose of prescribed medication. He recovered well, but it hampered his ability to campaign and gave people doubts about his overall health. It was only the first of many setbacks faced by the Democratic-Republican party leaders.

Adams, the son of the nation's second president, who had formerly been a Federalist, was clearly gathering support from the old Federalists in the Northeast. Meanwhile, Jackson was beginning to look like the people's choice in the South and in the West.

Of the two candidates, the Democratic-Republican party leaders thought Jackson would be the easiest to discredit. They published many articles in Democratic-Republican newspapers that said Jackson had **no real national political experience,** that he was **nothing but a frontier backwoodsman**. But that didn't work because it made people think Jackson was "one of them."

Then the Adams backers **said Jackson was a murderer.** They said they had proof that he had executed captured Indians without a trial and had even executed captured British troops. There may have been some truth to those charges, but many people saw those incidents as just part of war. After all, Jackson was known as a military hero. As a last resort, Jackson's political opponents said he had killed men in unfair duels, and that he was an adulterer living with another man's wife. While there may have been some truth to those charges, Jackson's support among the "common men" in the West and the South never wavered. In that era, although adultery was a serious matter and did hurt Jackson's reputation, duels were seen as matter of honor between gentlemen.

STORY

Although killing a man in a duel these days would certainly hurt a presidential candidate's chances of winning an election, it might well have been **a political advantage** in Jackson's time. Jackson was rumored to have killed many men in duels, and it was a sign of the times that he never disputed the charge. His reputation of having great prowess with a pistol made a lot of the men of that era look up to him (and remember, at that time, only men could vote). However, had the real truth about his dueling history been known at the time, it would have been considerably less flattering. While it was true that he was hot tempered and quick to challenge a man to a duel, the fact is his duels usually didn't take place. The problem was that he had a habit of challenging men to duels in the heat of the moment, only to find out later that his prospective opponent was a skillful and experienced duelist.

For example, at the tender age of 21, Jackson was trying to learn how to practice law. In one of his first court cases, an experienced lawyer ridiculed Jackson's judicial knowledge. Jackson immediately challenged the man to a duel. The duel was scheduled, but in the meantime, Jackson had learned more about the man's reputation as a duelist and had second thoughts. The details are lost to time, but the outcome on the field of honor was that both men agreed to fire into the air.

Over the next several years, other duels were offered, but never took place. But then Jackson made an enemy of John Sevier, the governor of Tennessee. The story is that the two feuded for years until a duel was finally scheduled. However, before the day of the scheduled duel, they happened to meet on the trail. In a scene right out of one of that era's notorious Western "dime novels," Jackson dismounted and pulled out his pistol. Sevier dismounted and drew his sword. Quite a few insults were exchanged before they both got back on their horses and went on their way. The scheduled duel never happened.

The one duel that did happen, was a deadly one. It was again a feud between lawyers, but it came to a head in a bar fight. After some fisticuffs, Jackson challenged a young lawyer named Charles Dickinson to a duel. The duel took place at Harrison's Mill, Kentucky. Unfortunately for Jackson, the young man turned out to be quite a good marksman, and when the command to fire was given, the young man shot Jackson square in the chest. Jackson managed to stay on his feet and shot Dickinson in the stomach, killing him. Jackson survived, but **he was to carry Dickinson's bullet in him for the rest of his life**.

The attacks on John Quincy Adams by Jackson's supporters were quite different. They said Adams was out of touch with the people. They called him an **Eastern elitist,** and they said he might even secretly be a royalist. They constantly brought up Adams's former involvement with the Federalists.

Those kinds of attacks didn't erode Adams's support in the Northeast and in the urban areas of the country, but they did hurt him with the voters Jackson was reaching out to, the so-called "common man" elsewhere.

Meanwhile, one of the best known candidates for president, Henry Clay, was getting left behind. Although he was a well-known politician, it was clear he was not popular among the people. He could only count on some support from his home state of Kentucky and neighboring states.

Jackson racked up victories in Alabama, Indiana, Mississippi, North Carolina, Pennsylvania, and Tennessee.

Adams won in the Northeast states, Connecticut, Maine, Massachusetts, New Hampshire, and Rhode Island

It showed that national sentiment was becoming divided by region: Jackson was generally favored in the rural states, and by a large margin, but Adams was favored in the more populous states of the Northeast.

The only two states Crawford won were Delaware and Georgia. However, that doesn't mean Crawford was the people's choice in those two states. **Delaware and Georgia did not allow a popular vote. In those states, the electors were chosen by the legislature. They were Democratic-Republican party loyalists who did their duty and cast their Electoral College votes for whoever the party leaders told them to.**

The final Electoral College vote was Jackson 99, Adams 84, Crawford 41, Clay 37.

Since no candidate had the required absolute majority of 131 electoral votes, the selection of the president once again went to the U.S. House of Representatives which had to choose from the top three candidates.

Interestingly, a vice president *had been* elected in the Electoral College: **John Calhoun** of South Carolina won the majority of votes for vice president and therefore took the office.

STORY

Because **Henry Clay** had come in fourth in the Electoral College voting, he was eliminated from consideration. However, he was still the **Speaker of the House**, and that placed him in a position of great influence in the House where the election would be decided.

At the time, Inauguration Day was in March. That meant the House should have acted quickly. But they didn't. First, there had to be the usual back room bargaining and arm-twisting. Some **representatives were putting the word out that their votes could be "bought" in exchange for a cabinet post.** or maybe an important ambassador assignment.

Clay was the best at making such deals. He had been collecting political debts for many years, and now it was time to call them in. His main goal was to set himself up for the next presidential election. He knew Andrew Jackson, having won both the popular vote and the Electoral College vote, would be his main opposition in the next presidential election; therefore, **his goal was to manipulate the vote in the House to make sure Jackson didn't get to be president** this time.

In those days, the usual stepping stone to the presidency was the cabinet position of Secretary of State. Many suspected Clay might try to accomplish his goal by working a deal with Adams. The deal would be that if Clay could convince enough representatives to vote against Jackson, Adams would be elected president, and in exchange, Adams would select Clay as his Secretary of State. **Clay believed that would put him in line for the presidency next time**. In actuality, **Clay disliked Adams, but he thought he would have a better chance against Adams than Jackson in the next election.**

As soon as the other representatives saw Clay meeting privately with Adams, they knew the deal was on.

Once the deal was made, it was Clay's job to get representatives to change their votes and go for Adams. It wasn't easy be-

> cause few liked Adams. But **with threats and promises, Clay was able to pull it off**.
>
> The House met to vote on February 9, 1825, and John Quincy Adams won the votes of 13 states, exactly the number needed to win the presidency.
>
> Adams immediately named Clay as his Secretary of State.
>
> Jackson and his supporters were furious. **They called the deal Clay and Adams had made a "corrupt bargain."** The term stuck, and in the end, undid all of Clay's attempts to set himself up for the presidency in the next election.

When the word of the House's vote and the corrupt bargain got out, the people who had voted for Jackson were outraged. They saw him as the rightful president-elect, and they could not be consoled by the politicians telling them that it had all been done according to the rule of law as specified by the Constitution's section on the Electoral College.

Jackson came right out and said the whole thing was a travesty. He and his supporters asked what kind of system it was where the person who won both the popular vote *and* the Electoral College vote did not get to be president. He said the rights of the people had been bartered away, and **called for an immediate end to the Electoral College system** of electing the president. **He demanded to know why the nation's most important office should not be elected *directly by the people.***

Although just about everyone agreed that the method of selecting a president was not fair, the smaller-population states were completely united in keeping the Electoral College system. In the first place, the two extra electoral votes each of the smaller states automatically got gave them an advantage in determining who the president would be. They didn't want to change the system of letting the House of Representatives decide close elections, because in the House, **every state got one vote, no matter how large or small the state was**. That disproportionate advantage pretty much guaranteed **Jackson's demand for an end to the Electoral College system would be ignored by the smaller states**. And because such a change would require an amendment to the Constitution and ratification by three-fourths of the states, even Jackson knew changing it was not going to happen.

The dissatisfaction with the results of the election of 1824 led to a significant change in the American political landscape. Jackson declared that he would run again in 1828, and because of the unfair way the 1824 election had turned out, many predicted he would win this time.

The senator from New York, Martin Van Buren, saw the people's anger at the way Jackson had been denied the presidency through back-room dealings as an opportunity to enhance his own fortunes. In the 1824 election, he had been a supporter of Crawford, but when it became clear that the people wanted the "outsider" Jackson instead of the usual Washington insider, he switched his allegiance and declared it was time for a new Jacksonian democracy. He said it would be **a democracy of the common man instead of a political monopoly by the eastern elites** (although he himself might accurately have been described as being part of that cadre).

Van Buren and Jackson broke with the all-powerful Democratic-Republican party. (**Modern day Democrats now see that moment as the starting point of the Democratic party, and they claim Andrew Jackson as the party's founder**.)

Leading up to the 1828 presidential election, the so-called **Jacksonian movement** gradually grew in political strength. It was a coalition of farmers and low-wage Irish-Catholic laborers. It was strongest in the states with the largest populations, which in those days included Virginia, New York, and Pennsylvania. This new "**democratic**" party was "for the people" and quite vocally against the "rich and the powerful."

In line with that belief, **they fought to get rid of voting rules that said only men of property, or men who paid taxes, were allowed to vote**. They said all white men should be allowed to vote. It took many more years to accomplish that goal, but by

1850, *nearly* all the "property requirements" had been eliminated in the *majority* of the states.)

The Jacksonian Democrats also believed America had a "**manifest destiny**" to expand throughout the American West, possibly all the way to the Pacific coast. However, they were against the expansion of slavery into the West. The Jacksonians were against unlimited expansion of centralized federal power, but they could not be called states' righters because they believed the power should be in the hands of the people, not in the hands of the rich and powerful who normally ran politics. They strongly believed **the Electoral College took power away from the people and put it into the hands of powerful politicians**. They were also against the idea that it was the rich and powerful who got to appoint the members of United States Senate. But the South was against direct election of either presidents or senators because **they were afraid the voters in larger states of the North would vote for men who might try to end slavery**.

The Jacksonian democrats favored a *laissez-faire* approach to economics; that is, they believed the federal government should not try to regulate businesses. They also believed in a "**hard money system**" in which only gold and silver could be considered true currency. They were suspicious of banks, and were against the idea of a government bank.

The Jacksonian Democrats were also in favor of the "**spoils system**." The basic concept of the spoils system was that **to the victor shall go the spoils**; that is, a newly elected government official had the right to fire all of the previous administration's political appointees and bring in their own people.

COMMENT

The Jacksonian Democrats' innovation of **the spoils system is still in place today**. Whenever new presidents come into office, they feel they have the right to get rid of any or all of the former administration's top-level employees. The newly elected leader usually brings in party loyalists who helped him win the election. The reasoning of the Jacksonian Democrats was that only through the adoption of the spoils system could an administration be held accountable for their failures. It's the "buck stops here" concept, meaning **the president makes all the personnel appointments; therefore he should be responsible for their failures**. However, although modern day presidents still use the spoils system to replace most of the nation's top government officials as soon as they get elected, they now seem less willing to take the blame when things go wrong.

The Presidential Election of 1828

As a result of the national outrage over the fact that Andrew Jackson did not get to be president despite winning the popular vote in 1824 pretty much assured him the win in 1828. He and his running mate, John C. Calhoun from South Carolina, won easily. It would mark the beginning of an era of "**Jacksonian democracy**" that tried to take political power out of the hands of the rich and powerful "elitists."

STORY

In response to Jackson's being elected president in 1828, Henry Clay and John Quincy Adams put together an opposition coalition in Congress to fight against Jackson's new **Democratic Party**. Eventually, they took on the name "**Whigs**." (There was a Whig party in England that fought against the absolute rule of monarchy, and in America the term had been taken up as a reference to those who fought against tyranny.)

However, at first, the Whigs were unable to persuade the people that their plans for the nation were better than those of the Democrats. For one thing, **they were against the popular**

idea of westward expansion, insisting that modernization of the still-undeveloped nation in the East was more important. **They felt Jackson and the Democrats were holding the nation back from modernization.**

The Whigs *did* find support among the professional classes, business owners, and the owners of large plantations. Also, the Whig's plans to modernize the cities and the nation's manufacturers struck a chord in the cities that depended on manufacturing.

On the other hand, the Democrats continued to describe the **Whigs as the party of the rich and powerful**, and that message resonated with the Irish-Catholic immigrants that had tended to settle in the eastern cities.

Some Protestant ministers, favoring the Whigs, tried to discredit the Irish-Catholics, telling their congregations that Jackson and his followers were immoral, and that a vote for the Democrats was a vote for immorality. **Protestant reformers railed against drinking and whoring, and they proposed a national prohibition on sales of alcohol that would put an end to what they saw as "the liquor problem" in America.**

Nevertheless, within a generation, the Whig Party was able to put up a candidate in nearly every election, and they gradually began to have more success.

The main agenda of the Whigs was to create an "**American system**" of rapid industrial growth and government support for manufacturers. **They proposed high tariffs against foreign imports that might compete with American manufactured products.** They were also in favor of government support of banking, and they felt the government should get involved in the expansion of the nation's infrastructure of roads and canals and railroads, anything that would make America more of a manufacturing country instead of an agrarian country.

> The Whigs also felt America's educational system was in great need of modernization. They wanted the national government to get involved in creating a better public school system.
>
> It soon became apparent that the main difference between the two political parties was that **the Whigs felt the national government should be stronger** and more involved in developing the future of the nation as a whole, while the Democrats felt such things should be left to the states.

The Presidential Election of 1832

The presidential election of 1832 saw the origination of national nominating conventions. The **Anti-Masonic Party**, the **National Republican Party**, and the **Democratic Party** all held conventions in Baltimore.

> ### STORY
> In 1832, most assumed that President Jackson would run for reelection along with his vice president, John C. Calhoun. But Jackson had a falling out with Calhoun over the issue of tariffs in Calhoun's home state of South Carolina. The highly protective Tariff of 1828 (nicknamed "the tariff of abominations" by South Carolina detractors) was designed to help American manufacturing win over European manufacturing, but many in the South blamed it for the gradual economic downturn the South had been suffering.
>
> As a result of the disagreement, Jackson dumped Calhoun and replaced him with New Yorker, Martin Van Buren.

The Republicans nominated **Henry Clay, a slave holder from Kentucky** who had served both as a senator and in the House of Representatives. He had also served as Secretary of State under President John Quincy Adams.

Jackson, won the presidency easily, winning 219 of the 286 electoral votes cast. However, a number of other candidates also received electoral votes, mostly from their own states. They included **Hugh L. White**, a Whig from Tennessee who won 47 electoral votes, and another Whig, **Daniel Webster,** who won 23 electoral votes. The electors from South Carolina, refused to vote for Jackson, and instead **cast their 11 electoral votes for John Floyd, the governor of Virginia, who wasn't a candidate**.

After Jackson was reelected, **the outrage over the Electoral College was soon forgotten.**

During the period, new political parties were developed and new ideologies sprang up. For the next decade, the national political argument would be mainly focused two issues, slavery and about how much power the national government should have.

The Presidential Election of 1836

In 1836, President Jackson supported his vice president, **Martin Van Buren,** for the presidency. Kentucky Senator **Richard Mentor Johnson** was chosen as Van Buren's running mate.

STORY

The selection of Richard Mentor Johnson as the Democratic vice presidential candidate in 1836 was surprising to many because he was known to be having a sexual relationship with one of his female slaves. He was quite open about it. Although it was well known that some slave owners had sex with their slaves, it was not seen as appropriate to discuss it openly. Johnson's first sexual relationship was with a slave named Julia Chinn. He described her as his common law wife and admitted that he was the father of her two daughters. When Julia Chinn died in 1833, Johnson started a new relationship with another female slave, but she left him for another man. Johnson sent his men to capture her, sold her at auction, and took up with her sister.

> **In political circles, there was much talk about Johnson's history of sex with his slaves, and even more talk about his unwillingness to keep quiet about it.** As a result, when Van Buren ran for reelection in 1840, **the Democratic party refused to endorse Johnson as Van Buren's running mate**. Nevertheless, Van Buren stuck with him.
>
> After Van Buren was defeated in his bid for reelection, Johnson went back to Kentucky where, in 1850, he was again elected to the Kentucky House of Representatives.
>
> Johnson saw to it that both of Chinn's daughters were provided with an education and arranged for them both to marry white men. Nevertheless, when Johnson died, the local judge ruled that he left no legal children and divided Johnson's considerable holdings between his brothers.

The Whigs, knowing they would have little chance against Jackson's Democrats, came up with a unique strategy: they nominated several candidates. The hope was to **take advantage of a "localism" bias in the Electoral College** so that the various Whig candidates could collect enough electoral votes from their home districts to keep Van Buren from getting the 148 electoral votes he would need to win. That would throw the election into the House of Representatives. They nominated **William Harrison**, the popular former U.S. Senator from Ohio, **Daniel Webster**, a U.S. Senator from Massachusetts, **Willie Person Mangum**, a U.S. Senator from North Carolina, and **Hugh L. White**, a U.S. Senator from Tennessee.

The Whig plan almost worked. Van Buren won the election, but he only got 170 electoral votes, just two votes more than the required number. Harrison came within a few thousand votes of winning Pennsylvania, which would have given him the state's 30 electoral votes. That would have once again sent the decision about who would be president to the House of Representatives

The Presidential Election of 1840

In 1940, **President Van Buren** ran for reelection. However, **the economy had been hurt by the panic of 1837,** and the people blamed it on **the restrictive economic policies of the Jacksonian Democrats.** As is common today, when the economy turns bad, the people vote against whatever political party is in power.

> **STORY**
>
> **President Van Buren** ran for reelection along with his controversial vice president, **Richard Mentor Johnson.** But his party **refused to go along with the nomination of Johnson for fear that his sexual exploits with his slaves would be used against both of them in the general election.** However, they couldn't agree on an alternative, and so **they nominated no one, something that had never happened before.**

The Whigs put up **William H. Harrison** from Ohio. He chose **John Tyler**, a senator from Virginia to be his vice president. The nomination of Harrison brought the candidate's age into the discussion. He was 67 at the time he was nominated, which made him the oldest major party candidate nominated up to then. Some questioned his ability to preside over the country at what was then seen as an advanced age. Harrison was seen as a military hero for his role in victories against the Indians in the Northwest Indian War, and in the United States, military heroes have often been popular presidential candidates. Harrison's campaign mainly focused on the economic policies of the Democrats, and that worked. He was able to defeat Van Buren, overwhelming him in the Electoral College, 234 to 60. However, Harrison died from pneumonia after only 32 days in office, and **Vice President Tyler** served out the rest of his term.

When **Harrison died after only 32 days in office**, there was no precedent about what to do. The question was, if a president dies in office, should a vice president take over for a short time until a new president could be elected, or should he serve out the rest of the president's term? And if it is decided that the vice president gets to serve out the remainder of the presidential term, **should he have all the power of a president, or only be seen as an "acting president."**

Tyler and the Whigs were determined to hold onto the presidency. **Tyler refused to sign any document that referred to him as an "acting president."** However, he was eventually convinced to go through the formal process of being sworn in as president. Tyler moved into the White House and assumed full presidential powers. To make sure, the Whigs got both houses of Congress to adopt a resolution confirming that Tyler truly was the President of the United States. (That resolution served as the official mechanism for a vice president assuming the office after a president's death, until **the issue was clarified by the 25th Amendment in 1967.**)

Tyler's time in the office of the presidency was not without controversy. Although he had been elected as a Whig, Tyler disagreed with many of their positions, especially their position against the expansion of slavery. **He was thrown out of the Whig Party while he was still serving as president.**

The Presidential Election of 1844

The election of 1844 began with the odd circumstance that President Tyler was no longer a member of the party under which he had been elected. Instead of supporting Tyler the Whigs chose Henry Clay, a former Congressmen and senator from Kentucky.

Former president, Martin Van Buren, wanted to make another run for the office, but at the Democratic National Convention, he was rejected by the Southern Democrats because he would not pledge to annex Texas and thereby expand slavery into the West. Instead, they again chose a Southerner, James K. Polk, a former Congressman and Governor from Kentucky. As a result, the issue of slavery soon became the predominate campaign issue.

> **STORY**
>
> In the early 1800s, the Mexican government was having a hard time enforcing their laws in the area we know as Texas. They had an especially hard time enforcing their strict laws against slavery. As a result, they tried imposing stricter control over Texas, including military occupation. But that only encouraged rebellion. In 1835, the Mexican Army rode into Texas in an attempt to quash any attempts at self-government. On March 2, 1836, the Texans responded by declaring their independence from Mexico. The Texans, under Texas General Sam Houston, soon drove the Mexican army out of Texas. Of course, the Mexican government still refused to recognize its independence from Mexico.
>
> In 1844, President Tyler, hoping to make a run for reelection as an independent, declared himself to be the pro-slavery candidate. He pressed the issue by signing a treaty with Texas, and he submitted a proposal for the annexation of Texas. His plan was to ally with Southern Democrats who would present the North with an ultimatum: support Texas annexation and allow slavery there or risk the chance that the entire South might leave the Union. When the people of the United States found out the Senate was considering such a bill, they saw it as yet another attempt to spread the institution of slavery to the West. Public support of the bill threatened to become a liability to both of the other candidates, so they opposed it. However, both Polk and Clay were from Southern slave-holding families, so behind the scenes, they too were in favor of the annexation of Texas as a slave state. Once Tyler had assurances of their support for the bill, he dropped out of the race.

In a fairly close election, Polk won over Clay, and that ensured **statehood for Texas and the spread of slavery into the Western territories.**

Mexico still refused to accept the loss of Texas, and that led **the Mexican-American War.**

> **STORY**
>
> **Unlike the War of 1812, the American people *were not* solidly behind the Mexican-American War.** Democratic president Polk encouraged **the annexation of Texas** as part of his plan to expand the United States all the way to the Pacific Ocean even though such a plan was almost sure to result in a war with Mexico. Anti-slavery groups, hoping to stop the spread of slavery into the West, were totally against the annexation of Texas.
>
> **One of the main reasons the Texans had declared their independence from Mexico was that the Mexican government had tried to enforce its government policy forbidding the practice of slavery.** As soon as the declaration of Texan independence was official, **many of the larger Texas landholders began bringing in slaves from the American Sout**h to use in their farming and ranching enterprises. By **1845, slavery was a well-established practice in Texas**.
>
> At that time, most of the territories petitioning for statehood were in the North. The Southern states feared there would soon be enough non-slave states to outvote them in Congress, and that could well mean the end of slavery in the United States.
>
> **Mexico had warned President Polk that if Texas was granted statehood, it would definitely lead to war.** President Polk sent representatives to Mexico City to try to forestall hostilities, even offering Mexico huge amounts of money as compensation. But Mexico would not negotiate. They felt reclaiming what they saw as the theft of a piece of their country was a matter of national honor.
>
> After the failure of negotiations, **President Polk sent troops to establish a fort on the banks of the Rio Grande River. In response, Mexico sent 2,000 cavalry troops to the area.** Ac-

cidentally, they ran into a small U.S. Army patrol, and they killed 16 U.S. soldiers.

In response, President Polk declared, "Mexico has passed the boundary of the United States, has invaded our territory and shed American blood upon American soil." **He demanded Congress grant a declaration of war against Mexico**. After a short, but bitter, debate, they did so, with the unanimous support of the Southern slave states.

Americans were divided over the war. Many in the North felt it was a war designed to spread slavery to the West. But others, knowing that Mexico also controlled California, thought **it might be a chance to grab California as well. There was much talk about "manifest destiny," the belief that the United States should extend from "sea to shining sea."**

The Whigs, including Abraham Lincoln, lobbied against the war. Nevertheless, preparations for battle went on unabated. President Polk soon sent troops into Mexico under the command of **General Zachary Taylor**, and **ordered naval forces to the Mexican coast in support**.

As General Taylor drove deeper into Mexico, Mexican General Santa Ana brought troops north from Mexico City to meet him. After extended fighting, Santa Ana was forced to retreat.

President Polk also sent a second army under General Winfield Scott to invade Mexico by sea. Santa Ana's army rallied to meet that advance, but was again routed.

Scott pushed on deeper into Mexico and soon captured Mexico City. Faced with the possibility of losing even more territory, **Mexico had no choice but to surrender**. Mexico signed **the Treaty of Guadalupe Hidalgo**, agreeing to the Texas boundaries specified by the United States.

At the same time, **U.S. forces invaded California, and within a year, they controlled California from San Diego to San Francisco**. On January 13, 1847, the **Treaty of Cahuenga,** signifying the surrender of California, was signed near what is now Los Angeles. Despite the relatively easy victory over Mexico, the people of the United States were still divided over the war and over the issue of slavery being expanded into the new Western territories. It is worth noting here that **President Ulysses S. Grant, who fought in Mexico under General Taylor, said in his later memoirs that the Civil War was largely the outgrowth of the Mexican-American war.**

The Presidential Election of 1848

In 1848, the nation was becoming more and more divided over the issue of slavery, which led to the creation of a new political party, the **Free Soil Party** which put up anti-slavery candidates at both the local and national level.

STORY
The Free Soil Party focused on one issue, slavery. After the annexation of Texas had spread slavery to the American West, there was a general assumption that even more states would eventually join the union in the West. The Free Soil Party was determined to keep them from being slave states. In 1848, the Free Soil party nominated former president, Martin Van Buren, to be their presidential candidate. He ran under the motto, "Free Soil, Free Speech, Free Labor, and Free Men." **They maintained that slavery was not only fundamentally undemocratic, it was holding the nation back.** At the New York State Democratic convention, a large number of the delegates walked out and joined the Free Soil party because the Democratic party wouldn't take an anti-slavery position.

After President Polk decided against running for reelection due to health problems, the Democrats nominated **Lewis Cass**, the former Governor of the Michigan Territory who had been President

Jackson's Secretary of War. (In that position, he had implemented the Indian Removal Act of 1830.) **He said he believed it should be up to the people of a territory to decide whether or not they would permit slavery.** That satisfied the Southern Democrats.

Zachary Taylor, a Virginia slave owner, was nominated by the Whig Party. Taylor's position on the issue of slavery was unclear, but he was seen as a war hero, having defeated the Mexican Army in the Mexican-American War, and the voters of the United States had long favored military heroes.

Taylor defeated **Lewis Cass** in yet another close election, with each candidate carrying 15 states. **If Cass had been able to carry New York, the Electoral College vote would have ended in a tie and the decision about who was to be president would have again been sent to the House of Representatives.**

The Presidential Election of 1852

At the 1852 Democratic presidential nominating convention, there was **constant arguing about how to deal with the issue of slavery**. When they finally did get around to the nominations, there were four strong candidates, and therefore the voting got nowhere. Finally, **Franklin Pierce**, who was not one of the four main candidates, was put up as a compromise candidate, and he was eventually selected as the Democratic party's nominee. Pierce was from the small state of New Hampshire, a non-slave state. However, he was known to favor allowing slavery to be practiced in the new western states. His main attribute, as far as the Democrats were concerned, was that **he had fought in the Mexican-American War** and had been so valued as a leader of men that he had risen to the rank of brigadier general of volunteers.

The Whigs nominating convention also had to deal with disagreement over the slavery issue. In the end, the party leaders decided to support the **Compromise of 1850,** which was a compromise that forced Texas to surrendered its claim to New Mexico, and allowed California to come in as a free state. However, the South added language to the compromise that **allowed new states**

to decide for themselves **whether to allow slavery** or not. That threatened to overturn the prior **Missouri Compromise** of 1821 which made slavery illegal north of the **Compromise Line** (any territory north of latitude 36° 30' North, which marked the northern border of Missouri). The South was also able to insert a **Fugitive Slave Act** into the compromise, which made it illegal for slaves to run away to the north and specified that if they did, the North had to return them to their rightful owners.

After much contention, the Whigs finally nominated **Winfield Scott, another Virginian from a slave-holding family**. He had made his name as a general in the Mexican-American war. Although his family still owned many slaves, he made it known that **he was against expanding slavery into the West.**

The issue of slavery was to play a big role in the presidential election of 1852. People were not sure of the Whig position on slavery. Scott was a slave owner, but he said he was against expanding slavery into the new Western states.

Because Scott's stated position on slavery was not in line with the wishes of the Southern states, he did not get the solid support from Southern voters he expected, and as a result, **Pierce, a relative unknown, won the election.**

STORY

Most people thought **General Winfield Scott** would be elected president simply because he was **a military hero** in the Mexican-American War and in the Indian Wars.

However, the Mexican-American War was not fully supported by most Americans because of the slavery issue in Texas. And there were rumors that his **"victories" over the Indians** included almost-unbelievable **cruelty to non-combatant Native Americans**.

Although **most Americans supported the idea of moving the Indians off their land and onto reservations**, the citizens of the East did not support excessive cruelty while doing it. News about the terrible treatment of the Indians leaked out, diminishing Scott's reputation as a military hero.

However, in Scott's defense, it should be pointed out that he was just carrying out policies that had been around for a long time. **A policy of "civilizing" American Indians had been in place since the presidency of George Washington.** Under that policy, **Indian agents were assigned to make the Indians give up their nomadic hunting and gathering ways and settle down to farming**. They Indian tribes were also encouraged to break up the communal lands and assign property ownership to individual Indian families. The problem was, as soon as that was done, the land could be sold by those families, and through various means (some legal and some not so legal), **much of what had been Indian lands ended up in the hands of white settlers**. Many Indian tribes, including the Cherokee, Chickasaw, Choctaw, Creek, and Seminole, resisted resettlement, so Congress passed the **Indian Removal Act**. President Jackson signed it into law at the beginning of the summer of 1830. The act deemed that the tribes would have to resettle in unclaimed land far to the west, into what is now Oklahoma, The area was deemed to be "Indian lands," and by law, the Indian lands were considered sovereign. That meant they were not under the control of the United States, and therefore could only be acquired by the United States through treaties. However, pursuant to the Indian Removal Act, **the Indians were put into a position of either signing treaties that would give them *some* payment for their lands and the right to settle in new land in the West, or face the prospect of being forcibly removed and getting nothing**. Many signed, but many others refused to leave their ancestral lands. Some used the services of sympathetic lawyers to try to fight the act, but they had little success. **A key 1823 Supreme Court decision stated that Indians** could only *occupy* land within the United States. That meant they could not legally hold title to those lands.

In 1838, General Scott was sent to forcibly move the Indians off their lands and into holding camps. General Scott wanted to use regular troops to do the job, hoping they would treat the Indians more humanely than the locals. But none were available, so he had to use the local militia. **Almost all of the 7,000 militiamen that participated were local citizens who were glad to get rid of the Indians so they could take over their lands.**

By the time it was over, the newspapers were proudly reporting that Scott's troops had **captured or killed every Indian in Alabama, Georgia, North Carolina, and Tennessee**. Those that were captured were sent to concentration camps near the U.S. Indian Agency near Cleveland, Tennessee. Eventually, they were sent farther West. In the dead of winter of 1838, most of the remaining Native Americans, including almost all of the 15,000 Indians that were part of the Cherokee nation, were **forced to walk one thousand miles to new reservations in the West**. Most had little warm clothing and some were barefoot. Many had contracted smallpox while being held in the concentration camps, and as a result, untold thousands died on the trail. It became known as the **Trail of Tears**.

The Presidential Election of 1856

By the time the election of 1856 came around, the Whig Party had been torn apart by the issue of slavery. A new party, **the Republican Party**, emerged specifically to fight slavery. The **Kansas Nebraska Act** of 1854 had created the new territories of Kansas and Nebraska, but the South had again used its unfair voting advantage in Congress to force language to be inserted into the law to allow the new states to determine for themselves whether or not to allow slavery. President Pierce's handling of the contention over slavery in Kansas proved to be his undoing. His party, sensing defeat at the polls, refused to grant his request to be nominated for a second term. Instead, they nominated **John C. Fremont**, a Mexican-American war hero from the new state of California.

In opposition to **John C. Fremont**, the Whig's candidate in the 1856 election, the Democrats nominated Senator **James Buchanan** from Pennsylvania. Buchanan won the election, however, the relatively unknown Fremont managed to carry 33% of the popular vote, which is remarkable given that he got **no votes at all in the South**.

STORY

The **Kansas Nebraska Act** created immediate **contention**, especially in Kansas. Slave holders in Missouri flooded into Kansas and created a territorial legislature in a town near the Missouri border. **One of their first acts was to pass a law making Kansas a slave state.** In response, a "**free soil**" group set up an opposing legislature in Topeka, Kansas. They declared the slave holder's legislation invalid. The "free soil" advocates opposed what they called "**slave power**," which was the idea that the small-population Southern slave states had so much power in Congress and in electing the president, they could make any new state a slave state.

An armed group of pro-slavery men attacked the free-state town of Lawrence, Kansas to destroy the offices of the anti-slavery newspaper. They burned several buildings and stole everything they could get their hands on.

Senator Charles Sumner of Massachusetts denounced the attacks in Kansas, and in response, **Preston Smith Brooks**, a congressman from South Carolina came into the Senate chambers and attacked Sumner with a cane. Some senators tried to stop the attack, but Southern representatives pulled out pistols to hold them back. **Sumner was beaten so badly he was bedridden for years and was unable to return to the Senate.**

Soon, **John Brown, a well-known anti-slavery advocate**, went to Kansas to enter the fray. One of his first acts was to lead an attack on a pro-slavery settlement at Pottawatomie Creek where he and his supporters killed five men.

As the tensions escalated, **Congress passed a resolution declaring the pro-slavery legislature illegal in Kansas** and the resolutions they had passed as improperly done. But **President Pierce ignored the congressional resolution and continued to recognize pro-slavery legislatures**. He then sent in federal troops to end any anti-slavery legislatures. Emboldened by the support of the president, **Missouri pro-slavery men formed an army and marched into Kansas**. In what was to become known as the time of **Bleeding Kansas**, battles between the pro-slavery forces and the anti-slavery forces continued for years, foreshadowing the Civil War that was to come.

Chapter Seven
A Country Divided Against Itself

The Presidential Election of 1860

The presidential election of 1860 **led to the Civil War**. While almost all other nations had already outlawed slavery, the South knew that if they allowed a majority of even one free state to exist in Congress, that would make it likely that slavery would be outlawed. For that reason, **the South had tried to maintain enough of a voting advantage in Congress** to block new free states from joining the Union. The control the slave states held over both Congress and the Electoral College went all the way back to the founding of the nation. They had refused to join the Union unless they got enough voting power to control future elections. Eight of the original thirteen states, Delaware, New Jersey, Georgia, New York, Maryland, South Carolina, Virginia, and North Carolina had slaves. However, as the nation grew in the mid-1800s, more free states joined the Union.

By 1848, there were fifteen slave states, and fifteen free states. But then, as a result of the Mexican-American War, in 1850, **California was brought in as a free state, and that upset the balance**. Soon, other western states petitioned to join the Union, and the Kansas Nebraska Act of 1854 made it possible that these new states might become slave states. The Republican Party was formed to fight against that possibility. In 1856, to make their point, the Republicans had nominated **John C. Fremont** for president simply because he was from the new free state of California. After two more western states, **Minnesota and Oregon, joined the Union** in 1858 and 1859, they chose not to become slave states, and that meant the handwriting was on the wall. The slave states had lost their voting advantage in both the Senate and in the Electoral College, and it was clear that sooner or later, the non-slave states would elect a president that would abolish slavery.

That was the situation leading into the presidential election of 1860. and **it was clear that slavery would be the main issue in the election.** New political movements were springing up as special-interest groups fought to gain control over both local and national political interests.

The Democrats held their 1860 presidential nominating convention in Charleston, South Carolina, and that resulted in a lot of agitation from the local pro-slavery groups.

Senator Stephen A. Douglas was from the free state of Illinois, but he had been a key proponent of the Kansas Nebraska Act. Many in the Democratic party thought he would make a good compromise candidate for president. Also, Douglas had made a name for himself as a capable orator in his campaign against **Abraham Lincoln** for an Illinois Senate seat. In that election, Lincoln had narrowly won the popular vote, but the state legislature chose Douglas.

Nevertheless, the Democratic Party was deeply divided. The **Supreme Court's Dred Scott decision** of 1857 had shocked the nation by declaring that once a person had been a slave, they could never be a citizen of the United States, even if they had been legally freed.

STORY

The Supreme Court's Dred Scott decision of 1857 caused an uproar throughout the North.

The court had been asked to decide if Dred Scott, a slave who had been taken by his master to the free state of Illinois, was then free due to his having lived there for an extended period of time. Scott had been legally married while in Illinois, even though in the South, slaves were not supposed to have any legal rights, not even the right to marry.

> The court, in a seven to two decision, shocked the anti-slave forces by stating that slaves were not legal citizens of the United States and therefore had no legal right to appeal to the court. The majority members of the Supreme Court went on to state that **slaves were private property even if they were taken to a free state**. They said a slave could not be taken away from his or her owner.
>
> **The court's decision triggered the economic panic of 1857** because investors and businesses got worried about the implications of the decision.

The Democratic party leaders knew that the nation's voters would be paying as much attention to the party's stance on slavery as to what candidate they nominated.

But many Southern hard-liners insisted that the Democratic party should openly take a pro-slavery stance and try to elect a president that would **fight for legislation to make slavery legal in *all* states**. But **now that the South had lost their advantage in the Electoral College, the party leaders knew that would all but guarantee a loss in the upcoming election**.

By the time balloting began, six major candidates had been put forward for the Democratic nomination. In the first ballot, Douglas led, but not by enough to be the nominee. There were just too many staunch pro-slavery delegates against him. The balloting went on and on with much pro-slavery agitation, until finally, after 57 ballots, the delegates voted to adjourn the convention and meet again later in a Northern city. When the Democrats met again in Baltimore, two months later, there was contention about whether the troublesome pro-slavery delegates from the South should be even be admitted. In the heated debate that resulted, all of the Southern delegates walked out, thus assuring Douglas's nomination. **Senator Benjamin Fitzpatrick** of Alabama was nominated for vice president. But he refused to run with Douglas. He was replaced by former **Senator Herschel V. Johnson**.

The Southern delegates who had walked out held their own convention. They nominated **John C. Breckinridge** from Kentucky and North Carolina's **Joseph Lane** as his running mate.

The 1860 the Republican presidential nominating convention was held in Chicago a month after the debacle of the multiple Democrat conventions. The favorite candidate going into the Republican convention was former **New York Governor William H. Seward**, and he led after the first two ballots. But when he failed to rally any more delegates to his side, **a local Illinois dark horse, Abraham Lincoln, was put forward.** Lincoln had gained some national notoriety as a calm and effective orator in his series of debates with **Stephen Douglas** during their race for an Illinois Senate seat. With some aggressive tactics on the convention floor by Lincoln supporters, and some clever back-room bargaining, Lincoln was able to squeak out the nomination.

Of special note was the Republican Party's written platform: it stated that **slavery would not be allowed to spread any further**.

In the 1860 election, the voters were presented with ballots that included not only the Republican and the Democratic candidates, but also the alternate Southern pro-slavery candidates. The result was that the Southern votes were split, **leading to a relatively easy victory for Lincoln**.

As a result of Lincoln's election, **seven Southern slave states, South Carolina, Mississippi, Florida, Alabama, Georgia, Louisiana, and Texas, quickly seceded from the union, and hostilities commenced. Their forces attacked Fort Sumter in South Carolina, and four additional slave states, Virginia, Arkansas, North Carolina, and Tennessee then seceded from the union. Thus, the Confederacy was formed and the Civil War began**.

COMMENT
Discussion of the **American Civil War** is beyond the scope of a book about how U.S. presidents are elected. Thousands of other books have discussed the Civil War, and its causes and

consequences have been covered in great detail. But I should point out that it was the biased Electoral College system that gave the Southern state **extra votes in the U.S. Senate**, plus the extra votes the South got in the House of Representatives **by counting millions of slaves as part of their population**, that kept the South in the Union as long as they were. **The South's extra voting power in the Electoral College resulted in ten of the first twelve presidents being Southern slave holders, and each of those presidents made sure slavery continued to be the law of the land.**

Even after a few Northerners were elected president, the South was able to use their voting power to keep a balance between slave states and free states.

As a result, **the U. S. became the last major country in the world to abolish slavery**.

President Lincoln took a hands-on approach to managing the war. He personally supervised the North's war strategy and selected the generals to fight it.

Whenever he was disappointed with the performance of a general, he replaced him. Eventually, he settled on the very aggressive General **Ulysses S. Grant,** a military leader who had been having great success in the West.

Lincoln knew he was going to have to try to hold the nation together throughout a war that was pitting friends and family against each other, but **he was determined to end slavery**. He used his position as commander-in-chief, along with the war powers granted to him, to announce an **Emancipation Proclamation** which declared slaves to be free. He appointed five judges to the Supreme Court that were well known for their anti-slavery positions. But he did not want the nation to be forever divided, so he also worked on plans for the reconstruction of the South.

The Presidential Election of 1864

Despite the terrible loss of human life in the ongoing war, Lincoln was again nominated by the Republicans for reelection in 1864. He was unhappy with his vice president, **Hannibal Hamlin**, so he replaced him with **Andrew Johnson,** a man that might be more acceptable to Southerners. (It was a decision that was to have a profound effect on the nation later in the post-war period.)

The Democrats put up General **George B. McClellan**, a general Lincoln had demoted early in the war. McClellan won only a few states, and **with no Southern vote, Lincoln won easily**.

STORY

In the days after Lincoln's reelection, the war dragged on into yet another spring.

However, Lincoln was sure the war would soon be over. The Confederate Army was exhausted and in retreat, but the Southern leadership was still not ready to give in.

The Union Army marched deeper into the Southern states, freeing millions of slaves as they went.

At Lincoln's request, some of the slaves were recruited into the Union Army, forming special regiments. Extended Union Army forays into the South, such as Sherman's infamous **March to the Sea,** destroyed much of the South's ability to continue the war. Lee understood that continuing to fight would only result in more pointless bloodshed, so he finally **surrendered his army to General Grant at Appomattox**, Virginia on April 9, 1865.

As the nation celebrated the end of a long and terrible war, the news came that Lincoln had been assassinated. The assassin was **John Wilkes Booth,** a well-known stage actor.

It was later learned that Booth was a spy being supported by the Confederate secret service and by Canadian anti-union forces.

Lincoln's vice president, **Andrew Johnson**, was sworn in as president the next morning, and for the next four years, he oversaw the rebuilding of the nation.

However, he was a Southerner, and he repeatedly vetoed Congressional bills that were designed to punish the South or to give more rights to the freed slaves.

His actions during the post-war period, known as "reconstruction," enabled Confederate leaders to regain power, and they used it to suppress the rights of the former slaves.

When Congress passed the bill to create the Fourteenth Amendment which provided civil rights to all U.S. citizens, including freed slaves, Johnson vetoed it.

Congress quickly overrode Johnson's veto, and the House began formal impeachment charges against him.

He was charged with committing high crimes and misdemeanors.

The resolution to impeach him passed in the House, 122 to 4. Thus, Andrew Johnson became **the first U.S. president to be impeached**.

However, in the Senate, after a lengthy trial, the vote to remove him from office was 35–19.

The constitutional threshold for removing a president from office requires a two-thirds majority in the Senate, which meant **the vote to remove him from the presidency was one vote short**.

Chapter Eight
Democrats Versus Republicans

The Presidential Election of 1868

The presidential election of 1868 took place during the postwar reconstruction period. Johnson ran for reelection, but his Republican Party didn't want him because they saw him as being too soft on the South. Instead, they nominated Civil War hero, **General Ulysses S. Grant,** and they nominated Indiana Congressman, **Schuyler Colfax**, to be his running mate.

President Johnson sought support from the Democrats, but they didn't want him either. Instead, they nominated **Horatio Seymour**, the former governor of New York. **Francis Blair**, a Congressman from Missouri who had also served as a general in the war, was named as his running mate.

STORY

After the war, Congress passed several Reconstruction Amendments, and none of the breakaway Southern states were allowed to participate in the presidential election until they ratified the Fourteenth Amendment. By the time the election took place, Mississippi, Texas, and Virginia had not done so, and they were left out of the election process.

Another aspect of the new reconstruction laws was that the vote of the Electoral College should be "based on" the vote of the people. Most states put in place some kind of system to do that. In Florida, the state legislature still cast the electoral votes.

Grant wanted citizenship and full civil right for the freed slaves, but the Democrats held fast to the "states rights" position.

Grant easily won both the general election and the Electoral College vote. However Seymour surprised everyone by **winning his home state of New York.** An accusation of voter fraud in New York was put forth and a Congressional investigation was initiated, but in the end, no action was taken. It was said **if all of the Southern states had been allowed to vote, the outcome of the election might have been quite different**.

The Presidential Election of 1872

In 1872, the Republicans nominated President Ulysses S. Grant for re-election. However, because Colfax had been implicated in a scandal, they were no longer willing to accept him as the vice president. Instead, they nominated Senator **Henry Wilson** of Massachusetts.

STORY

During the presidential election of 1872, a group of Republicans split off from the main party and formed the **Liberal Republican Party**. They nominated New York publisher **Horace Greeley** as their presidential candidate and Missouri Governor **Benjamin Brown** as vice president.

Another Republican-leaning group formed the **Labor Reform Party**, and they nominated **David Davis**, a Supreme Court Justice from Illinois who had been placed on the court by President Lincoln.

However, he refused the honor, so they turned to **Charles O'Conor**, a well-known New York lawyer. He also refused, but the Labor Reform Party decided to go ahead and put his name on the ballot anyway. It was a mistake that was to spell the end of the Labor Reform Party.

> The Democrats wanted to defeat Grant and try to overcome some of the sanctions that had been put in place against the South. Surprisingly, **they nominated the same two men the Liberal Republicans had nominated**, Horace Greeley and Benjamin Brown.

Despite reported scandals during his tenure, Grant easily won reelection, but **five other men also received votes in the Electoral College.** Horace Greeley, came in second in the popular vote, but died before the Electoral College met. Three electors voted for him anyhow.

The Southern states all voted against the Republicans because it was "the party of Lincoln."

> **STORY**
> In the election of 1872, there were accusations off widespread voter fraud designed to keep African-American voters away from the polling places. The votes from five Southern states were questioned, and **the electoral votes of Arkansas and Louisiana were rejected due to clear evidence of voter fraud and intimidation of African-American voters.**

The Presidential Election of 1876

The election of 1876 was one of the most controversial in the history of the United States.

For president, the Republicans nominated **Rutherford B. Hayes**, the former governor of Ohio. He chose as his vice president, **William Wheeler**, a U.S. Congressman from New York. Hayes was a compromise, selected after many ballots.

The Democrats nominated Governor **Samuel J. Tilden** of New York, with **Thomas A. Hendricks**, governor of Indiana, to be his running mate. Tilden had gained national recognition for sending

New York's corrupt **Boss Tweed** to prison.

STORY

Politics during the eighteenth century was a rough and tumble business. Although some may say politics in our current era is mostly run by the rich, it was clearly so in New York in the mid 1800s. William Tweed, known as "**Boss Tweed**," was one of the largest landowners in the state of New York, and he was a director of railroads and banks. He was elected to Congress in 1852, and later served in the New York state Senate.

After that, **he got himself appointed to various city positions in which he could dispense political favors -- for a price**. By controlling New York City boards and commissions, he was able to gain great influence over local politics, and even more influence over how public money was spent. Over time, he was able to create a political machine that controlled much of New York's politics. **He became known as the "Grand Sachem" of Tammany Hall.**

The end of his "reign" came when **Governor Tilden worked with local prosecutors to convict him of stealing millions of dollars of public money** through various schemes. The prosecution said he paid "workers" huge payments for mostly nonexistent city building projects just to get kickbacks. They gave examples such as the **plasterer who had been paid over a hundred thousand dollars for a day's work and a carpenter who had been paid over three hundred thousand dollars for supposedly doing woodwork carpentry in a building that turned out not to have any woodwork in it** (at that time, the average urban worker made about $300 per year).

Tweed was imprisoned, and a million dollar bail was set. He had no trouble raising that much money and was therefore released. **Unbelievably, while all this was going on, Tweed was re-elected to the state senate.**

> However, he was soon arrested again, and this time the bail was raised to eight million dollars, an astounding amount of money in that era. Again, he had no trouble raising it.
>
> But it was clear his empire was falling apart. His associates were also being arrested, and some of them were being convicted despite Tweed's attempts to subvert the legal process.
>
> Tweed was finally convicted of corruption and graft and given a prison sentence of twelve years. But when **the local jailers allowed him out for a "home visit," he escaped and fled to Spain.** He was eventually caught there and put on an American warship to be brought back to the United States.
>
> Now apparently out of money and desperate to get out of prison, he said he would tell prosecutors all about how his corruption system worked if they would release him. The agreement that was reached resulted in the prosecution of many members of Tweed's inner ring.
>
> After confessing, Tweed was ready to get out of prison, so he could to try to reestablish his empire. **But Governor Tilden refused to let him go, and Tweed was held in a local New York City jail until his death in 1878.**

Everyone knew the election of 1876 was going to be close. The Democrats were resurgent, especially in the South, and with the retirement of President Grant, they felt they had a good chance to take the presidency back from the Republicans. The Democrats tried to paint the Republicans as involved in graft and political manipulation, and contrasted them with Tilden who had a reputation as a reformer.

The Republicans main approach to the campaign was to remind the people that it was the Democrats that had caused the Civil War through their support of slavery. The Democrats referred to the Republican tactic of associating them with the Civil War as "**waving the bloody shirt**." They pointed out that not every Democrat had been a rebel, and they reminded the voters that both Tilden and his running mate, Hendricks, were Northerners. They called for "a return to normalcy, which would mean **an end to the repressive rules of reconstruction**.

During the election, Southern paramilitary groups such as the **Red Shirts** and the **White League** disrupted Republican rallies. They **used violence and intimidation to try to stop Republicans, and especially blacks, from voting**. When the results of the popular vote were in, Tilden, the choice of the Southern states, had apparently won by 252,666 votes, the closest national vote in US history. However, there were cries of fraud with regard to the counting of votes in the South. The Republicans claimed their voters in Florida had either not been allowed to vote or had been tricked into voting for the wrong candidate by deceptively designed ballots. They cited **numerous instances of voter intimidation and fraud in Florida**, pointing out that documents certifying the election there had been signed by the state attorney-general, a Democratic, and by the Florida governor, also a Democrat.

Reports of voter intimidation and ballot fraud were also raised in Louisiana, and South Carolina. One of the tricks used by the Democrats was to print a picture of Abraham Lincoln on the Democratic ballot to try to get the votes of illiterate voters.

When the ballots of the Electoral College voters were counted, it appeared that Hayes had won by one vote. But neither candidate had the requisite 185 electoral votes that were required for a majority. It appeared that once again the selection of the president would take place in the House of Representatives, and at that time, the House was controlled by the Republicans.

However, because of the many accusations of voter fraud in the South, Congress created **a special commission** to review the results of the 1876 election. All that did was lead to more **contention about who should be appointed to the special commission**. In the end, the Democrats, who controlled the Senate, were allowed to appoint five members, and the Republicans, who controlled the population-based House of Representatives, were also allowed to appoint five. Four Supreme Court justices were added to the commission, two with Republican leanings, and two with

Democratic leanings. Those four Supreme Court justices were allowed to select one more justice to serve on the commission, and they chose **Justice David Davis** who they saw as politically independent. Hoping to gain a deciding vote on the commission, the Democrats who controlled the Illinois senate immediately appointed Davis to fill their vacant U.S. Senate seat. The four justices then selected **Justice Joseph P. Bradley** who was supposed to be another impartial member of the court.

In January of 1877, the special Congressional commission met to examine the results of the Electoral College votes from Florida, Louisiana, Oregon, and South Carolina. If the commission hoped for easy answers, they were disappointed: those states each presented **two conflicting sets of Electoral College results**, one from the Republicans and one from the Democrats.

After much debate, the Congressional members of the commission voted right along party lines. That meant the vote was a tie. The decision was up to Justice Bradley. He voted with the Republicans, making the decision 8-7 in favor of giving the disputed Electoral College votes to Hayes. **That gave Hayes a 185-184 Electoral College victory**.

It is not clear under what authority Congress made their decision about the winner of the 1876 election. **According to the Constitution, the winner of the Electoral College vote is supposed to become the president**.

The South thought the election had been stolen from Tilden by the North, but the people of the North felt it was the right decision because they were sure that **large numbers of former slaves in the South had not been allowed to vote for Hayes**.

The Presidential Election of 1880

In 1880, the incumbent president Rutherford B. Hayes did not seek reelection. That left the race wide open. For the Republicans, Tilden, their candidate from the previous election, was seen as the favorite. But the Republican National Convention was very divided, with U.S. Senator **James G. Blaine** and Treasury Secretary

John Sherman, among others, vying for the nomination. A surprise candidate was **Ulysses S. Grant** who had decided to seek an unprecedented third term. In the first ballot, Grant almost won: he got the most votes, but didn't have a majority. Many other ballots followed, but neither Grant nor Blaine could get a majority. Finally, a compromise candidate, **James A. Garfield**, a U.S. Congressman from Ohio, was put forward, and he was able to get enough votes to win the nomination. **Chester A. Arthur**, a party regular from New York won the nomination for vice president.

When the Democrats held their national convention, Tilden was assumed to be the favorite. But he was not sure he was willing to undergo yet another grueling election campaign.

Among the many other candidates, **Major General Winfield Scott Hancock** from Pennsylvania and U.S. Senator from Delaware, **Thomas F. Bayard**, were seen as the favorites.

On the second ballot, Hancock was nominated with **William Hayden English**, from Indiana, as vice president.

STORY

As the presidential election of 1880 approached, the Democrats rallied around the concept that the election of 1876 had been stolen from them by the North. The Democrats in the House of Representatives spent much of their time trying to prove it. By the time the new election rolled around, they had no new evidence, but they were still convinced of it, and that turned out to be their main argument in favor of their presidential candidate.

As in the previous president election, new political parties sprang up. The **Greenback Party** favored safety regulations in factories, an eight-hour work day, and an end to child labor. They nominated **James B. Weaver**, a U.S. Congressman from Iowa who had been a general in the Civil War.

A new **Prohibition Party** entered the fray, with the avowed purpose of ending the sale of alcoholic beverages. They nominated **Neal Dow**, a Civil War general from Maine. With the North and the South still divided politically, the idea emerged, for the first time, that "**swing states**" (states that tended to swing back and forth on which party they supported) could determine the outcome of an election.

In the general election, the vote was extremely close. Republican **Garfield** got 4,453,337 votes to Democrat **Hancoc**k's 4,444,267 votes. **With a tiny national margin of only 9,070 votes, you would expect the Electoral College to end in a tie**, but because of the strange winner-take-all system which had by then been accepted by almost every state, Garfield won in the Electoral College, 214 to 155. He had won all the Northern states, and Hancock, the Democrat, had won all the Southern states. However, now that there were more Northern states in the Union, they had enough Electoral College votes to give Garfield the victory. Interestingly, if only a few thousand voters in a handful of Northern states had voted for Hancock, he would have won both the popular vote and the Electoral College vote.

STORY

During his first year in office, Garfield was assassinated by a mentally ill man who had failed to get a job in the Garfield administration. Vice president, **Chester A. Arthur** served out the remainder of his term. Despite the fact that he was a Republican Party regular who had grown rich off of patronage jobs given to him, **President Arthur soon became known as a reformer**. He signed **the Pendleton Act** into law and strongly enforced its provisions. The Pendleton Act created the United States Civil Service Commission and attempted to undo the spoils system in which government positions were given out based on political affiliation rather than on merit. Today, Arthur is one of the least known of all our past presidents.

The Presidential Election of 1884

As the 1884 presidential election season began, there were questions as to whether President Arthur would run for reelection. There was also speculation that Lincoln's son, **Robert Todd Lincoln**, would run. He had been serving as the U.S. Secretary of War. Another possible candidate was Civil War general **William Tecumseh Sherman**, but he soon made it clear that he was not interested. **Robert Todd Lincoln** also declined.

By the time the Republican National Convention started, **President Arthur also declined to run for reelection due to health problems** (he had been keeping his health problems secret for a long time). As a result, several prominent Republicans came forward to seek the nomination. The two leading figures were U.S. Congressman from Maine, **James G. Blaine** and Vermont Senator **George F. Edmunds**. After several ballots, Blaine was nominated, with Illinois Senator **John A. Logan** as vice president.

By the time the Democratic National Convention started, **New York Governor Grover Cleveland** was the front runner. As the balloting began, several other candidates names were put in, but it only took two ballots to nominate Cleveland. He selected **Thomas A. Hendricks**, from Indiana to be his vice president.

STORY

Alternative political parties were again involved in the presidential election. The **Greenback Party** nominated candidates, as did the **Prohibition Party**.

In addition, two new parties emerged, the **Anti-Monopoly Party** and the **Equal Rights Party**.

The Anti-Monopoly Party focused on one issue, being against the emergence of huge monopolistic corporations.

The Equal Rights Party was formed to bring voting rights to women in the United States. They held a national convention in San Francisco and nominated **Belva Ann Lockwood**, an attor-

> ney from Washington, D.C., for president. In the general election, even though women couldn't vote for her, it is estimated that she received over four thousand votes.

Cleveland won the general election by a very narrow 57,579-vote margin, and the Electoral College vote was also close, 219 to 182. He was to be the first Democratic president since before the Civil War. **He did it by winning the South**, and by winning Indiana, New Jersey, and most importantly, New York. **He won the popular vote in New York by only 1,149 votes**, thereby gaining all of New York's 36 electoral votes. Had those 1,149 votes gone the other way, **Blaine would have been elected the nation's 20th president in the Electoral College**.

The Presidential Election of 1888

The 1888 presidential election campaign began with the Democrats nominating President Cleveland for reelection. However, his vice president, Thomas A. Hendricks, had died in office, and a replacement had to be found. They chose former U.S. Senator **Allen G. Thurman** of Ohio.

The Republican national convention did not go as smoothly. The presumed nominee, **James G. Blaine**, a former U.S. Congressman and Secretary of State from Maine, withdrew in an attempt to promote harmony within the party. Nevertheless, it still took eight ballots to secure the nomination for Senator **Benjamin Harrison** of Indiana. In the end, part of the reason Harrison was nominated was because he was from Indiana which, at the time, was considered to be a key swing state.

Levi P. Morton, a former U.S. Congressman from New York was chosen to be his vice presidential nominee.

> **STORY**
> Once again, the **Prohibition Party**, the **Equal Rights Party**, and the **Greenback Party** also nominated candidates.
>
> Another new party, the **Industrial Reform Party** favored an increase in the money supply and women's right to vote.
>
> The **American Party** opposed immigrants and members of the Catholic faith, who they saw as possibly being more loyal to the Pope than to the United States.
>
> Two labor parties, the **Union Labor Party and the United Labor Party, also nominated candidates**.

Again in 1888, it was the strange workings of the Electoral College, not the will of the people, that determined who would be president. Democrat **Grover Cleveland won the popular vote, but Republican Benjamin Harrison got more Electoral College votes** and was therefore elected president.

> **STORY**
> In the 1888 popular vote, Cleveland got 5,538,163 votes to Harrison's 5,443,633—Cleveland had won the election by 94,530 votes. But Cleveland was not to be the next president because **Harrison won the Electoral College vote by squeaking out narrow popular vote margins in states with a lot of Electoral College votes**. He won Illinois with its 22 electoral votes, Michigan with its 13 electoral votes, and Missouri with its 16 electoral votes. He won the people's vote in each of those states, but by very slim margins. Nevertheless, all three of those states were winner-take-all states.
>
> Harrison's win in New York, with its 36 electoral votes, was the key to his victory in the Electoral College. He got only 14,373 more popular votes than Cleveland, out of 1,319,748 votes cast, but he got all of New York's electoral votes. There-

fore, **for the second presidential election in a row, a few voters in one state determined who would be president, and it *was not* the candidate who won the people's vote.**

Unlike the election of 1824 when there was national outrage over the fact that Andrew Jackson did not get to be president despite winning the popular vote, there was little public outrage this time. The reason the people of the North didn't complain about the election's outcome was because it was common knowledge that hundreds of thousands of former slaves had been kept away from the polling places in the South. It was reasoned that those voters would have voted for Harrison if they had been given the opportunity, and so he would have won the popular vote anyway. Nevertheless, **the outcome of the election made it clear that close elections would continue to reveal the flaws of the Electoral College system**.

The Presidential Election of 1892

By the time the election of 1892 rolled around, many in the Republican Party were unhappy with President Harrison.

At the 1892 Republican National Convention, there was a dump-Harrison movement. In fact, many believed Harrison didn't want to serve another term.

Even before the Republican convention got started, **James Blaine's name was being put forward**. Not wanting Blaine to win, Harrison actively sought reelection, and as a result, he was quickly nominated for another term.

Most expected the incumbent vice president, Levi Morton, would also be re-nominated, but Harrison wanted a different vice president because he suspected Morton had secretly been supporting Blaine. Harrison chose **Whitelaw Reid** of New York to be his vice president, mainly because he was a fellow graduate of Miami University in Ohio. Reid had formerly served as U.S. Ambassador to France, and at the time of his nomination, he was the editor of the New York Tribune.

The election results again demonstrated that **voters don't like it when the candidate they chose through popular election does not get to be president. They voted against the incumbent Benjamin Harrison and returned Grover Cleveland to the presidency**. He was the only person to be non-consecutively elected to a second term as president.

Although the South was still solidly in the Democratic camp, **six new Northern states, Idaho, North Dakota, South Dakota, Montana, Washington, and Wyoming voted for the first time** in a presidential election, and they mostly supported the Republicans. That made all the difference.

In the presidential election of 1892, new political parties put forward candidates. In addition to the Prohibition Party and the various labor parties, the **People's Party** was created. It was mainly made up of farmers, and they allied in purpose and in principle with the labor parties against the capitalists. Some of the populist parties actively included women.

STORY

After the Civil War, women were allowed to vote on some matters in the state of Wyoming, and soon thereafter, they were allowed to vote in the Utah and Washington territories. The men of Wyoming may have had more personal reasons for trying to draw more women to their state; at the time, there were about 6,000 men living in Wyoming and only about 1,000 women. However, **Women's suffrage** in the rest of the United States did not come as easily. There had been no serious movement in the United States to allow women to vote until 1848 when Gerrit Smith, a candidate for president, made the women's vote part of his Liberty Party's platform. The idea didn't get much traction, and by the mid 1850s, there was still no concerted effort on the part of the all-male political establishment to allow women to vote. However, women were starting to get some legal rights. In some states, a woman could file for divorce, and a few states passed laws that said working women didn't have to turn over their wages to their husbands.

Some states, especially southern and rural states, were unwilling to give women *any* legal rights. A famous legal case in North Carolina made the point. A woman had appealed to change the state law so a woman could file for divorce if she had been badly beaten by her husband. The state Supreme Court turned down her appeal in 1862, stating "The law gives the husband power to use such a degree of force necessary to make the wife behave and know her place."

After the Civil War, there was some talk of women's suffrage, but it took female activists like **Susan B. Anthony** to bring the issue to the public's attention. She and others like **Elizabeth Cady Stanton** organized women's rights gatherings and wrote books about the lack of women's legal rights in the U.S. Their books were intended for women, but some men also read them. Some men voiced approval, but others tried to ban the books, saying giving a women rights would be against the will of nature. And there was considerable resistance among women's groups. Many women felt the suffragettes shouldn't be trying to change traditional women's roles.

Movements were formed to fight against the very idea of women gaining *any* legal rights, let alone the right to vote. One prominent organization was the **National Organization Against Women's Suffrage,** and it counted many women as members. In 1869, Susan B. Anthony and Elizabeth Cady Stanton formed the **National Woman Suffrage Association (NWSA)** which lobbied for women's rights and an amendment to the Constitution giving women the right to vote.

In 1890, several women's rights organizations came together to form the **National American Woman Suffrage Association** which was headed by **Carrie Chapman Catt**.

After Wyoming gave women the right to vote, lobbying efforts by Susan B. Anthony and others encouraged some of the other Western states to follow suit, apparently in hopes of attracting more women to the still untamed and almost all male Western territories. Utah territory was one of the first places to allow women the vote, but it was not activist women who were behind the effort; it was activist men who were trying to stamp out the practice of polygamy. A group of men known as **Godbeites** left the Latter Day Saints (Mormon) church and took up the fight against the church-condoned practice of men having multiple wives. They hoped women, if given the right to vote, would be freed from the male dominance officially sanctioned by the Mormon Church and would vote to end polygamy. **The practice of men having multiple wives was part of the Mormon religion**, but the church's leader, Brigham Young, got behind the women's suffrage movement effort in hopes it would help change the image of Utah women as oppressed, and maybe even sidetrack anti-polygamy legislation that was working its way through Congress. With Brigham Young's support, there was no resistance to the idea, and in 1869, the territorial legislature passed an act giving women the vote (but not the right to run for office).

Paradoxically, the U.S. Congress overrode the new Utah act by passing the **Edmunds-Tucker Anti-polygamy Act**, which specifically banned voting by women in Utah.

The movement to stamp out polygamy in Utah was gaining momentum across the nation, and it was becoming a major issue in every presidential election. There was even a call to send U.S. Army troops to Utah to put a stop to the practice.

In 1890, the Mormon Church leaders declared that the church would no longer sanction the practice of polygamy. With that controversy out of the way, Utah was granted statehood in

1896 and **the right of Utah women to vote was written into the new state's constitution**.

In 1865, Republicans proposed the **Fourteenth Amendment** to the Constitution that would give the vote to the millions of **newly-freed black men, but not women**.

It was not until 1915 that Congress passed the **Nineteenth Amendment** to the Constitution which prohibited the states from denying the right to vote based on sex.

Even at that late date, with the country becoming more and more industrialized and all of the lower 48 states now part of the Union, only some Western states and a few Midwestern states had granted women the right to vote.

The Presidential Election of 1896

As the presidential election of 1896 began, the nation was still recovering from the panic of 1893, a nationwide economic depression that had started with a run on the U.S. gold reserves. Many banks closed and many businesses failed.

As a result, the election campaign mainly focused on economic issues. One contentious issue was about whether the United States should remain on **the gold standard**, and the Democratic Party was split over the issue.

After much contention, the Democrats nominated **William Jennings Bryan** who was against the gold standard and in favor of liberalizing the nation's banking standards.

Famous as an orator, Bryan used the Democratic National Convention as a forum to deliver a powerful speech that became known as the "Cross of Gold" speech. It accused big business of profiting on the backs of factory workers and farmers that had been hurt by the economic depression and the closing of banks. He called for an end to the gold standard and government relief efforts for the poor. After the conclusion of his speech, the delegates hoisted Bryan to their shoulders and carried him around the convention hall. Bryan won the nomination to become the youngest presidential nominee in American history; he was only one year older than the constitutional minimum of 35. To serve as his vice president he chose **Arthur Sewall**, a New England industrialist. The Republicans nominated **William McKinley** who had served in the U.S. House of Representatives from Ohio, and as that state's governor. The election of 1896 was also one of the first elections in which campaign money played an important role. **The Republican campaign outspent the Democratic campaign by sixteen to one**. With little money to mount an effective national advertising campaign, Bryan took to the railroads and went on a nationwide **whistle-stop campaign**. Up to that time, **it was seen as unseemly for presidential candidates to actively go out and campaign for themselves**, and the novelty of seeing a presidential candidate in person drew large crowds to Bryan's campaign stops. Outside of the large Eastern cities, few had ever had the chance to listen to the powerful oratory of a skillful speaker.

In the end, money won out, but the election was fairly close because the South again voted solidly for the Democrat, as did a few of the Western states. McKinley won by only about 600,000 votes out of almost 14 million votes cast.

STORY

The presidential election of 1896 is considered significant in that it signaled a change in American politics. New coalitions were becoming the key to winning elections. There was a new alignment of voters, with the voters in the cities responding to issues that were in marked contrast to the issues favored by voters in rural areas of the country.

As part of the new political alignments, new political parties appeared. The **Gold Democratic Party** was formed in response to Bryan's anti-gold speech. They saw themselves as the only legitimate heirs to Jeffersonian principles.

> The **Populist Party** agreed with Bryan's attack on big business and was mainly supported by farmers.
>
> Presidential candidates were again put forward by the **Prohibition Party**, but like the rest of the country, they were split over economic issues. A "broad-gauge" group called for woman suffrage and generous pensions for war veterans, arbitration of international disputes, and other measures. A "narrow-gauge" group limited their platform to calling for the prohibition of liquor.

The Presidential Election of 1900

The first presidential election of the new century in 1900 turned out to be a rematch of the 1896 election, McKinley versus Bryan. This time, William McKinley chose New York's governor, **Theodore Roosevelt**, as his running mate. Although Roosevelt didn't want to give up his powerful position as the governor of the nation's most populous state just to be vice president, he finally relented. It was a decision that was to have significant ramifications for him and for the country.

Although **Bryan again carried the South**, which was still solidly voting against "the party of Lincoln," McKinley won by carrying more of the Western states in addition to the North.

> ### STORY
>
> In light of recent assassinations of public figures by anarchists in Europe, there was extra security in place for McKinley's planned visit to the Pan-American Exposition in Buffalo, New York during the fall of 1901. While in Buffalo, McKinley stayed at Milburn House, the expansive home of the Exposition's president, **John G. Milburn**.
>
> On his first day at the exposition, McKinley spoke to a huge crowd of some 50,000 people and there was no trouble. How-

ever, the next day, at the request of Milburn, McKinley again visited the exposition to help build the gate receipts This time, instead of giving a speech, he planned to meet the public. That gave a man named **Leon Czolgosz** an opportunity to get close to the president. Czolgosz was a peripheral member of some American anarchists groups, and he believed the design of the government of the United States was perpetuating social injustice against poor people like himself. He was aware that an anarchist had killed King Umberto I of Italy and that the killer said he had done it for the sake of the common man. Czolgosz decided to do the same thing.

At a large ornate building named the Temple of Music, space was cleared to make room for a line of people who would get to meet the president and shake his hand. McKinley was a skilled hand-shaker who had developed a practiced technique of gripping peoples' hands firmly and guiding them past him so he could greet a lot of people and shake a lot of hands.

Czolgosz procured a pistol and got himself into the greeting line. He waited patiently for his turn to shake hands with the president, and when he got close, he quickly pulled out his pistol and shot McKinley twice in the stomach.

Czolgosz shouted, "I done my duty." The crowd immediately attacked him, but McKinley told them to stop.

Even as McKinley was guided to a chair, he tried to tell his staff that he was not seriously injured. Mostly, he was worried about how his ill wife would take the news.

The president was taken to an local infirmary where a local doctor probed the president's stomach wound, but could not find the bullets. McKinley was taken to Milburn's home where he seemed to recover somewhat, and doctors assured the public that the president was going to be fine.

After news of the shooting went out by telegraph, members of the cabinet rushed to Buffalo and Vice President Roosevelt hurried back from a camping trip in the Adirondack Mountains.

A large crowd stayed near the Buffalo police headquarters threatening to lynch Czolgosz.

Unfortunately, the doctors were wrong about their rosy prognosis. The president's condition soon began to deteriorate due to the gangrene that was growing around the bullets that were still lodged in his intestines. Thomas Edison sent a newly-invented X-ray machine to Buffalo to try to determine the location of the bullets inside the president, but the attending doctors would not allow its use. Within a few weeks, McKinley died, and Roosevelt was sworn in as the new president.

Czolgosz was quickly put on trial for the murder. He was found guilty and sentenced to death. He was executed by electric chair only a month later.

The Presidential Election of 1904

At the Republican National Convention of 1904, **Theodore Roosevelt**, who had assumed the office of president upon the death of president William McKinley, easily won the nomination on the first ballot. Republican conservatives, feeling Roosevelt might be too liberal to get elected, pressured him to accept Indiana Senator **Charles W. Fairbanks** of Indiana as his vice presidential candidate. Roosevelt went along with the "old guard" to avoid a floor fight. Because Roosevelt had already served most of McKinley's term in office, he promised, if elected, he would not run for another term.

STORY

The Democratic National Convention of 1904 foreshadowed what twentieth-century politics was going to be like.

When the delegates were unable to talk former president Grover Cleveland into running again, they turned away from the presumed favorite, William Jennings Bryan, and instead put

> forward the name of a relative unknown, Judge **Alton B. Parker,** who had been out of politics for twenty years.
>
> Bryan, still a force in the Democratic Party, strongly opposed Parker because he had been one of the "Gold Democrats" who had opposed Bryan in 1896. He said Parker was "a tool of Wall Street," pointing out that Parker had been one of the New York Court of Appeals judges who had declared the eight-hour work day law unconstitutional. Bryan went so far as to suggest that if Parker was nominated, he would encourage Democrats not to vote for him. Bryan said the delegates should go for New York publisher **William Randolph Hearst.** (Hearst's newspapers had endorsed Bryan in his bid for the presidency.) Hearst's newspapers were known to be on the side of labor and against the monopolies of big business.
>
> The Democratic delegates were so worried that a labor candidate like Hearst might take over the Party, they all rallied behind Parker.
>
> However, the strife of the convention was not over. Parker was upset that the Democratic platform didn't include anything about the monetary issue. He said the platform would have to include support of the gold standard or he would not accept the nomination. It was a bold move, and it worked. The Democratic platform also called for reduced government spending, an end to big business monopolies, an eight-hour work day, and oddly, the extermination of polygamy. It also called out the Roosevelt administration as "spasmodic, erratic, sensational, spectacular, and arbitrary."

After the Democrats had nominated Parker for president, they nominated former Senator **Henry G. Davis** of West Virginia for vice president, hoping he could deliver the vote in his home state. Davis was 80 years old, the oldest major-party candidate ever nominated for national office. The relatively unknown Parker had little chance against the popular president, Roosevelt. **He was** only able to carry the South, which continued to vote against the Republicans no matter who they put up. In essence, **they were still voting against Lincoln**. In Florida, Louisiana, Mississippi, and South Carolina, Roosevelt was only able to get a few thousand votes despite his overwhelming popularity elsewhere.

The Presidential Election of 1908

The 1908 president campaign began with the popular Republican incumbent president, **Theodore Roosevelt**, staying true to his pledge not to run for another term. Although that could have led to a wide-open race for the Republican nomination, it was not to be: Roosevelt made it clear that he wanted his Secretary of War and good friend, **William H. Taft**, to be the Party's nominee.

STORY

In 1904, the Democrat Party in Florida had held a primary election to elect delegates to their national convention.

In 1908, **the Republican Party decided to also hold primaries**. Four states participated, California, Ohio, Pennsylvania, and Wisconsin. It resulted in a larger than normal number of candidates being presented at the Republican National Convention, many of them local favorites from the four states.

Despite the large number of potential candidates brought forward by the primary election method, the Party leaders still held sway, nominating their man, **William H. Taft.**

The Democratic National Convention was held in Denver, Colorado. It was the first time the national convention of a major party was held in a Western city. At the convention, populists, labor parties, and even socialist parties tried to make their voice heard. However, in the end, it was again the great orator, William Jennings Bryan, who prevailed. Bryan chose U.S. Senator **John W. Kern** from the "swing state" of Indiana, to be his running mate.

> **STORY**
> Although William Randolph Hearst had lost his bid for the presidency in 1904, he was not the type to give up easily. In 1908, rebuffed by the Democrats, Hearst decided to create a new party, **the Independence Party,** to attract votes from populist voters. When his new party didn't get much attention, Hearst abandoned the idea. Nevertheless, he took an active role against Bryan at the convention.

Although Bryan was by then a very experienced presidential campaigner, his campaign was under funded. He was only able to carry the South and a few of the Western states, and **Taft was elected by a comfortable margin**.

The Presidential Election of 1912

The presidential election season of 1912 began with the threat of war in Europe. However, that threat was not to play a very large role in the election. Instead, the nation's attention was fixed on the domestic issues of monetary supply, the gold standard, and labor versus big business.

> **STORY**
> By 1912, **some states had adopted the primary elections approach to choosing delegates** to send to the Republican National Convention. Even though President Theodore Roosevelt had originally endorsed William Howard Taft to be his successor, **Roosevelt had begun to feel that Taft was moving the party away from Populist principles**. Roosevelt took the surprising step of challenging Taft and announcing that he would once again seek the office of president. As a result, Roosevelt

> won most of the primaries. Taft only won Massachusetts; he even lost his home state of Ohio.
>
> At the Republican National Convention, **both Roosevelt and Taft worked behind the scenes to sway delegates**, and when it seemed that Taft was going to be victorious, Roosevelt cried foul. He said that **he had proof that a number of state delegations had been illegally taken over by Taft forces, and he refused to participate in the convention any longer.**
>
> After Taft won the nomination and selected his incumbent vice president, **James S. Sherman**, Roosevelt started his own progressive political party. It was eventually nicknamed the "**Bull Moose Party**."

With the splitting off of Roosevelt from the Republican Party, the Democrats felt they had a good chance to oust the incumbent president. However, they struggled to select a candidate. U.S. Congressman **James "Champ" Clark** from Missouri was serving as the U.S. Speaker of the House, and many thought he would be the Democratic nominee.

At the Democratic National Convention, Clark did receive the most votes on the first ballot, but he didn't get the two-thirds majority that was required to win the nomination. Part of the reason why he didn't get the required number of votes, was because **he didn't have the support of William Jennings Bryan** who was still considered to be one of the movers and shakers of the Democratic Party. Bryan favored New Jersey Governor **Woodrow Wilson**.

That led to neither candidate getting enough votes to win, and when ballot after ballot failed to yield a winner, **Thomas R. Marshall**, the Governor of Indiana, ordered his state delegates to switch their allegiance to Wilson

That led to Wilson finally getting being nominated. Not surprisingly, he selected Marshall to be his running mate.

> **STORY**
> Another political party, **the Socialist Party of America**, became better known during the presidential election of 1912. The party had been growing in stature after it managed to pull together coalitions of trade unionists along with other populist groups such as factory workers, immigrants, and farmers. They declared themselves "at war" with capitalism with its subjugation of workers. They nominated **Eugene V. Debs**, a former U.S. Congressman from Indiana, along with **Emil Seidel**, the mayor of Milwaukee, to be his running mate.

With the split in the Republican Party and the emergence of the Socialist Party, the presidential campaign of 1912 created a situation that made the unseating of an incumbent president more and more likely.

Although Roosevelt and Taft received more votes in the general election than Wilson, together they won only 96 Electoral College votes. Wilson received 453 Electoral College votes and was therefore elected the nation's 28th president. **It was the worst defeat of an incumbent president in U.S. history.**

Chapter Nine

The Politics of War

The Presidential Election of 1916

The **presidential election of 1916** took place against the backdrop of an ongoing bloody war in Europe. Wilson ran for reelection as a **Democrat** on a platform of **keeping the U.S. out of the war**. It was a popular position in 1916.

The **Republicans** put up Supreme Court Justice **Charles Evans Hughes**. He received the support of former president, Theodore Roosevelt.

The **Socialists** again put up a candidate, **A. L. Benson**, and although the socialist ideas were gaining some popularity, there was little chance he would win any Electoral College votes.

The popular vote was close, with 9,126,868 votes going to Wilson and 8,548,728 votes going to Hughes. The Electoral College vote was also close, but Wilson, helped by the fact that women were now allowed to vote in some 30 states, was able to prevail 277 to 254.

His slim 23 vote majority in the Electoral College meant it would have taken only one or two states to swing the Electoral College in the other direction.

STORY
Despite the ongoing war in Europe, after the election of 1916, most **Americans wanted the United States to maintain**

its neutrality. However, part of Germany's war effort was to use their fleet of U-boats (submarines) to attack and sink any ship that might be bringing supplies to England. At that time, the United States was very dependent on its trade with England and other European countries that were allied with Britain. When the U.S. tried to maintain that trade despite the war, the **German U-boats began to sink U.S. ships**, and **President Wilson threatened retaliation**.

At about the same time, American officials learned **Germany was trying to use the memory of the Mexican-American war to get Mexico to join Germany's war effort**.

When that information was published by several U.S. newspapers, Americans were outraged. Although Wilson had promised in his campaign for the presidency to keep the United States out of the war in Europe, he now went before Congress to ask for a declaration of war against Germany.

Many Americans still wanted to stay out of the war, but **throughout history, few members of Congress have dared to vote against going to war if a president requests it**. On April 6, 1917, the Senate voted 82 to 6 to declare war on Germany. The House followed suit, 373 to 50. and the United States entered **World War One**.

The Presidential Election of 1920

By 1920, President Wilson had not only failed to keep the United States out of the "European War," he had also failed to rally the country behind his hope for the League of Nations. He decided against running for reelection. As a result, the Republicans felt they had a good chance of regaining the White House.

However, The Nineteenth Amendment giving women the vote had been ratified earlier that year, and the Republicans were worried about how to get the women's vote. The women that had been allowed to vote in 1916 had mostly voted Democratic.

STORY

The presidential election of 1920 was the first to be held after the ratification of the Nineteenth Amendment. Therefore, it would be the first presidential election in which women would be voting in all 48 states. In 1920, most political analysts believed the women would simply vote the way their husbands did, because in 1916 that had been true in most Midwestern and Eastern states. But it was not true in the West; many women in the West had voted for the Democrat Wilson, even if their husbands voted Republican. When women were asked why they voted for Wilson, they said because "He kept us out of war." This distinction was especially notable in California where 400,000 women had voted. They mostly voted Democratic, even though the National Woman's Party had endorsed the Republican candidate. However, in 1920, after Wilson had failed to keep the U.S. out of the European war, most women turned against the Democrats and voted Republican. In the South, however, the dominate issue was not war, but white supremacy. That meant the white women in the South mostly voted Democratic, and few women of color were allowed to vote.

Leading up to the **presidential election of 1920,** there was much turmoil in the country. Not only was the country war-weary, but more than half a million U.S. citizens had died in the **1918-19 flu pandemic.** Also, **labor unions were gaining considerable power,** and they began **using strikes as a tactic for improving wages and working conditions.**

Racial issues were also becoming more of a problem. **In East St. Louis, Illinois. a race riot, resulted in the deaths of more than one hundred African-Americans**. Another riot erupted in Chicago when **Irish groups fought African-Americans** attempting to find work at the city stockyards.

Because several previous elections had been close, the political parties were **becoming more aware of the problems of the Electoral College system**. As a result, **both of the leading political parties tried to pick candidates from states with the most Electoral College votes**. At that time, Ohio had 24 electoral votes, and both parties ended up picking candidates from that state. The Democrats nominated Ohio Governor **James M. Cox with Franklin D. Roosevelt as vice president**, and the Republicans chose Ohio Senator **Warren G. Harding with Calvin Coolidge as vice president. Both presidential candidates were newspaper publishers** in an era when newspapers were becoming powerful political tools.

The Socialist party again put up **Eugene V. Debs.**

The election did not turn out to be as close as everyone expected. Harding, campaigning on a "return to normalcy" platform, won most of the large states. Cox, being a Democrat, carried the Southern states. The Socialist Eugene V. Debs won almost a million votes, but he was unable to win any Electoral College votes. Warren G. Harding won the Electoral College vote and became the 29th president.

In 1923, Harding died in office. His vice president, **Calvin Coolidge**, former governor of Massachusetts, served out his term.

The Presidential Election of 1924

In 1924, it was a given that **incumbent president Coolidge** would be nominated by the Republicans. However, things were not so clear on the Democratic side. Harding's Secretary of the Interior, **Albert Bacon Fall**, had been convicted of receiving bribes from the oil companies in the so-called **Teapot Dome scandal**. However, **there was no proof that Coolidge was involved.**

Going into the 1924 **Democratic National Convention** in New York City, it seemed as if **William Gibbs McAdoo,** a lawyer from California and the son-in-law of former president Wilson, was the overwhelming favorite due to his support from labor. Also, it was hoped that the voters would associate the Republicans with the Teapot Dome scandal. However, as more information about the scandal came out, it soon became clear that Democrats had also been involved, and it was leaned that **McAdoo also had a lawyer-client relationship with one of the central players in the scandal**. Also, **McAdoo was supported by the Ku Klux Klan, and he was not willing to come out and say he did not welcome their support**. Even though the Democrats were the party of the South and the Klan was active in trying to keep African-American voters away from the polling places, there was growing distaste for the Klan.

William Jennings Bryan was still a key player in the party, and when some said the Democrats should come out against the Ku Klux Klan, **he suggested avoiding the issue altogether so as to not lose the votes of the rural South**.

In the first ballot, most of the votes either went to McAdoo or New York Governor **Al Smith**, But neither was able to get the required two-thirds majority. **Smith failed to get any votes from the Southern delegates because he was a Catholic.**

In ballot after ballot, the votes swung back and forth between McAdoo and Smith, and the **observers in the galleries were getting more and more rowdy.** Many began to complain about New York rowdyism. Bryan even suggested the convention should be halted and moved to another city.

After the sixtieth ballot, the delegates began to look for a compromise candidate. Indiana Senator **Samuel Ralston** was one name put forward, and **he had the full support of the Ku Klux Klan.** But like the other candidates, he couldn't get enough votes to win. Finally, on the one hundred and third ballot, the delegates settled on another compromise candidate, U.S. Congressman **John W. Davis** from West Virginia. He chose **Charles W. Bryan**, governor of Nebraska and brother of William Jennings Bryan, to be his running mate.

In the election, **Robert M. La Follette,** a candidate representing the progressives, also ran. **He was to become the most successful third-party candidate in the modern era**. He won 4,831,706 votes and carried his home state of Wisconsin with its

13 Electoral College votes. However, **this time, the election was not close enough for the presence of a third-party candidate to throw the decision into the House of Representatives.**

Of course Davis, the Democrat, once again carried the entire South, but he won no other electoral votes.

Coolidge won the Electoral College with a large majority.

The Presidential Election of 1928

In the presidential election of 1928, Coolidge chose not to run for reelection, and the Republicans nominated **Herbert Hoover** from California. He had been the nation's Commerce Secretary under president Harding.

The Democrats nominated Governor **Al Smith** from New York. Smith was a Catholic which meant the Ku Klux Klan would not support him, and that would cost him a lot of Southern votes. Also, there was widespread concern among Protestants that, if elected, he might take orders from the Pope. (**Religion** had rarely played a role in presidential elections because nearly every previous candidate had been a Protestant.) Despite Smith's religion, he was still a Democrat going up against a Republican, so he won all of the South except for Florida. **After 68 years, the South was still voting *against* the Republicans, the party that had elected the hated Abraham Lincoln, even if it meant voting for a Catholic.** Hoover won the presidential election by one of the largest pluralities in any modern presidential election.

The Presidential Election of 1932

The **presidential election of 1932** took place in the middle of **the Great Depression**. The Republicans put **Herbert Hoover** up for reelection and Kansas Senator **Charles Curtis** for vice president. However, with the economy being in such bad shape, few believed the incumbent Republicans would be able to win.

The Democrats nominated **Franklin D. Roosevelt**, the wealthy governor of New York. He chose **John Nance Garner IV from Texas** as his running mate.

> **STORY**
> During the campaign, there was some talk about Roosevelt's health being an issue. **Roosevelt had contracted polio in 1921 and the infection left him permanently paralyzed from the waist down.** At that time, polio (poliomyelitis) was a common childhood disease and outbreaks of the disease were all too common during the summer months, especially in large cities.
> Roosevelt learned to get around a bit with the help of leg braces and canes. At home he used a wheelchair, but he was careful to never be seen by the public in that wheelchair. The most famous pictures of him, such as in the back seat of his convertible, or on the deck of the USS Quincy at the end of WWII, always showed him sitting down.

Hoover's chances looked grim from the start. It was the first election in which many leading members of the Republican Party refused to support the party's nominee. Hoover only won the Northeastern states, Connecticut, Delaware, Maine, New Hampshire, Pennsylvania, and Vermont, and even in those states his margin of victory was very slim.

The election was a landslide for Roosevelt who became the first Democratic presidential candidate to win since Wilson won in 1916. Roosevelt won the South, of course, but he also won the Midwest and the West, which was quite a change in national voting patterns; only four years before, Republican Hoover had won every single Midwestern and Western state.

The Presidential Election of 1936

With the depression still going on, **Roosevelt** ran for reelection in **1936**. His running mate was again John Garner.

The Republicans nominated **Alf Landon**, governor of Kansas.

For the Democrats, there was some concern that Roosevelt might lose the South in 1936 because **Southern Republicans had**

started calling him a socialist. They claimed his "**New Deal**" policies, including Social Security and unemployment relief, were taking the United States down the road toward socialism.

But Roosevelt needn't have worried about losing the South. In the Southern states where African-Americans were systematically kept from voting, **the Republican candidate hardly got any votes at all**. For example, in Mississippi, Landon got only 4,443 votes, and in South Carolina he only got 1,646 votes. It was clear that **even 76 years after Lincoln's election, the South was still voting *against* Lincoln and the Republicans, even if it meant voting for a very liberal (and some said, *Socialist*) candidate.**

Roosevelt carried every state except Maine and Vermont. His Electoral College win was an overwhelming 523 to 8.

STORY

The Great Depression influenced several presidential elections. The poor economy was the main reason Hoover was overwhelmingly rejected by the voters in 1932.

Roosevelt's voter "mandate" meant he was able to enact many radical "New Deal" programs. (However, some of his programs were later declared unconstitutional.)

Although there were some fundamental problems in the U.S. economy before 1929, generally the depression is thought to have begun on "**Black Tuesday**," October 29, 1929. That day the U.S. stock market dropped dramatically. **The downturn had actually begun the week before** when stock market instability scared some investors, causing them to get out of the stock market entirely. Then on "Black Tuesday," a huge number of shares were traded with most stocks falling.

William C. Durant and **the Rockefeller family** saw the fall in stock prices as an opportunity to buy at historically low prices, so they stepped in and bought stocks in large quantities.

That helped convince some investors that the market was safe. But after a bit of recovery, the market began to fall again.

Although investors like **John D. Rockefeller** tried to talk about a stock market comeback, the problem was that many ordinary citizens had begun to invest in the market, and many had lost money in the downturn.

At that time, **in order to attract investors, stock brokers were in the habit of lending small investors money to buy stock**s, so it was not just stock speculators that were wiped out.

Many people reacted to the economic downturn by spending less. That started **a cycle of business slowdown and job lay-offs, which led to even less spending**.

It didn't help that the Midwestern plains states were suffering from an extended drought that eventually led to what was referred to as the "**dust bowl**" (the drying out and blowing away of rich agricultural soil).

President Hoover's response to the economic slowdown had been to try to pressure businesses to keep workers employed and to keep wages high. That didn't work very well because the businesses were under too much pressure from decreasing sales.

Hoover did lower some taxes, but at first he was opposed to the government getting involved in job programs or putting money into the economy in any other way. Instead, **he believed churches and private charities should take up the challenge**. As for government back-to-work programs, he said that was up to local and state governments.

When the depression worsened, Hoover *did* begin to institute some large government job-creation programs. The huge Hoover Dam project on the Colorado River is one example.

The Presidential Election of 1940

By the time the presidential election of 1940 came around, the economy was improving and all attention was on the ongoing World War II in Europe. The country was divided as to whether the U.S. should go to the aid of England and France to try to stop Hitler's German aggression.

John Garner, Roosevelt's vice president, **assumed Roosevelt would stick to tradition and not run for a third term**, so he decided to make a run for the presidency on the Democratic ticket. He was much more conservative than Roosevelt and disagreed with much of the New Deal agenda. As a result, he had much wider support in the South and in the conservative rural states.

However, President Roosevelt **decided to break with tradition and run for a third term**. He chose his Secretary of Commerce, **Henry Wallace** from Iowa to be his vice president.

When the Republicans were unable to agree on a candidate, a surprising dark horse named **Wendell Willkie** came forward. He was an industrialist from Indiana who had not been much involved in politics.

Throughout the election, the Republicans focused on Roosevelt's perceived failure to end the depression and his willingness to get the United States involved in the ongoing war in Europe.

Roosevelt responded by saying it was his New Deal programs that were ending the Great Depression, and **he said he had no intention of getting involved in the European war**.

Again, there was talk that Roosevelt was too liberal and might lose the conservative South. In 1940, it seemed possible that a Republican could win the South because a "conservative coalition" had emerged in Congress that brought together conservative Southern Democrats with conservative Republicans. By election time, they had already been successful at defeating *some* of Roosevelt's liberal New Deal policies. Many thought the two groups would work together to defeat Roosevelt in the next election.

> **STORY**
> Nationally, there was little notice that during the second Roosevelt administration there had been a dramatic shift in how African-Americans were voting in presidential elections. In the North, Midwest, and West, African-Americans had been voting Republican since the election of Abraham Lincoln. However, in the South, even as late as 1932, many African-Americans were still either being kept away from the polling places or being discouraged through the use of poll taxes and literacy tests (**The 24th Amendment, which prohibited poll taxes, wasn't passed until 1964.**)
>
> In the 1930s, **the Ku Klux Klan was still a powerful political force in the South**, especially in rural areas. The Klan always supported Democratic candidates, and they used intimidation and/or violence to keep African-Americans from going to the polling places to vote Republican. However, by the time the 1934 election was underway, many African-Americans had seen the benefits of Roosevelt's New Deal policies and were starting to shift their loyalties away from the Republicans. It was the beginning of **a strange coalition of Southern Whites and Southern Blacks that supported Roosevelt**.

As it turned out, there was no shift away from the Democrats in the South: **white Southern voters were still unwilling to vote for the hated "Lincoln-Republicans,"** no matter how liberal Roosevelt was.

The East also went for Roosevelt, except once again, conservative Maine and Vermont voted against him.

The Presidential Election of 1944

By the time the presidential election of 1944 came around, the nation was at war. Germany's ally, **the Japanese, had attacked the U.S. naval base at Pearl Harbor in Hawaii** and that immediately drew the United States into **World War Two**.

As the fall election approached, the entire country was focused on winning what was turning out to be a very difficult war. **Nearly every family had somebody involved "over there,"** and casualties were high. Most of the families in America dreaded the arrival of the telegraph delivery boy, sure that any news from Europe would be bad news about their loved one. In addition, **nearly every family in the country was either working on something related to the war effort, or suffering restrictions because of it.** Although the war was taking place far away, there was a feeling that if the Germans and the Japanese were not stopped they would eventually arrive on our shores. As a result, the people were probably less involved in the election of 1944.

For the 1944 presidential election, the **Republicans** put up **Thomas E. Dewey**, the governor of New York. He chose **John Bricker**, the Governor of Ohio, as his running mate. It was no surprise when **Roosevelt ran for reelection in 1944**, this time with **Harry S. Truman** as his vice president. With the U.S. in the middle of a war, most assumed Roosevelt would be reelected.

Dewey campaigned hard against Roosevelt, saying four terms for a president was too many. Some accused the president of trying to become a king. Others tried to **paint him as a socialist**, pointing out that some of his New Deal programs had been declared unconstitutional and others had been overturned in Congress, mostly through the efforts of the conservative coalition).

COMMENT

When Franklin D. Roosevelt ran for a third term it was unprecedented in U.S. presidential election history. The Republicans pointed out the fact that George Washington had declined to run for a third term as president. They said President Washington's decision indicated the founding fathers wanted to limit the time a president could serve.

Based on that reasoning, they introduced a measure to amend the Constitution to limit the number of terms a person could

> hold the presidency. It was passed and the result was **the Twenty-Second Amendment which limited any one individual's term of presidency to two terms**.

By the time the election campaign was underway, the economy was improving, helping Roosevelt's chances. In addition, U.S. troops had landed on the beaches of Normandy on June 6, 1944, and although American casualties were heavy, **the invasion of Europe was being seen as a success**. By the end of August, U.S. troops were in Paris, and there had also been a string of successful battles against Japan in the Pacific.

By election day, U.S. troops were at the Germany border. The military successes of that summer were enough to convince most U.S. citizens that Roosevelt was running the war properly, and he was reelected for a fourth term, again winning all of the Southern states.

However, much of the conservative Midwest voted against Roosevelt, and Dewey also got quite a few votes in some Southern states. **The conservative versus liberal message was beginning to gain some traction in the South.** For example, although Roosevelt won North Carolina, Dewey managed to get 263,155 votes. In West Virginia, which Roosevelt had easily won in 1940, Dewey got 322,819 votes. However, in South Carolina, Republican Dewey only got 4,610 votes. In Mississippi, he only got 11,601 votes.

Nationwide, the popular vote was fairly close, 25,612,916 for Roosevelt and 22,017,929 for Dewey. But the Electoral College vote was not close at all. It came out 432 for Roosevelt and only 99 for Dewey.

Roosevelt died after only a few months into his fourth term. His vice president, **Harry Truman,** was sworn in as president. He presided over the last few months of the war, and he approved the two atomic bomb attacks on Japan.

The use of such a horrific weapon on innocent civilians was controversial, especially when it appeared that Japan was already defeated, but Truman defended it by saying it saved many American soldiers because they didn't have to invade Japan.

STORY

World War Two did not play as much of a role in U.S. presidential politics as we might have expected. Although the war did influence the voting that took place prior to the election of 1940 when Wendell Willkie accused Roosevelt of trying to get the U.S involved in what people saw as "a European war," Roosevelt's promise to keep the country out of the war defused Willkie's attack.

But when Japan attacked the American naval base at Pearl Harbor, nearly all Americans supported Roosevelt when he went on the radio to tell the country he was asking Congress for a declaration of war on Japan. **His "day of infamy" speech** was a rallying cry for the U.S. to enter the war. He issued a presidential order that said any government agency that was in any way related to the war effort would report directly him. **He ordered many corporations to modify their manufacturing lines to make war materials,** and he established a goal of producing 10,000 new fighter airplanes per year. **He also ordered emergency shipbuilding in order to quickly build ships** to carry troops and war materials.

The **Selective Service Act** was passed with Roosevelt's help, meaning all men in the United States between the ages of 16 and 65 were required to register for the draft.

Millions of young men were drafted into the Army and millions more voluntarily signed up to serve in one of the military branches. It is a little known fact that the Selective Service Act even provided a role for those who were, for reasons of religion or personal belief, unwilling to fight in wars. It

> said they would not be required to undergo combat training but would instead undergo training for noncombatant support roles.

The Presidential Election of 1948

In 1948, Truman was nominated for reelection. He chose Senator **Alben Barkley** as his running mate.

The Republicans again nominated **Thomas Dewey** and his running mate, **Earl Warren**, the Governor of California.

Henry A. Wallace, Roosevelt's former vice president, was also on the ballot as a **Progressive Party** candidate.

Despite the national joy that the war was finally over, Truman was not all that popular. There was trouble brewing in Asia, and elsewhere, as an aftermath of the war, and there was **unease about the fact that Truman had ordered atomic bombs dropped on innocent Japanese civilians when many thought the war was all but over anyhow**. There was also concern about what was going on in Europe. The division of Berlin between the Eastern and Western powers was still unsettled, and Russia's blockade of Berlin was an **indication that a "cold war" was developing between Russia and the United States.**

> ### STORY
> The election of 1948 was the first in which the Democratic stranglehold on the South began to loosen. Four terms of a liberal president had not deterred Southern voters from voting against the Republicans, the hated party of Lincoln. But when the Democrats began to talk about civil rights for Southern Blacks, many in the South saw unwanted change coming
>
> At the Democratic national nominating convention, Truman promised that if he was elected, he would introduce **civil rights legislation**. Hearing that, the **Southern Democratic delegates all got up and walked out**. They held their own convention in

Birmingham, Alabama and **nominated Senator Strom Thurmond** from South Carolina as a States' Right Democrat. **Thurmond, running on a segregationist platform,** won Alabama Mississippi, Louisiana, and his home state of South Carolina.

With the loss of some of the South, the first results showed the election was very close. Truman had also lost some of the Midwest, but he won the Northeast and the West coast. Some newspapers came out the morning after the election with mistaken banner headlines declaring **"Dewey Wins,"** but when the long process of counting the ballots was finally finished, Truman had won after all with 24,179,347 nationwide popular votes over Dewey's 21,991,292 votes.

The final Electoral College vote was Truman 303, Dewey 189, and Thurmond 39.

Thurmond's wins in the South **marked the first time in the modern era that a third-party candidate had won a significant number of electoral votes**. Had only a few states in the rest of the country gone for Dewey, **it would have meant that no candidate would have reached the required majority**, and that would have thrown the decision about who would be president into the House of Representatives.

Chapter Ten

Postwar and Cold War Politics

The Presidential Election of 1952

In 1952, the Republicans finally managed to convince **World War Two hero**, **General Dwight D. Eisenhower**, to run for president. They had tried to convince him to run in 1948, but he had refused. This time they told him it was his duty to the country, and he finally accepted.

Because the **Cold War** with Russia was bound to be one of the main election issues, Eisenhower chose noted anti-communist, **Richard Nixon**, from California, as his running mate.

The Democrats were in a quandary because **Truman, the incumbent, had decided not to run**. By 1952, primary elections to select a party's candidate were becoming the norm, and in the Democratic primaries, Governor **Adlai Stevenson II** of Illinois did well. He was nominated at the 1952 Democratic national presidential nominating convention in Chicago. In **an attempt to recapture the Southern vote**, he selected **John Jackson Sparkman from Alabama** as his running mate.

There was little doubt about the popularity of General Eisenhower, but some of his opinions were very controversial. He was a strong believer in the United Nations, and he thought that organization could control the expansion of nuclear weapons better than the United States could.

Those kinds of opinions were strongly opposed by **Republican Senator Joseph McCarthy** who was beating the drums of nationalism and stirring up anti-communist "witch hunts." His congressional committee claimed to be finding anti-American communist spies ("commies") everywhere, in the entertainment industry and even deep inside the U.S. government.

Two years before, the **Korean War** had flared up as a result of the postwar division of that country. The conflict could expand into a showdown with China, and maybe even with Russia. Having just been involved in a horrific world war, this time the **people of the United States were not so enthusiastic about getting involved in yet another war.** By 1952, **Russia had developed its own atomic bomb**, and Joseph Stalin, the Russian Premier was making threatening comments toward the U.S. In the face of such threats, what the United States needed was a hero. Eisenhower, the famous Army general, fit that bill. **He was elected by a large popular majority and won the Electoral College, 442 to 89. He was to be the first Republican in the White House in 20 years.**

As usual, the South mostly went to the Democrats. Stevenson won most of the Southern states by large majorities. However, for the first time in many years, a few Southern states, Florida, Tennessee, and Virginia, went for the Republican candidate, although by narrow majorities in each case.

After 92 years, cracks in the anti-Lincoln, anti-Republican Southern attitude were beginning to show.

STORY

The **Korean War** was one of the Asian conflicts that flared up after World War Two over **who would control the country after the Japanese were forced to withdraw.**

Without consulting the Koreans, the allies decided to divide the country north and south. In 1950, armed conflict broke out between the divided sections.

As the conflict escalated, the North Koreans were supported by the People's Republic of China and the USSR, while the South Koreans were supported by the United States. It was to become **the first armed conflict of the so-called "cold war"** that pitted the U.S. against what was seen as a communist agenda to control the post-war world. From the U.S. point of view, the "war" was mostly against Russia, but there was also talk about a threat from communist China.

With the support of the U.S. military, the South Koreans invaded the North, only to be pushed back when the Chinese army came to the aid of the North Koreans.

In 1953, an uneasy stalemate was reached along the 38th parallel that divided the country north and south.

A **Demilitarized Zone** along that line still maintains the stalemate to this day. Democratic South Korea has developed a thriving economy based on manufacturing and export, while North Korea has retreated into a secretive communist dictatorship which has, reportedly, pushed most of its citizens into poverty. Nevertheless, many South Koreans still hope for eventual unification.

The Presidential Election of 1956

In 1956, **Eisenhower** again ran against **Adlai Stevenson**, and for the first time, **political television advertising played a significant role**. Much of the TV advertising was aimed at women.

The cold war was still going on, but Senator McCarthy had been discredited, leaving most Americans less worried about communist infiltration here at home.

Nevertheless, despite the country being in a period of peace and prosperity, the U.S. military was **actively pursuing development of even more powerful nuclear weapons** in response to a perceived threat from Russia.

Meanwhile, Russia was doing the same, and the proliferation of nuclear weapons continued until it actually became a policy known as **mutual assured destruction.** Many hoped that would keep either side from being the first to use such weapons.

With the Korean War becoming only a memory, and the economy doing well, most thought Eisenhower would win again.

Despite the traditional strength of the Democratic Party in the South, some voters there were beginning to rebel against that. The main issue in the South was civil rights, and they worried that Northerners, if elected, might pass new legislation that would break down the established Southern policy of strict segregation. As a result, some Southern Democratic leaders broke with the national Democratic Party and tried to manipulate the Electoral College outcome by getting a slate of "**unpledged**" electors onto the ballot. (**An unpledged elector is one that has not pledged to support any particular candidate for President**.) In Alabama, the unpledged electors got 20,150 votes. In Louisiana, they got 44,520 votes. In Mississippi, they got 42,266 votes (seventeen percent of the total vote), and in South Carolina, they got 88,509 votes (almost thirty percent of the total vote). It was clear voting patterns were changing in the South, and even though the unpledged electors were unable to win any states, it was a sign of things to come.

In the end, the Republican Eisenhower was soundly beaten by Stevenson in the traditionally anti-Lincoln, anti-Republican states of Mississippi and South Carolina, but he won every state outside of the South and managed to pick up a few of the border states that he had lost in the previous election.

The Presidential Election of 1960

In 1960, Eisenhower's vice president **Richard Nixon was nominated by the Republican Party**.

Despite his being defeated twice before, the Democrats seemed poised to again nominate **Adlai Stevenson**. He still had the support of many in the party, despite his having picked a segregationist VP in a prior election. But he had a reputation of being "too intellectual for the average voter, and **many of the party leaders wanted to put forward John Kennedy, the charismatic young Senator from Massachusetts** who had been wining some of the primaries. Stevenson refused to withdraw, setting up a convention fight. Behind the scenes, party analysts were trying to decide what position the party should take regarding the issue of segregation. By taking a neutral position on segregation in the past, they could count on winning the South, because the South was still voting against the Republicans, the party of Lincoln. Now they weren't sure which position would cost them the most votes nationwide. They even put the question to a brand new invention, the mainframe computer, and in the end, they decided to have Kennedy take an anti-segregation stand.

COMMENT

In 1960, the economy was not doing all that well, and **the Russian launch of the world's first satellite, Sputnik**, gave Americans the feeling that the U.S. was falling behind Russia. The **"space race"** was a notable milestone in **"the cold war"** that would dominate politics for decades.

There was a movement underway in the South against Kennedy because he was Catholic. They were also afraid that he might introduce legislation that would outlaw segregation.

Nixon, despite having served as vice president under the fairly liberal Eisenhower, was becoming known as a conservative "cold warrior." Many of his speeches were attacks on Russia, and he positioned himself as being the most anti-communist candidate.

STORY

The **1960 election introduced televised debates.** Many wondered if that would change how people voted, and if it could overcome the influence of local party machinery. **Some thought the election would be won or lost by how well the candidates came across on the small screen**, and that turned out to be at least partly true. Analysis of the four televised debates revealed an interesting fact: **those who heard the debates on the radio thought Nixon did very well, but those who watched the debates on television thought he did very poorly** against the calm and polished (and handsome) Kennedy. **It was becoming clear that television was now the way people learned about the candidates.**

The first televised debate was watched by an estimated 77 million people. **At the time, that was over sixty percent of the adult population in the U.S.** Four prime-time debates, in which journalists asked the candidates to respond to questions, were shown on TV in September and October, and **Kennedy was well prepared for the debates**. He looked directly at the camera and spoke not to the journalists in the hall, but to the TV audience. Nixon, on the other hand, seemed to be having a private dialogue with the journalists.

In the post-debate analysis, the overall appearance of the candidates was much discussed. Kennedy, who was considerably younger than Nixon, seemed athletic and at ease. Nixon, who was recovering from the flu, seemed unsteady and uncomfortable. He refused to wear make-up, which made him look pale and drawn as compared to the tanned Kennedy.

In the 1960 presidential campaign, **television advertising was also becoming more important**. Kennedy was one of the first to use television clips in his ads. He used an excerpt from one of President Eisenhower's press conferences in which a reporter had asked what contribution Vice President Nixon had made to his two terms in office. Eisenhower joked that if you gave him a week, he might think of something. It got a good laugh from the assembled reporters, but in the campaign, Nixon had been making much of his experience in government.

By 1960, Alaska and Hawaii had been admitted to the Union. However, with only six electoral votes between them, they didn't get much attention from the two candidates.

The real election battleground was in the South. To help him win the Southern States, Kennedy chose **Texan Lyndon B. Johnson** as his running mate. As a result, despite his being a Catholic, Kennedy was able to win the predominantly Protestant Southern states of Georgia, Louisiana, North Carolina, and South Carolina. But his anti-segregation speeches cost him Florida, Kentucky, Tennessee, and Virginia.

In Mississippi, Southern conservatives again put up a slate of unpledged electors as a protest against voting for either candidate. In that state, **the unpledged electors received more votes than either Nixon or Kennedy, winning Mississippi's eight electoral votes**. In Alabama, Nixon received more votes than Kennedy, but **the majority of the state's voters voted for the six unpledged conservative electors** who, it was clear, were not going to cast their Electoral College votes for either Kennedy or Nixon.

When the Electoral College met to cast their ballots, **all of the unpledged electors cast their votes for segregationists, Harry F. Byrd and Strom Thurmond**.

Nevertheless, Kennedy managed to win enough Electoral College votes elsewhere to be elected president. **The final Electoral College vote was Kennedy 303, Nixon 219, and Harry Byrd 15.**

COMMENT

As in most close elections, there were **accusations of voter fraud in favor of Kennedy, especially in Mayor Daley's Chicago, and in Johnson's home state of Texas**. Investigators later found that in some counties in Texas, more votes were cast for the Kennedy-Johnson ticket than there were voters.

As soon as Kennedy was elected, he instituted new domestic programs and set about to change the nation's foreign policy. At home, he reinvigorated the space program and promised a balanced budget.

The Republicans said Kennedy was soft on communism, but in the spring of 1961, **Kennedy authorized a plan to try to overthrow the communist government of Cuba**. The CIA and the U.S. military landed 1500 former Cubans near the **Bay of Pigs** on the remote south side of the island of Cuba. They had been trained by the U.S. military in guerrilla tactics and were supposed to rally the people against Fidel Castro's government. However, the Cuban military soon killed or rounded up all of the guerrillas, and **the U.S. was forced to pay a ransom to get the survivors back**.

Then, in October of 1962, **CIA U-2 spy planes photographed missile sites being built by Russian technicians in Cuba**. It was possible the missiles could be used in a future nuclear attack on the United States. It was **the greatest crisis of Kennedy's administration**. The military wanted to immediately bomb the missile sites, but Kennedy was afraid that would lead to a direct confrontation with Russia, with the potential that it could escalate into nuclear war. Instead, Kennedy decided on **a naval blockade of Cuba** until the missiles were removed. Eventually, a deal was secretly struck: Russia's Premier, Nikita Khrushchev, agreed to dismantle the missile sites in Cuba if the U.S. would dismantle its missile sites in Turkey and promise never to invade Cuba. Kennedy agreed.

The "**Cuban Missile Crisis**" as it came to be known, **quieted Republican criticism of Kennedy**.

In November of 1963, President Kennedy was on a visit to Dallas when **he was shot and killed by Lee Harvey Oswald**, a former Marine marksman who had positioned himself above the president's motorcade in a 6th floor window of a building.

Oswald claimed he was "a patsy," and then, when he was assassinated by **Jack Ruby**, a local nightclub owner, many conspiracy theories were put forward about who might have been behind Kennedy's murder. A commission was put together, and after hearing many witnesses and reviewing amateur video of the shooting, they said Oswald had acted alone.

Chapter Eleven

The Politics of War and Antiwar

The Presidential Election of 1964

In 1964, sitting president **Lyndon Johnson,** having served out the remainder of President Kennedy's term, was nominated for re-election by the **Democrats**. Johnson's only serious competition in the primaries came from **Alabama's governor George Wallace** who had come to national prominence when he **stood in the doorway of the University of Alabama** to block the entrance of black students. Wallace's name appeared on the ballot in three of the sixteen states that were holding Democratic presidential primaries that year, Wisconsin, Indiana, and Maryland. **Running on a segregationist platform, Wallace won a surprising number of votes in those states.**

STORY

George Wallace's infamous "**stand in the schoolhouse door**" came about after the United States Supreme Court handed down a decision that state taxpayer-supported universities could not legally refuse to admit students because of their race. Most states complied to one degree or another, but the University of Alabama, with the support of the state's governor and other leading politicians, **found ways to reject a student application if they found out the student had *any* African-American heritage**. When the University of Alabama refused to accept the applications of three fully-qualified African-American students, the students went to court. A federal judge

> ordered them to be admitted. When the three student arrived on the opening day of classes, Governor Wallace was there in the doorway with local police to block their entrance. He had made sure there would be plenty of news media present to record the confrontation. Knowing ahead of time what was going to happen, President Kennedy federalized the Alabama National Guard and ordered them to make sure the students were admitted, by force if necessary. The students were admitted, but **it gained Wallace a big following throughout the South and that emboldened him to later make a run for the presidency of the United States.**

Despite Wallace's presence in the race, at the Democratic national nominating convention, Johnson won easily. He chose U.S. Senator **Hubert Humphrey** from Minnesota as his running mate.

The Republicans nominated **Barry Goldwater**, a conservative from Arizona. He chose Congressman **William E. Miller** from New York as his running mate.

In 1964, the candidates primarily used television to get their message across to the public, and **television "attack" ads began to evolve**. Johnson's ads used skillfully done movie-like scenarios to portray what might happen if Goldwater was elected. The infamous **Daisy Girl ad** showed an innocent-looking little girl picking petals from a daisy in a field of flowers. As she counted the flower's petals, the screen morphed into a missile launch countdown followed by a dramatic nuclear explosion. The ads were in response to **Goldwater's statement that nuclear weapons might have to be used in some circumstances**. Although the ad didn't come right out and accuse Goldwater of being an advocate of nuclear war, it effectively made the point that Goldwater's militaristic opinions could lead the country in that dangerous direction.

Paradoxically, Johnson was already secretly getting the country more deeply involved in the cold war against the communists. As the election campaign progressed, U.S. forces were beginning to engage enemy forces in Vietnam. President Johnson was fully aware of the worsening situation there, but as he was presenting himself as the anti-war candidate, he kept it quiet.

Johnson won most of the nation in a landslide, but Goldwater carried his home state of Arizona, plus Alabama, Georgia, Louisiana, Mississippi, and South Carolina. It was the first time a Republican had carried that much of the deep South, and it **marked the end of a one hundred year dominance of Democrats in the region**. That change in voting preferences was to have a profound effect on future presidential elections.

STORY

By the time Johnson won the election in the fall of 1964, **U.S. forces were secretly becoming more engaged in combat in Vietnam**.

Years before, President Eisenhower had told President Kennedy that he believed the U.S. would end up having to send troops to Vietnam. After soviet Premier Nikita Khrushchev said Russia would support the North Vietnamese communists, Eisenhower predicted Vietnam would be the next hot spot in the escalating "cold war."

In 1961, Johnson, as vice president, had visited President Diem in South Vietnam and hailed him as the "Winston Churchill of Asia." Soon after that visit, skirmishes with troops from North Vietnam began. In response, President Kennedy sent a few hundred Green Beret '"advisors" to South Vietnam to help train the South Vietnamese Army. When more attacks on South Vietnam came from North Vietnam, the South Vietnamese President Diem requested more military aid from Kennedy. In response, Kennedy sent General Maxwell Taylor to Vietnam to access the situation. Taylor came back alarmed at what he had seen. He told Kennedy that if Vietnam fell into the hands of the communists, all of Southeast Asia could eventually fall. The Pentagon advised Kennedy's Defense Secretary Robert McNamara that a massive show of force was needed in Vietnam. McNamara concurred and suggested to Kennedy that the U.S. should send at least 20,000 troops there. Kennedy decided against it, and to this day there is discussion about **whether the U.S. would have gotten so deeply involved in Vietnam had Kennedy not been assassinated.**

Kennedy *did* continue to send advisers to Vietnam (eventually more than 16,000), and he also sent helicopter units. In the fall of 1961, he guaranteed President Diem that the United States would help Vietnam "preserve its independence."

In 1962, a reporter asked President Kennedy if any Americans in Vietnam were engaged in the fighting there. The president said no, but in fact, they were. U.S. pilots were participating in bombing runs using U.S. aircraft, and in some of the attacks, civilians were being killed, leading to much ill will among the locals toward the American presence.

Defense Secretary McNamara visited South Vietnam during the summer of 1962 and came back to tell President Kennedy that **the South Vietnamese war against the northern invaders was going well** because of U.S. help. **Soon after that visit, the first U.S. Special Forces base was secretly established at Khe Sanh.**

When Buddhist rioters in South Vietnam took to the streets in Saigon to protest a government crackdown on religion, they were fired on by South Vietnamese troops. **Several Buddhist monks publicly burned themselves to death as an act of protest,** and the worldwide publicity from those acts brought Vietnam to the attention of American citizens for the first time. Some citizen groups began asking what we were doing over there, and reports began to circulate that the U.S. was supporting a corrupt government in Vietnam.

Soon, a coup was mounted against President Diem, resulting in the assassination of Diem and his brother. Later evidence suggested that the CIA had at least tacitly supported the coup.

By the time Kennedy was assassinated in November 24, 1963, the situation in Vietnam had become very unstable. **Viet Cong guerrillas, fighting for North Vietnam, were occupying more and more of the countryside**.

As soon as President Johnson was sworn in, he took over management of the war. At press conferences, **he began making strong statements that the U.S. would not allow the communists to take Vietnam**.

At first, President Johnson made sure most of **the U.S. involvement in the Vietnam War was being done covertly**. Secret U.S. bombing raids, using U.S. airplanes and "volunteer" American pilots, were attacking Viet Cong bases both in Vietnam and in Laos. Defense Secretary McNamara began making more and more public statements indicating that the U.S. would support the new South Vietnamese military government. He said, "**We'll stay for as long as it takes.**"

After that, America was committed. Johnson believed the reputation of the U.S. (and his personal reputation) was on the line. But when word leaked out that our "support" of the South Vietnamese was already **costing the U.S. more than two million dollars a day**, more people began to ask if it was such a good idea to be committing those kinds of resources in a tiny and relatively unknown country halfway around the world.

Johnson continued to try to keep the war low profile, mainly because **he knew he didn't have the support in Congress for another Asian war so soon after the debacle in Korea**. He mostly used the CIA to conduct secret operations out of Saigon, and he used U.S. Navy warships to harass North Vietnamese installations along the coast. But the increasing success of the Viet Cong was causing political instability in Vietnam. **In one year, South Vietnam saw five different governments**

come into power. In the summer of 1964, President Johnson was preoccupied with running for election. He named Lt. Gen William C. Westmoreland to oversee operations in Vietnam.

Senator Barry Goldwater, who had been Johnson's Republican opponent in the last election, tried to use the lack of more aggressive action in Vietnam to paint Johnson as "soft on communism."

Only a few months before the next presidential election was to take place, the **"Gulf of Tonkin Incident"** took place. It involved U.S. warships that were supporting South Vietnamese speed boats that were staging attacks on North Vietnamese coastal installations. North Vietnamese torpedo boats came out to respond and were shelled by the USS Maddox, a Sumner-class destroyer. It was reported that at least one of the torpedo boats fired back, and that one 14.5 mm round hit the destroyer. The round didn't cause any serious damage on the Maddox, and no one was injured. Later that same day, a second attack was reported. **As minor as the incident was, it was nevertheless the excuse Johnson had been looking for to show he was not soft on communism.** He went on the radio to describe **two attacks by North Vietnamese vessels against U.S. Navy ships "on the high seas."** He said the U.S. could not allow such brazen attacks. In his speech, he did not indicate that the U.S. was already involved in Vietnam in any way other than in a supporting role. The implication of his speech was that the North Vietnamese had launched an unprovoked attack on a U.S. ship that was just minding its own business in international waters, and therefore, the U.S. had to respond.

The truth, as we later learned, was that **neither Johnson nor McNamara were sure there really had been an attack**, and later the captain of one of the ships involved said the second attack might have actually been a false radar image.

There was resistance in Congress to getting involved in Vietnam, but after some deliberation, they passed the **Tonkin Gulf Resolution** which authorized President Johnson to use "conventional" military force in Southeast Asia **if necessary**. Significantly, **it was not a formal declaration of war**. The "Vietnam War" was never actually designated as a war; it was termed a "**police action.**" Looking back, the term "police action" is an inappropriate euphemism for a conflict that is estimated to have **cost the lives of 266,000 Army of the Republic of Vietnam soldiers, 1,100,000 North Vietnamese Army and Viet Cong soldiers, 58,272 American soldiers, and 843,000 Vietnamese civilians**. In addition, **303,644 American soldiers were wounded in action,** not counting those that suffered from **post-traumatic stress disorder (PTSD)**.

As the U.S. involvement in Vietnam escalated, there were some protests against it back home in the United States, and later, as the news media began showing footage of Americans fighting and dying over there, the protests increased. **Eventually, some of the antiwar protests attracted as many as half a million people.**

In 1968, the **Viet Cong's Tet offensive** further undermined U.S. support for the war. Popular CBS anchorman Walter Cronkite visited Vietnam and went on TV to say that in his opinion the U.S. was mired in a stalemate in Vietnam. He was one of the first public figures to suggest that the U.S. might actually lose the war.

On March 31, 1968, **President Johnson went on live television to announce that he would not seek reelection**, saying, "There is division in the American house now."

> His 1964 campaign promise of creating a "great society" had been ruined when his focus turned to combating communism. It caused him to escalate a pointless war in Vietnam that ended in complete failure. By the end of his presidency, there was no great society, only a divided nation that was deeply involved in a war that was costing the country untold amounts of money and many thousands of American lives.

The Presidential Election of 1968

Johnson's decision not to run for reelection meant the 1968 race for the presidency would be wide open.

Richard Nixon, Eisenhower's former vice president threw his hat into the ring. His two main rivals were Michigan Governor **George W. Romney** and California Governor **Ronald Reagan**.

Everyone knew the election would be a referendum on the Vietnam War, and there were clear choices between the candidates. Nixon and Reagan were both saying America had to be tough on communism, and that Vietnam was a key test of America's resolve. Romney had voted for the **Tonkin Gulf Resolution,** and he had been an early supporter of the war, but now he said Vietnam was a mistake. **He said he had been "brainwashed" by the military into supporting the Vietnam War**. That remark cost him a lot of votes in the Republican primaries.

Both Nixon and Reagan knew the Democrats were likely to run somebody who would make ending the Vietnam War a priority. In order to make the election about fighting communism, **Nixon and Reagan tried to show they would be tougher on communism, and that they would win the war in Vietnam as part of that**. Much of Nixon's oratory was to rail against the anti-war protesters that he characterized as un-American supporters of worldwide communism.By the end of the Republican primaries, it was clear Republican voters were responding to Nixon's pro-war, anti-communist message.

There were a few antiwar protests at the **Republican national presidential nominating convention**, but most of the Republicans in attendance were in favor of continuing what they saw as a fight against communist aggression in Vietnam. Nixon was nominated, and as part of the new Republican "**Southern strategy**," he selected **Maryland Governor Spiro Agnew** as his running mate.

The **Democratic national presidential nominating convention** was anything but peaceful. Held in Chicago, it attracted many **thousands of antiwar protesters who gathered outside the convention center**. Mayor Richard Daley brought in 23,000 police and National Guardsmen to control the situation, and **many of the protesters were beaten and arrested**. Unfortunately for the Democrats, all this was shown on live TV, disrupting the coverage of the convention and making the Democrats, or at least the Chicago police, seem unnecessarily cruel. The **Walker Report**, a federal investigation of what happened, characterized it as "a police riot." The report blamed Mayor Richard J. Daley for what it called "unrestrained and indiscriminate police violence."

Hubert Humphrey, Johnson's vice president had won the most votes in the Democratic primaries, but when **Martin Luther King and presidential candidate Senator Robert F. Kennedy were assassinated. the anti-war candidate, Minnesota Senator Eugene McCarthy,** began to get a lot of votes.

Despite the divisive nature of the convention, Humphrey won the vote for nomination. Surprisingly, instead of doing the usual thing of picking a Southerner as his running mate, he picked **Edmund Muskie**, a senator from Maine.

The 1968 presidential election took place in an atmosphere of ongoing antiwar protests. Although Nixon worked hard to get Southern votes by appealing to conservatives, the segregationist **Alabama Governor George Wallace** managed to get himself on the ballot in the Southern states as the presidential nominee of the **American Independent Party**. He chose the militaristic Air Force **General Curtis LeMay** as his running mate. Wallace's main strategy was to try to get enough Electoral College votes in Southern states to send the decision to the U.S. House of Representatives. He aggressively campaigned against the anti-segregation policies of Johnson. He also pledged an immediate withdrawal of U.S. troops from Vietnam, but he made sure nobody thought he supported the antiwar protesters. Far from it; he said he was simply against the waste of money and lives in a pointless war in faraway Asia (which, of course, was exactly what most of the antiwar protesters were saying).

During the election, Wallace's running mate **Curtis LeMay got a lot of attention by saying he did not fear using nuclear weapons in the fight against communism**. He was widely quoted when he said the U.S. had the capability to **bomb Vietnam "back into the stone age."**

In the general election, because of the strong showing of third-party candidate George Wallace, Nixon's "Southern strategy" failed to win many Southern states. But Nixon was able to get enough votes in the Midwest and West to win the election, even squeaking out a win in his home state of California. Nixon's seemingly contradictory message of being *for* the war but promising to *end* the war (with honor), had somehow resonated with the American people.

The national popular vote was one of the closest ever, with 43.42% of the popular vote going to Nixon and 42.72% going to Humphrey. Wallace got almost ten thousand votes. Nevertheless, in the Electoral College, Nixon won 301 votes, Humphrey won 191, and Wallace won 46.

COMMENT

The very close 1968 election once again prompted Congress to try to get rid of the Electoral College. The House overwhelmingly passed a Constitutional amendment to change to a popular vote of the president. President Richard Nixon was behind it, and many of the states were deemed likely to approve it. However, Southern senators and conservatives from small states quickly filibustered to keep the proposal from being vot-

> ed on. Out of at least **700 attempts in Congress to alter the presidential-election system**, it came the closest to making an actual constitutional change to get rid of the Electoral College.

Many observers felt Humphrey had lost a lot of votes because he didn't try hard enough to dissociate himself from Johnson's failed Vietnam policy. In addition, he had failed to follow through with the Democratic "Southern strategy" to win votes in the South by supporting some of their demands.

Wallace's strategy of getting enough electoral votes to deny either Nixon or Humphrey the majority and send the decision to the House of Representatives failed, but it would have worked if Humphrey could have accumulated more votes in the West and in the South. If Humphrey would have toned down his talk about civil rights legislation, and if he would have selected a running mate from the South, he might have been able to win the more moderate states like Georgia, where he lost to Nixon by only 45,671 votes (Wallace got 535,550 votes there). **If Humphrey could have won even a few of the Southern states the Democrats had traditionally won, he would have won the presidency**. Wallace's role as a spoiler showed that **a third-party candidate could have a dramatic effect on the outcome of the presidential race**.

It didn't take Nixon long to grab hold of the same "**Vietnam tar baby**" that had ruined Johnson's presidency. By the time Nixon entered the White House, **over 500,000 troops were stationed in Vietnam and American soldiers were dying at the rate of 1200 a month**. With the antiwar protests mounting and public opinion turning against the war, many expected Nixon to deescalate U.S. involvement there. But he didn't. In fact, he did the opposite. The new Secretary of State, Henry Kissinger had convinced Nixon that the war was not "winnable" in the traditional sense, but **Nixon knew withdrawal would be political suicide**. He had been elected to "win" the war in Vietnam and to win it "with honor." That meant at least some kind of military victory in Vietnam was mandatory. Nixon and Kissinger came up with a two part strategy: they would build up South Vietnam's military and get them to take over more of the actual combat. At the same time, Nixon would order an increase in the intensity of the war, including bombing civilian areas in North Vietnam, in hopes it would bring the North Vietnamese to the bargaining table. **Nixon also ordered U.S. troops into the neighboring neutral countries of Cambodia and Laos.** At home, **Nixon tried to paint anti-war groups as supporters of communism,** and as the antiwar protests grew, he tried to appeal to **the "silent majority," the majority of Americans he said were quietly supporting what he was doing in Vietnam.** He tried to paint anyone who disagreed with him as **radical communist sympathizers. He also railed against the** "liberal media," saying they were trying to discredit him.

In response to the protests at Kent State University in Ohio, the governor of Ohio, James Rhodes, **sent in the National Guard with live ammunition** in their rifles, and they **fired into a crowd of demonstrating students. Thirteen students were hit, and four died.** Some of the students who were killed were shot intentionally as they tried to run away. Other students who were not part of the demonstration were killed some distance away as they were walking to their classes. When the details of the killings at Kent State were reported, many American Universities were shut down in sympathy.

Even though a presidential commission harshly criticized the guardsmen, concluding that "the indiscriminate firing of rifles into a crowd of students and the deaths that followed were unnecessary, unwarranted, and inexcusable," the killings dramatically increased the popularity of Governor Rhodes in Ohio and helped rejuvenate his flagging campaign for reelection. It was a clear indication of how divided the country had become during Nixon's presidency.

Eventually, Nixon said **the U.S. would begin to pull out of Vietnam by training and equipping the South Vietnamese Army, and thereby leave the war in the hands of the South**

Vietnamese. It was a complete failure. When the North Vietnamese continued to invade, the South Vietnamese military was unable to hold them back.

President Nixon had stated publicly that if the South Vietnamese needed our help, we would again intervene. But when his Secretary of Defense, James R. Schlesinger, stated that he was **ready to recommend resumption of the U.S. bombing of North Vietnam, the U.S. Senate quickly passed the Case-Church Amendment to prohibit any more United States military involvement in Vietnam**.

STORY

In 1970, news leaked out that **the Army had been covering up massacres of Vietnamese civilians. It was learned that the military had successfully hushed up a U.S. Army massacre of 504 Vietnamese women, children, and old men in a South Vietnamese village called My Lai**. The massacre had taken place in the spring of 1968 and had been systematically covered up by the Army brass at all levels of command. Later **interviews with some of the soldiers present at the massacre said they had been under orders to kill everybody in the village as part of a new "search and destroy" approach to the war**. They said the mission was not an unusual one and that **such things had been going on for some time**. They said that in addition to the murders at My Lai, **rapes and torture had also taken place, and that there was some mutilation of the civilian's bodies in revenge** for American soldiers that had been killed or wounded earlier.

Although the details of the mission were well known (several officers where on the ground during the massacre, and Colonel Oran K. Henderson, the brigade commander who had ordered the attack, observed it all from a helicopter hovering over the village), no action had been taken against the soldiers involved. **Everyone involved had been ordered to cover it up**.

> Years later, **a military trial brought criminal charges against 26 American soldiers who had been involved in the My Lai massacre**, but **the charges were eventually dropped, and only one officer, Second Lieutenant William Calley, a platoon leader, was found guilty**. Even though he said he was only following direct orders that had been given to him by his superiors, he was convicted of the premeditated murder of 22 Vietnamese civilians. He was given a life sentence, but the next day, **President Richard Nixon canceled the sentence and ordered Calley to be held under house arrest in his home at Fort Benning**.
>
> While today we might think the news that U.S. soldiers had killed innocent women and children and tortured and raped civilian women would lead to public outrage, **many in the U.S. rallied to the defense of the soldiers**. It was yet another indication of how divided the country was over the war in Vietnam. Indiana's governor asked that all **state flags to be flown at half-staff in support of Calley** and his men. **The governors of Utah and Mississippi came out publicly in support of Calley** and against his being sentenced to house arrest. The state legislatures of Arkansas, Kansas, Texas, New Jersey, and South Carolina **voted to request clemency for Calley**. Alabama's governor **George Wallace visited Calley to express his support**, and he requested that Nixon pardon Calley.
>
> **Calley stayed in his personal quarters at Fort Benning for three and a half years until President Nixon quietly arranged a pardon for him.**

The Presidential Election of 1972

In 1972, it was clear that once again, the election was going to take place while the war in Vietnam dragged on.

In the Republican primaries, Nixon's only serious competition came from **Congressman Pete McCloskey** of California who ran as an antiwar candidate. At the Republican national presidential nominating convention, Nixon won easily.

The Democratic race was wide open with fifteen men and two women declaring their candidacy. The 1972 election also saw the emergence of several third-party candidates vying for the presidency. Conservative U.S. Congressman **John G. Schmitz**, a member of the ultra-conservative **John Birch Society**, ran as a representative of the **American Party** which George Wallace had run on in 1968. Schmitz got onto the ballot in 32 states and received 1,099,482 votes, but he won no Electoral College votes.

Linda Jenness was nominated by the **Socialist Workers Party**, with Andrew Pulley as her running-mate.

Dr. Benjamin Spock was nominated by the **People's Party**.

1972 was the first time the **Libertarian Party** fielded a candidate. They nominated **John Hospers**, but he was only able to get on the presidential ballot in Colorado and Washington (every state had their own rules about how to get onto the presidential ballot, and Colorado and Washington were among the easiest.) Hospers received only 3,573 votes, but he did get one Electoral College vote in Virginia from a "**faithless elector**."

COMMENT

The term "**faithless elector**" refers to a member of a state's Electoral College who does not vote for the presidential candidate who won the state's popular vote. **The U.S. Constitution does not say members of the Electoral College are required to vote for the candidate that wins the popular vote**. In fact, in the Constitution, there is no mention of a popular vote. From the beginning, electors have been free to vote for anyone they wanted to in case **the people wanted "the wrong person"** to be their president By freeing members of the Electoral College to vote for anyone they chose to, *even if that person was not a candidate,* they **assured that political**

leaders in the states would have the final say about the presidency.

Faithless electors have never overturned an election, but over the years, there have been many who tried. Below is a brief description of each incident.

In 1796, Samuel Miles, a Federalist elector from Pennsylvania, refused to vote for the winner of the popular vote, Federalist candidate **John Adams**. Instead, he voted for **Thomas Jefferson**, the Democratic-Republican candidate. The Electoral College voting was so close, that had only a few more Federalist electors done the same thing, it would have changed the outcome of the election.

In 1808, six Democratic-Republican electors refused to support **James Madison**, their party's candidate for president, and instead, voted for **George Clinton**, the Democratic-Republican candidate for vice president.

In 1812, three Federalist electors refused to vote for the Federalist vice presidential candidate **Jared Ingersoll**. Instead, they voted for **Elbridge Gerry**, the vice presidential candidate from the opposing Democratic-Republican Party.

In 1820, James Monroe would have received all of the Electoral College votes if **William Plummer, the governor of New Hampshire,** acting as a Democratic-Republican elector, hadn't decided at the last minute to cast his vote for his friend, **John Quincy Adams,** even though Adams was not a candidate in that election. Supposedly, Plummer was protesting against the "wasteful extravagance" of the Monroe Administration and **he used his Electoral College vote to bring attention to that issue**. He also voted against **Daniel D. Tompkins**, Monroe's vice presidential choice, saying the man did "not have the weight of character which that office requires."

In 1828, seven of the nine electors from Georgia refused to vote for **John Calhoun, Andrew Jackson**'s choice for vice president. Instead, they voted for **William Smith**, a senator from South Carolina who was a vocal opponent of Calhoun. (In 1837, President Andrew Jackson nominated Smith to the Supreme Court, but he declined the honor.)

1832 saw the largest rebellion of electors in history. Thirty-two electors from Pennsylvania and Maryland refused to vote for the presidential candidate that had won the popular vote. Two Republican Party electors from Maryland **refused to vote for anyone** rather than cast their votes for **Henry Clay,** the candidate who had won their state. **In Pennsylvania, all 30 electors refused to vote for vice presidential candidate, Martin Van Buren**, even though he had won the popular vote. Instead, they voted for **William Wilkins**, the senator from their home state of Pennsylvania (Andrew Jackson and Martin Van Buren won anyhow).

The election of 1836 saw something happen in the Electoral College that changed the election's outcome and could have set a precedent that would change all future presidential elections: **some electors refused to vote for the candidate that won the popular vote, just because they didn't like his personal behavior**. Twenty-three Democratic electors from Virginia refused to cast their votes for the winning Democratic vice president, Richard M. Johnson of Kentucky, because **they'd learned he was involved in a sexual relationship with one of his African-American slaves**. Johnson caused much consternation because he openly admitted he was the father of that slave's child. Furthermore, after that slave woman died, **he took up sexual relationships with some of his other female slaves**, and he was perfectly willing to brag about it.

With the loss of those 23 votes, there was no majority in the Electoral College for vie president, so as specified in the U.S.

Constitution, the decision about who would be vice president was sent to the U.S. Senate for a "contingent election." In the Senate, with little debate, the senators voted strictly along party lines to name Johnson vice president.

An unusual situation occurred in **1872. Sixty-three of the sixty-six Democratic electors** who were from states Horace Greeley had won voted for somebody else because Greeley had died between the time the election was held and when the Electoral College met. **That was something the founding fathers hadn't considered when they created the Electoral College system.** Seventeen of the Greeley electors chose to cast no vote at all, but the other 46 electors voted for whoever they liked. They voted for four different candidates for president, and eight different candidates for vice president. **Three of the electors followed what they saw as their duty and voted for the dead man**. These votes were later disallowed by Congress, but it is not clear under what authority they disallowed the votes for Greeley because there is no provision in the Electoral College section of the Constitution specifying how such a situation should be dealt with.

As described earlier, the **presidential election of 1876** was the only election in which **Samuel J. Tilden, the candidate that won both the popular vote and the Electoral College vote did not get to be president**. A special Congressional commission, created after considerable contention, voted strictly along party lines to **invalidate many of the Electoral College votes from the South** due to perceived voter fraud. The commission declared the Republican, Rutherford B. Hayes, the Electoral College winner. It is not clear under what authority they had disallowed the Electoral College votes for Tilden. The Electoral College section of the Constitution does not mention any possible circumstance in which the winner of the Electoral College vote can be denied the presidency.

In 1896, four electors, unhappy with their winning vice presidential candidate, **Thomas E. Watson**, switched their votes to a different vice presidential candidate, **Arthur Sewall** from Maine.

In 1948, Preston Parks, a Southern Democratic elector from Tennessee, refused to cast his vote for the Democratic winner, Harry S. Truman. Instead, he cast his vote for Strom Thurmond, the segregationist States' Rights candidate. It was a remarkable moment in Electoral College history because **it showed that an elector could go so far as to vote for the opponent of the winner** of the popular vote if the elector had a personal disagreement with the policies of the winner. Strom Thurmond ended up getting 39 Electoral College votes, all from Southern electors.

In 1956, a Southern Democratic elector, **W.F. Turner from Alabama**, voted for his friend, Walter Burgwyn Jones, a U.S. congressman from Alabama (who was not a candidate). The elector didn't like Adlai Stevenson, the winner of the popular vote in Alabama, **so he simply refused to vote for him**.

In 1960, one elector planned a revolt that showed the danger of letting a few selected individuals decide who the nation's president would be. **Republican elector, Henry D. Irwin**, from Oklahoma, refused to vote for Richard Nixon, the candidate that had won his state. He simply said he "could not stomach" Nixon. And he went further: he tried to get all the other electors to reject both Nixon and Kennedy and vote instead for two of the most conservative members of the Senate, **Harry Byrd** of Virginia and **Barry Goldwater** of Arizona. He secretly tried to arrange a revolt among the Southern electors, but in the end, the other electors were not willing to go along with his plan (fourteen *unpledged* electors from Mississippi and Alabama *did* cast their presidential votes for Harry Byrd). Although Irwin's plan failed, **it did show what could happen if enough of the Electoral College members decided to get together**

and elect their own preferred candidate. If that ever happens, according to the wording of the Electoral College section of the Constitution, **there is nothing anyone will be able to do about it.**

In **1968, Republican elector, Dr. Lloyd W. Bailey of North Carolina,** refused to vote for Richard Nixon. Instead, he voted for George Wallace. Dr. Bailey pointed out (accurately) that the U.S. Constitution said nothing about him having to vote for the candidate who won his state. He also pointed out (accurately) that George Wallace had won his home district and that before the winner-take-all system had been instituted he would have been obliged to vote for Wallace.

In **1972, Republican elector Roger L. MacBride from Virginia** refused to cast his electoral vote for Richard Nixon, and instead voted for John Hospers, the Libertarian Presidential candidate. He also voted for the Libertarian vice presidential candidate, **Toni Nathan, making her the first woman ever to receive an Electoral vote.**

In **1976, Republican elector Mike Padden, a lawyer from Washington** refused to vote for the winner of his state, Gerald Ford, and instead voted for Ronald Reagan (who was not a candidate at that time).

In **1988, Democratic elector Margaret Leach from West Virginia** was shocked when she learned members of the Electoral College were not required to vote for the candidates they were pledged to. She decided to draw attention to this ridiculous situation by switching her votes for president and vice president. She cast her vote for Bentsen for president and Dukakis for vice president, and she tried to get the other electors to do the same in order to show the citizens of the United States what was possible with the nonsensical Electoral College system in place. But she was unable to convince any of the others to do what she had done.

In **2000, Democratic elector Barbara Lett-Simmons from the District of Columbia** refused to cast any vote at all. She intended it as a protest against the lack of Congressional representation for the citizens of Washington, DC.

In 2004, **an unknown Minnesota elector voted for someone he named John Ewards** instead of the Democrat that had won the Minnesota popular election, John Kerry. At that time, Minnesota's electors cast secret ballots. As a result of this incident, Minnesota now requires elector votes to be public.

In 2016, after it became obvious that Donald Trump was going to win in the Electoral College despite losing the popular vote by such a huge margin, there was a public outcry for the members of the Electoral College to rectify that unfair situation. Several electors said they were going to vote for a different Republican. **The group, which became known as "Hamilton Electors," said they would "vote their conscience for the good of America,"** and for a while it appeared that they might be able to get enough other electors to vote for someone other than Trump to throw the result to the House. When it became clear that they would not get enough other electors to go along with them, most of them backed out. However, a few of them did vote for Republican candidates other than Trump. **When they were punished with fines, they sued**, saying the state was acting against the will of the Constitution. **The case went all the way to the Supreme Court**, but that court was only willing to rule that the states **did** have the right to punish the faithless electors. They did not rule on the main issue of whether the electors had the right to vote for whoever they wanted to. Most historians believe the wording of the Electoral College section of the Constitution is no accident; **the founding fathers wanted to be sure the electors *did* have free rein to vote for anyone they wanted to.**

As the 1972 presidential election neared, it was clear that if Nixon was to win reelection, he was going to have to show progress was being made in Vietnam. The public's perception of the war in Vietnam was constantly growing less favorable. The country was ready for the war to be over. As a result, Nixon's campaign message was twofold: first, he tried to convince the American public that the war was going well; second, he had to convince them that his strategy was working to the degree that the war would soon be over. He added, that the U.S. had never lost a war, and "we are not going to lose this one."

Peace talks were going on in Paris, and just before the election, **Henry Kissinger returned to the United States and went before the press to announce that "peace is at hand."**

The polls indicated it was a winning strategy.

Before the election, newspaper stories appeared suggesting that the group that broke into Democratic headquarters in the Watergate building might be connected directly to Nixon. Either the people didn't believe the stories, or they didn't care, and **Nixon was easily reelected**.

STORY

The **Paris Peace Accords** were finally signed in January of 1973. Nixon had ordered intense bombing of civilian areas of North Vietnam in order to force North Vietnam to the peace table, but a much more important concession was that America was ready to leave Vietnam to the Vietnamese. **The country would remain divided. The U.S. would train and equip the South Vietnamese Army, but the U.S. military would leave the country.**

Although the peace accords ended America's involvement in the war, it didn't end the war. Nixon ordered a "Vietnamization" of the war, a program of training and equipping the Army of the Republic of Viet Nam (ARVN) to be sure they could hold South Vietnam without the presence of U.S. troops.

> The Vietnamization program was a complete failure, and when the North Vietnamese again invaded the south, the South Vietnamese military was unable to hold them back.
>
> In April of 1975, Saigon fell to communist forces, and the last few Americans still in South Vietnam were airlifted out of the country.

Chapter Twelve
Secret Presidential Power

After Nixon was reelected in 1972, Americans began hearing more about the group that had been arrested for breaking into the Democratic National Committee's offices in the Watergate office building. The group, that was to become known as the **White House plumbers,** claimed to be investigating "leaks," but diligent newspaper reporters eventually found out the group was tied to President Nixon's reelection committee.

STORY

On the night of June 17, 1972, a group **broke into the Democratic National Committee (DNC) headquarters in the Watergate building in Washington, D.C**. They looked for information about Democratic strategy, and they placed wiretaps in the DNC offices. A security guard noticed tape on a door that was being used to keep the door from locking. He called the police, and five men, Bernard Barker, Virgilio González, Eugenio Martínez, James McCord, and Frank Sturgis, were caught inside the Democratic National Committee offices and arrested.

As soon as Nixon found out about the arrests, he and his Attorney General John Mitchell began a cover-up to keep the American public from finding out what was really behind the break-in. Nixon's **presidential counsel, John Dean**, spearheaded the cover-up effort, and at first, Nixon was confident they would be able to distance themselves from it.

However, two reporters from the **Washington Post** newspaper,**Bob Woodward and Carl Bernstein**, kept digging and eventually managed to contact an informant who gave them information implicating the president. The two reporters refused to name their informant. They said the informant was known only by the code name, **"Deep Throat"** (many years later the informant was revealed to be **Federal Bureau of Investigation Associate Director Mark Felt**). Woodward and Bernstein were able to trace money that had been paid to the Watergate burglars. **It turned out to be money that had been donated to the president's reelection effort.** Piece by piece, Woodward, Bernstein, and other reporters ferreted out more information about the White House plumbers group. Despite intense efforts on Nixon's part to cover up the whole mess, information continued to leak out, and eventually, all five Watergate burglars were **tied directly or indirectly to Nixon's reelection committee**. In March of 1973, five **months after Nixon had been elected with an overwhelming Electoral College majority, his attorney, John Dean, fearing a prison sentence for himself, began cooperating with the U.S. Attorney's office. He implicated several of Nixon's aides.**

In May of 1973, **the U.S. Senate formed a committee to investigate** the whole Watergate affair. The hearings were televised live, and the entire country watched with rapt attention as the story unfolded through the testimony of **John Dean** and other members of Nixon's inner circle. One bit of tantalizing information Dean revealed to the committee was that Nixon secretly audio taped all of his meetings. **The committee asked Nixon to turn over the tapes, but he refused.** It took a series of court battles that eventually led to a decision by the U.S. Supreme Court that he had to comply with the request and turn over transcripts of the tapes. Although forensic analyses of the tapes showed that some conversations had been intentionally erased, they did reveal that Nixon was aware of hush payment to some of the Watergate defendants. The tapes also revealed that Nixon tried to get the CIA to claim that the Watergate break-in was part of a national security investigation.

In July, the House filed **articles of impeachment against Nixon, citing three articles: 1) obstruction of justice, 2) abuse of power, and 3) contempt of Congress.**

At first, **some Congressional Republicans stood firm in their support of Nixon**, but when more tapes came to light that showed how actively Nixon was involved in the cover-up, they too finally said they would vote for impeachment.

When Nixon heard that even the Republicans in Congress were abandoning him, he went on TV to announce he was resigning the presidency. He left the White House the next day. He was **the first, and only, U.S. President ever to resign.**

Vice President Gerald Ford succeeded him and soon **granted Nixon a full pardon for any crimes he might have committed while president.**

A total of 25 officials from the Nixon administration, including four cabinet members, were eventually convicted and imprisoned.

The Presidential Election of 1976

After Nixon resigned, **Gerald Ford** served out the remainder of the presidential term and ran for reelection in **1976**. Ford was handicapped both by Nixon's Watergate scandal and by the fact that he had never been elected to any national office

In 1976, more and more people were aspiring to be president. Fifteen candidates competed in the Democratic primaries, including governors, senators, U.S. representatives, an ambassador, and a housewife.

As the Democratic primaries went on, it became clear that **Jimmy Carter**, the former governor of Georgia was going to prevail.

He was nominated at the Democratic nominating convention, and he went on to mount an effective campaign as an outsider who would go to Washington to change the kind of dirty politics Nixon had been engaged in.

STORY

Although televised debates had played a significant role in the Kennedy-Nixon election of 1960, no televised debates occurred after that until the election of 1976.

In 1964, President Johnson was so far ahead of the Republican candidate, Senator Barry Goldwater, he saw no need to risk that lead by debating.

And then, in 1968, Johnson decided not to run for reelection. His vice president, **Hubert Humphrey**, wanted to debate candidate Nixon, but Nixon was not about to revisit his 1960 problems with television. And then, once Nixon had managed to win the White House, he was not about to risk losing it again by participating in any of those dreaded televised debates.

In 1976, after President Ford fell behind in the polls, he felt he had no choice but to debate Carter. Unlike the previous televised debates, the debates of 1976 were held before a live audience. The first debate began after a long delay due to technical problems with the television feed. Although both candidates had chairs available to them, neither of them sat down while they waited for fear that they would look weak.

When the debate finally got going, Carter launched the expected attack on President Ford regarding the weak economy the country was going through. Carter said the country was in an inflationary spiral, and there was no chance of balancing the budget until we found a way to get people back to work. He suggested tax cuts and some incentive programs. He said the present tax structure was a disgrace to the country, a welfare program for the rich. Ford said he also favored tax cuts and incentive programs. In fact, he said he had already made some of

> those kinds of suggestions to the Congress, but they had not gone along with his ideas. Ford was also challenged about how to deal with the many draft-dodgers who had refused induction because of the Vietnam War. Carter asked Ford why, if he had pardoned Nixon, he would refuse to pardon the draft-dodgers.
>
> The consensus was that although Carter had made some good points, Ford had adequately held his own.
>
> Unfortunately for Ford, he did not do as well in the second debate when he made a blunder about foreign affairs. He said, "There is no Soviet domination of Eastern Europe and there never will be under a Ford administration." He went on to say that he did not believe the people of Eastern Europe considered themselves to be "dominated by the Soviet Union."
>
> After the second debate, Carter surged ahead in the polls and President Ford was never able to recover.

Carter and his running mate, **Walter Mondale from Minnesota**, won all the Southern states except Virginia (which they lost by only 22,658 votes).

Ford won most of the Midwestern and Western states, but **his controversial full pardon of Nixon hurt him elsewhere**.

The popular vote was fairly close with 40,831,881 votes going to Carter and 39,148,634 votes to Ford. **The Electoral College vote was 297 for Carter and 240 for Ford.** Carter thus became the first president from the deep South since Zachary Taylor in 1848. **Eugene McCarthy**, a former Democratic senator from Minnesota. was known for his anti-Vietnam position. He ran as an independent and got 756,631 popular votes, but he didn't win any electoral votes.

The Presidential Election of 1980

As the 1980 presidential election season began, the American people were dismayed about the continuing poor economy, and they were upset about the taking of American hostages in Iran, an incident that became known as the **Iran Hostage Crisis**.

Many were also upset with Carter's decision not to allow U.S. athletes to compete in the 1980 Olympics in Moscow. It was his way of protesting the Soviet invasion of Afghanistan, but many felt the international Olympic movement was a venue to honor the world's best athletes and not a place for political statements. They felt if President Carter's Olympic boycott was allowed to stand, other countries would retaliate and every Olympics from then on would be marred by political posturing.

President **Jimmy Carter** led in most of the Democratic primaries, but **Senator Edward M. (Ted) Kennedy** of Massachusetts was also making a strong showing.

By the time the Democratic national presidential nominating convention came around, Carter had enough votes to win, but a strong anti-Carter mood on the convention floor resulted in a last minute "**draft Muskie**" movement to replace Carter with Secretary of State **Edmund Muskie** from Maine. It failed and Carter was nominated.

STORY

The **Iranian Hostage Crisis** took place in 1979 when a group of Islamist students and militant revolutionaries took over the American embassy in Tehran.

The revolutionaries were involved in a power struggle with Mohammad Rezā Shāh Pahlavī, **the Shah of Iran,** who was supported by the United States. With the support of Revolutionary leader Ayatollah Ruhollah Khomeini, the militants captured American citizens who had been in the embassy and held them as hostages.

As the months went by, President Carter came under increasing criticism for not doing something about it. Finally, Carter approved a rescue mission code named **Operation Eagle**. The plan was to use helicopters and U.S. Army Delta Force troops to fly into Iran and rescue the hostages. Unfortunately,

> some of the helicopters suffered mechanical problems and the mission was called off. And then, as one of the helicopters was being refueled, it collided with the refueling tanker aircraft causing the helicopter to crash, and soldiers aboard were killed.
>
> The new government of Iran, under the control of Ayatollah Ruhollah Khomeini, agreed to release the hostages if the U.S. would agree to release several billion dollars of Iranian assets that had been frozen in American banks when the hostages were first taken. President Carter was secretly working with various international banks to make the deal come about, but it took so long to finalize the details that **by the time the hostages were flown out of Iran, Carter had already been defeated.**

The early 1980 Republican primaries indicated that their nominee would likely be former **California Governor Ronald Reagan**. Reagan was fairly well known outside of California, because before being elected governor, he had been a movie actor and TV commercial representative. Barring any unexpected developments, Reagan was sure to win the Republican nomination at the Republican national nominating convention.

Reagan won the nomination and selected one of his opponents, **George H. W. Bush** of Texas as his running mate.

In the general election, Reagan based his campaign on what he called "**conservative values**," giving Carter ammunition for his accusations that Reagan was a dangerous right wing radical who would take the country down the wrong path.

> ### STORY
> Although Ronald Reagan had previously been a registered Democrat who supported Roosevelt's very liberal "**New Deal**" policies, his two terms in office as California's Republican

governor established his credentials as a **conservative**. His tenure as California's governor took place during a time of **great dissonance in the state over the Vietnam War**. California was a fairly liberal state, but Reagan soon showed that he was going to support the conservative side on most issues. He had plenty of liberal opposition in the state due to his defense of the Vietnam War and his frequent **sarcastic attacks on student antiwar protesters** (he called them "welfare bums").

There was a recall effort against him, but when it failed Reagan took that as a sign that his policies had the support of the people.

When the anti-Vietnam protests began to grow at California state universities, **Reagan began to crack down on the protesters, calling them "communist-inspired."** Reagan frequently used the California state police against the student protesters, and when a large **"people's protest"** was staged at the University of California campus in Berkeley, he called in National Guard troops. They occupied the area of the city around the university campus for two weeks. **When one student, James Rector, was killed by police gunfire, Reagan's response was, "If it takes a bloodbath, let's get it over with. No more appeasement."** His strong actions against the student protesters **had the approval and support of J. Edgar Hoover, the director of the FBI. (It was later learned that Reagan had secretly been working for Hoover when he was in the Hollywood actor's union** in order to root out "communists" in the movie industry. From then on, Hoover and the FBI were reported to have done everything they could to help Reagan's political career.)

The election of 1980 was not close. **Although Carter was a Southerner, the South was now mainly Republican.** Carter won his home state and a handful of Northern states, but Reagan won all the other Southern states and all of the Midwest and West.

Reagan's Electoral College win of 489-49 was the largest in U.S. history for a candidate running against an incumbent.

Republican Congressman John B. Anderson of Illinois also managed to get himself on the ballot in many states, running as an independent.

Carter refused to debate Anderson, but Reagan agreed, and most observers felt Anderson had done very well against Reagan. In the general election, **Anderson got 5,719,850 votes, but he won no electoral votes.**

The Presidential Election of 1984

In the presidential election of 1984, Reagan ran for reelection, but being **the oldest president in U.S. history**, there were questions about whether he should be elected for another term. Nevertheless, he dominated the primaries and easily won the nomination at the Republican presidential nominating convention.

After Senator Ted Kennedy again declined to run for president, the Democratic primaries indicated the nomination would come down to three candidates, former vice president, **Walter Mondale** of Minnesota, Senator **Gary Hart** of Colorado, and civil rights leader **Jesse Jackson** of Illinois.

At the Democratic nominating convention, Mondale won, and he chose **New York Congresswoman Geraldine Ferraro** as his running mate. **It was the first time a woman had been on the ticket of any major political party.** The Democrats hoped she would attract the women's vote.

Mondale and Ferraro immediately began an attack on Reagan's so-called conservative values, saying he was using the threat of communism to scare Americans into going along with his extreme right-wing policies. They also said **his so-called anti-socialist economic policies were being used to turn average Americans against the poor and minorities.**

The Reagan campaign focused mostly on his "cold war" foreign policy and on his approach to American economics that had became known as **"Reaganomics."** Reaganomics was the idea that if you get rid of business regulations and cut taxes on the rich, the resulting benefits to the most wealthy would "**trickle down**" to the middle class.

During the primaries, Reagan had little opposition, although another Republican candidate, George H. W. Bush, derided Reaganomics as "**voodoo economics**."

After the nominations, the nation tuned in to the **televised debates**. After the first debate, which was limited to domestic policy, most observers felt Reagan had done poorly against Mondale. **Reagan seemed hesitant and at times confused**. But in the second debate, which was about international policy and national defense, Reagan seemed more confident.

Even as the debates were going on, the Reagan campaign was producing **slick television ads that emphasized the threat from Russia** and fostered a "peace through strength" approach to foreign policy. The ads said it was the only way to **stop the spread of worldwide communism**.

COMMENT

Reagan's cold war foreign policy of fighting communism on all fronts was quite vividly demonstrated in 1983 when a military coup in Granada, a small island off the coast of Venezuela, replaced the government with one that was sympathetic to communist ideals. Reagan immediately sent in 7,000 troops, consisting of ranger battalions and airborne paratroopers to depose the new Granada government. Although most Americans supported the invasion as a necessary part of the fight against communism, it was criticized by the United Nations General Assembly as "**a flagrant violation of international law.**"

Reagan's campaign approach, plus his personal appeal, worked. **He won easily**. He even won 55 percent of the women's vote **despite the presence of a woman on the opposing Democratic ticket. The Mondale-Ferraro ticket won only Mondale's home state of Minnesota and the District of Columbia.

Reagan was a popular president, but information began to leak out that he had created a secret task force not unlike the one that had resulted in Nixon's resignation. Further investigation led to what is now known as the **Iran-Contra scandal** (sometimes referred to as **"Irangate"**).

STORY

The **Iran-Contra scandal** began when **President Reagan created a secret organization known as "the Enterprise."** It was originally created as a way to deal with Iran in order to gain the release of hostages being held by terrorists in Lebanon. **The Enterprise group** worked out a deal with the Iranian Army wherein the U.S. would sell weapons to Iran to help with their ongoing war with Iraq, and in return, they would try to secure the release of the hostages.

National Security Adviser Robert McFarlane told President Reagan about the potential deal, but **they were stymied because there was an embargo against selling arms to Iran. Reagan wanted to go ahead with the deal anyhow. Secretary of Defense Caspar Weinberger** and **Secretary of State George Shultz** opposed the deal, but McFarlane and **CIA director William Casey** supported it. With the backing of President Reagan, the plan was put into action. The result was that **arms, including thousands of missiles, were sent to Iran**, and in exchange, a few hostages were released. Unfortunately, they were soon replaced with new hostages. It appeared that Iran had discovered a way to get military arms from the U.S.—just take hostages and then trade them for weapons.

When the Lebanese newspaper, **Al-Shiraa**, printed an exposé of the deal in November of 1986, **President Reagan went on TV to vehemently deny any such deal had been made.** A week later, he admitted some kind of operation *had* occurred, but said it was definitely not an arms-for-hostages deal. Insiders in the Reagan administration continued to support him and defend him. Later, some said **President Reagan was having memory problems** at the time and may have simply forgotten the details of the operation.

Polls indicated most Americans **believed President Reagan was not telling the truth,** and his popularity declined. But he still had plenty of support among Republicans. They felt that **although what he had done might have been illegal, it had been done with good intentions**.

That might have been the end of the affair, but it was soon discovered that **eighteen million dollars out of the thirty million dollars the Iranians had paid for the American weapons had disappeared**. A member of the National Security Council, **Lieutenant Colonel Oliver North**, admitted he had been diverting funds from the arms sales to **the Contras**, a group that was fighting against the communist government in Nicaragua. Although **direct support of the Contras was against U.S. law**, Reagan was well known as a supporter of the Contras, calling them **"the moral equivalent of our Founding Fathers."** It was also revealed that **North had been working with drug smugglers and with Panamanian dictator Manuel Noriega** to assist the Contras. North said everything he did had been done **with the full knowledge of National Security Adviser Admiral John Poindexter and, he assumed, with the full knowledge of President Reagan.**

Poindexter resigned and North was fired, but Reagan continued to claim he didn't know anything about it.

To many members of the national media, the connection between the arms sale and the diversion of the money to the Reagan-supported Contra seemed like the same kind of secret White House operation that had driven Nixon out of office. They hounded the president about it at every press conference, but Reagan continued to deny any knowledge of what his closest advisers were up to.

Some of Reagan's aides were tried and convicted, but when Reagan's vice president George Bush was elected in 1988, **he pardoned most of them,** including **Secretary of Defense Caspar W. Weinberger. Oliver North was indicted on sixteen felony counts, but they were all later overturned.** Using the publicity he got during the Iran-Contra hearings, North ran for the U.S. senate in 1994 as a Republican against **Democrat Charles Robb**, son-in-law of President Lyndon B. Johnson.

North was able to raise over twenty million dollars to fund his campaign, but the Iran-Contra affair continued to haunt him, and he was defeated.

Since then, North has been a regular commentator on cable news programs and has written several best-selling books.

Chapter Thirteen
Foreign Wars and Presidential Scandal

The Presidential Election of 1988

The presidential election of 1988 saw Vice President **George H. W. Bush** winning **the Republican nomination** by promising to continue the policies of outgoing president Ronald Reagan. He chose Senator **Dan Quayle** from Indiana as his running mate.

With the Iran Contra scandal continuing to dominate the news, Democrats were optimistic that they could take back the presidency. **Due to the Iran-Contra scandal, they had regained control of the senate** after six years of Republican domination.

In 1988, a large number of candidates fought for the Democratic nomination. At first, Gary Hart seemed to be the most likely nominee, but questions were raised about his extramarital affairs.

Senator Edward M. Kennedy of Massachusetts again decided against running in 1988, and Arkansas Governor Bill Clinton also declined to run.

Eventually, the convention nominated **Michael Dukakis**, the governor of Massachusetts. He chose U.S. Senator **Lloyd Bentsen** as his running mate.

The 1988 campaign was one of finger pointing. Bush said Dukakis was too liberal, and Dukakis said Bush was too conservative and too militaristic.

Dukakis tried to tie Bush to the Iran-Contra scandal, saying Bush's involvement in the sale of arms to Iran showed Bush had "failed the test of leadership."

In the general election, Bush won the popular vote by about seven million votes (out of ninety million votes cast). **In the Electoral College vote, the margin was larger, 426 to 111**.

The Republican candidate, Bush, won the South, as was becoming the trend, but he also won California and most of the Midwestern and Northern states.

It turned out to be the last election in which a Republican presidential candidate would win California.

Libertarian Ron Paul from Texas and his running mate, **Andre V. Marrou** from Alaska were also on the ballot in many states. They gathered 431,750 votes nationwide, but no electoral college votes.

At first, Bush was a popular president. But a 1990 jump in the price of oil was tied to a brief war in **the Middle East** (now known as the **first Gulf War**). In addition, a weak economy and **huge government budget deficits** hurt his popularity.

As the 1992 presidential elections approached, his chances of being reelected seemed in doubt.

STORY

The **first Gulf War** was a military action waged by a United Nations authorized coalition of forces against Iraq in response to Iraq's invasion of Kuwait.

In August of 1990, **Iraqi troops invaded Kuwait with the intention of annexing the country**. The invasion was met by widespread condemnation and immediate economic sanctions against Iraq by some UN member nations.

President Bush sent American ships to the area and **deployed forces in Saudi Arabia** to gather near the Kuwait border. Saudi Arabia, Britain, and Egypt also sent troops and promised financial support.

Starting **in January of 1991, the U.S. began an aerial bombardment** on Iraqi positions. **Much of the aerial attack was shown on American television, and for some time, it dominated the news.**

Ground troops were sent in after the aerial attack, and within a few days, the **Iraqi forces had been pushed back into their** own country. At that point, President Bush ordered a cease fire. The war had lasted only a few days, and some in the U.S. criticized the president for not continuing the war. It was seen as a chance to oust the presiding regime in Iraq. However, both Bush and his Secretary of Defense, Dick Cheney, pointed out that **the UN mandate** was only to push the Iraqis out of Kuwait. They felt **further action would have made the United States, with its overwhelmingly powerful military machine, seem like an invading bully, and that might create new enemies in the Middle East**.

By the end of the hostilities, it is estimated that there were between 20,000 and 35,000 Iraq military fatalities plus an estimated 100,000 civilian deaths. According to the U.S. Department of Defense, **U.S. forces suffered 148 battle-related deaths, 35 of them from so-called "friendly fire"** (killed by their own troops). Another 145 deaths occurred in non-combat accidents. The United Kingdom reported 47 deaths, 9 to friendly fire. Other countries that were involved reported 37 deaths.

The Presidential Election of 1992

In 1992, **President George H. W. Bush ran for reelection** and was again nominated by the Republican Party. Although there was some discussion about replacing Dan Quayle as the vice presidential candidate, in the end, Bush stuck with him.

After a long and contentions primary season, with many well-known candidates vying for the nomination, the **Democrats** finally nominated the popular **Arkansas Governor, Bill Clinton.** He chose **Tennessee Senator Al Gore** as his running mate.

The Bush campaign chose a personal attack strategy. They accused Clinton of marital infidelity and draft dodging.

The **Clinton campaign focused almost entirely on the economy,** pointing out the fact that the Republicans had a long history of increasing the size of government and thereby increasing the national debt.

In the 1992 election, political polling was getting ever more sophisticated, and the polls were indicating that **Bush's personal attack strategy wasn't working**. People were more concerned with their own pocketbooks. **Another problem for the Republicans was that the cold war was cooling down**. A political moderate, **Mikhail Gorbachev**, had been named the General Secretary of the Soviet Union's Communist Party. As a result, **the usual Republican rhetoric about the worldwide communist threat fell on deaf ears**. By then, the Berlin Wall had come down and the phrase "Iron Curtain" was relegated to history. With no looming enemy abroad, all Bush had left to campaign on was his record, and many observers felt his campaign promise of "**Read my lips: no new taxes**" in the prior election hurt him because he'd been forced to raise taxes as part of a compromise with Congress.

STORY

The surprise of the presidential election of 1992 was the candidacy of **Texas billionaire Ross Perot**. At one point during the campaign, **Perot was leading both Bush and Clinton in the national polls**. It seemed as if the public was ready to consider an outsider for president. Midway through the 1992 race, Clinton was still leading in the polls, but when the presidential debates began, Ross Perot made some gains by attacking *both* Bush and Clinton. Some felt Perot would pull votes away from Clinton, improving Bush's chances for reelection, but Perot was also talking about the poor economy and pointing out how much the Republicans were running up the national debt.

In the end, **Perot managed to get 19,743,821 votes, but he wasn't able to win a single state** and therefore didn't get any Electoral College votes. **It seems Perot pulled votes away from *both* Clinton and Bush.**

Clinton's message about the Republican's poor handling of the economy won out and Clinton won the popular election by

5,805,256 votes (out of 104,423,923 votes cast). **He won the Electoral College vote even more convincingly, 370 to 168.**

The Presidential Election of 1996

By the time the election of 1996 rolled around, **Clinton was being credited with improving the economy**, and he was reducing the national debt. **He was also successful at keeping the U.S. out of any foreign wars**. The absence of a Russian threat, meant he was able to cut some military expenditures which helped reduce the national debt even more.

After **Clinton announced that he would seek reelection in 1992**, the Republicans began to criticize his "liberalism."

Ten serious candidates **fought for the Republican presidential nomination** during the Republican primaries.

Pat Buchanan, a well-known conservative, won some of the early Republican primaries, but eventually **Bob Dole** pulled ahead and was nominated as the Republican's 1992 presidential candidate. He chose **Jack Kemp**, a former congressman (and former professional football player) as his running mate.

Ross Perot again jumped into the race.

With no serious competition for the Democratic nomination, Clinton was able to get his campaign started early. **He raised a lot of money and mounted an intensive TV campaign**.

In order to secure the Republican nomination, Dole had to appeal to the more conservative elements of the Republican party, especially in the South. **That gave Clinton the ammunition he needed to paint Dole as a right-winger** who would cut popular social programs like Medicare and Social Security.

The relatively young and talkative Clinton came off well in the election debates. In contrast, Dole seemed more hesitant.

Ross Perot's chances of winning any Electoral College votes were dashed when he was left out of the televised presidential debates. (He later sued, claiming an unfair lack of coverage by the TV networks, but his lawsuit was thrown out of court.)

In the 1996 general election, because the Democrats were becoming known for pushing civil rights legislation, **Clinton lost the South.** He also lost much of the Midwest, but he was able to regain Democratic dominance in California and in the East. He won the popular vote by 8,201,370 votes and won the Electoral College vote 379 to 159.

In his second term, Clinton continued his policy of budget reductions and reduced military expenditures, but in 1998, **there was talk on the internet that he was involved in a sexual relationship with a 22-year-old White House intern named Monica Lewinsky.** At first, Clinton denied the affair, but eventually admitted he had engaged in some sexual "fooling around."

The Republicans, who were in control of the House of Representatives at that time, impeached him for trying to cover up the affair. Although a few past presidents have been threatened with impeachment, **President Clinton was only the second president in the history of the United States to actually be impeached** by the House of Representatives. However, the Senate did not confirm the impeachment.

STORY

The **Lewinsky scandal**, sometimes referred to as "**Monicagate**," came to light in the fall of 1997 when White House intern, **Monica Lewinsky**, confided to a coworker named **Linda Tripp** that she had been having a sexual affair with President Clinton. Tripp reported it to **literary agent, Lucianne Goldberg**, who advised Tripp to engage Lewinsky in more conversations and secretly record whatever Lewinsky said. When Tripp did that, Goldberg urged Tripp to take the tapes to **Kenneth Starr**. Starr had been appointed by President Reagan to a federal judgeship, but was at that time a private practice lawyer acting as an independent counsel to investigate some of President Clinton's past real estate investments. Goldberg began speaking to reporters about the existence of the tapes, and in January of 1998, the Washington Post reported the accusations.

Clinton immediately **denied having "sexual relations" with Miss Lewinsky, and his wife, Hillary Clinton, stood by her husband throughout the scandal, describing it as "a vast right-wing conspiracy against my husband."**

By the summer of that year, Lewinsky had been called before a grand jury and had received transactional immunity in exchange for her testimony. **She told the grand jury about the affair, and later turned over a semen-stained dress to Starr as DNA evidence proving she was telling the truth.**

When Clinton was called before the grand jury, he admitted he had had an "improper physical relationship" with Lewinsky that was "not appropriate." But he defended himself against the charge that he had lied about the affair when he said he had not had sexual relations with her by saying he had not understood that letting her perform oral sex on him could be included in the strict definition of "sexual relations." He said he had never been "the actor," in the affair and had never made physical contact with Lewinsky's "genitalia, anus, groin, breast, inner thigh, or buttocks." That argument didn't carry much weight with the Republicans in the House of Representatives. They were in the majority, and they initiated impeachment proceedings against him. **Almost all of the Republicans in the House voted for the majority of the articles of impeachment, and four Democratic representatives from the South voted with them**, as did Representative Paul McHale of Pennsylvania.

If a president is impeached by the House of Representatives, it must be confirmed by the Senate with a two-thirds majority.

After the televised senate hearings concluded, 45 Republican senators voted guilty, but all of the Democrats and 10 of the Republicans voted not guilty.

Chapter Fourteen

The Electoral College System Fails Again

The Presidential Election of 2000

Now we come to the very significant presidential election of 2000. In the preceding pages, I hope I have made clear the complex and unwieldy way U.S. presidents are elected via the Electoral College system. With that understanding in mind, let's closely examine the 2000 presidential election to try to understand **how a candidate could win the popular vote by 543,895 votes and yet not get to be president.**

After the revelation of President Clinton's sexual exploits in the White House and his impeachment by the House for trying to deny it, many wondered how much it would hurt the Democratic party in the next election. Everybody knew it would hurt, but no one knew if it would be enough to overcome the positive effect of the Democrats having been in power **during a time of peace with a good economy.**

Al Gore, Clinton's vice president, ran for president and took the position that the Clinton's affair had nothing to do with him. He won the nomination easily and selected **Joseph I. Lieberman,** a senator from Connecticut, as his running mate. Lieberman was the first observant Jew to be named on the ticket of any major party, and many wondered it that would be important in the election.

The **Republican primaries** were wide open. There were no fewer than 13 candidates vying for the nomination.

In the **Republican presidential primaries, Arizona Senator John McCain** took the early lead by winning the New Hampshire primary, but from then on it was mostly wins for George W. Bush.

At the Republican presidential nominating convention, Bush won easily. He named **Texan Dick Cheney, the CEO of**

military contractor **Halliburton Company** as his running mate. Cheney had been Secretary of Defense under Bush's father, George H. W. Bush.

When somebody remembered that the U.S. Constitution states that the presidential and vice presidential nominees cannot be from the same state, **Cheney quickly got a driver's license from Wyoming and put his Texas home up for sale.**

A third-party candidate, **Ralph Nader**, nominee of the **Green Party**, was on the ballot in Florida, and that **probably cost Gore the presidency.**

The 2000 presidential campaign was mainly **a battle of television ads**, many of them negative (meaning they attacked the opponent rather than extolling the virtues of the candidate who placed the ad). **The three October debates were also important.** In the first televised debate, **those present in the auditorium felt Bush had performed very poorly.** In fact, immediately after the debate ended, Bush's handlers went on TV to attribute his poor showing to the fact that he had been ill. They also said he had not had adequate time to prepare for the debate. **But when the polls came out the next day, a majority of the television viewing audience said they liked what they saw in George Bush.** They said he seemed like **"a regular guy."**

Gore accused Bush and the Republicans of being too "right wing" and too militaristic. There was also a lot of talk about where Bush's campaign funds were coming from. Gore talked about the tax breaks **the wealthiest one percent** were getting, pointing out that it was **the other 99 percent** that were responsible for the country's current prosperity and the budget surplus, so why should they have to pay more in taxes and the rich less?

The Bush campaign focused on the "Clinton-Gore" years in an attempt to tie Gore closely to the now-unpopular Bill Clinton.

Gore tried to distance himself from Clinton personally, but he did often make reference to how Clinton had turned the budget deficits of the Republican years into a budget surplus.

Bush responded by saying Gore was using "fuzzy math."

In the end, Gore won the entire West Coast accounting for 7,829,197 of his popular vote total. Gore also won **the East**, except for New Hampshire which he lost by only 7,211 votes.

In just three of the eastern states he won, New Jersey, New York, and Pennsylvania, he got 7,878,047 popular votes. Gore was racking up large pluralities in the large population states.

In **the Midwest, Gore won** Illinois, Iowa, Michigan, Minnesota, and Wisconsin, and Bush narrowly won the all-important state of Ohio with its 21 Electoral College votes.

It is important to note that in the states Gore won, **Nader was also strong. Without Nader in the race, it is likely Gore would have won the popular vote by more than a million votes.** However, Gore still wouldn't have won in the Electoral College.

Of course, the **Republican Bush won every Southern state**, including his home state of Texas, and he **won the Western states that had small populations**, including Colorado, Idaho, Kansas, Montana, Nebraska, Nevada, North Dakota, Oklahoma, South Dakota, Utah, and Wyoming which gave him **60 Electoral College votes**. The total number of voters in those states was 9,394,171. In comparison, **California had 10,965,856 voters, a million and a half more voters than all of the small Western states put together. However, California only gave Gore 54 Electoral College votes. It again showed the advantage the smaller-population states have in the Electoral College.**

COMMENT

The **Florida voting outcome in the 2000 presidential election** was very controversial. With Bush's conservative Republican brother, Jeb Bush serving as the governor in Florida, most observers thought Bush would win the state's presidential election easily. But Florida had **large Hispanic and African-American populations that traditionally vote Democratic**. Gore's running mate, Joe Lieberman, was Jewish, and that was expected to hurt them in the South, but the large Jewish population in Florida traditionally voted for Democrats.

Based on exit polling, **the national TV networks declared Gore the projected winner in Florida**. That meant Gore would have enough Electoral College votes to become the nation's forty-third president.

But a significant moment occurred when reporters asked Bush if he was ready to concede. **Bush said no, and reminded them that his brother was the governor of Florida. He said "We're working the phones."** When the reporters asked what good "working the phones" would do now that the polls were already closed, there was no answer from either George Bush or his brother, Jeb Bush. Later that night, more and more last-minute results began coming in favoring Bush. Somehow, inexplicably, Gore's big lead was being overcome.

In the end, Bush was declared the winner, but by only 1,784 votes out of the six million votes that had been cast in Florida. The vote was so close, a recount was legally required. When the careful recount was finished, Bush's lead had been cut to only 537. **Somehow, the recount had taken 1,247 votes away from Bush**.

The Democrats immediately began looking for voting irregularities, and they found quite a few. **In traditionally Democratic districts,** large numbers of votes had been thrown out for unexplained reasons. **In Escambia County, a predominately African-American district, 16% of the ballots were thrown out without explanation. In Columbia County, another predominately African-American district, 17% of the ballots had been rejected**. Another 54,000 Florida citizens, **the majority of them African-American, had not been allowed to vote.** The Democrats found that many of the African-American voters had been turned away from the polls, because on the official voting lists, **they had somehow mistakenly gotten listed as being ineligible felons.**

Something that drew special attention in the recount was a confusing type of paper ballot that became known as the "**butterfly ballot.**" The Democrats said voters had been confused by the odd design of the ballots that **made them mistakenly vote for Pat Buchanan of the Reform Party** when they thought they were voting for Al Gore. In one county, Buchanan received 3,407 votes on the so-called butterfly ballots, even though Buchanan had only expected to get 400 to 500 votes in that Democratic stronghold, and the exit polls had confirmed that expectation. Analysis of the butterfly ballots in that county showed **most of those who had voted for Buchanan had voted Democratic for all the other offices listed on the ballot.** After looking at one of the so-called butterfly ballots, Buchanan himself said he could see how voters might have mistakenly voted for him when they thought they were voting for Al Gore.

For all these reasons, the Gore campaign requested that **disputed ballots be counted by hand,** Under Florida law, such a recount was allowable. In fact, previously, thousands of spoiled absentee ballots from overseas soldiers (that mostly favored Bush) had been carefully recounted by hand to determine "**the voter's intent.**" Nevertheless, **the Bush campaign fought against a manual recount of the disputed ballots.**

The manual recount went on, and when it started to look bad for Bush, Katherine Harris, the Republican Secretary of State in Florida suddenly ordered the recount stopped. Of course, the Democrats went to court pointing out that under Florida law, a manual recount was required. **Harris argued against the recount** in the courts until the case was finally sent to **the Florida Supreme Court. They ordered the recount to go on, and recount was resumed.**

The problem for Bush was that the more the ballots were recounted, the more votes he lost. After careful scrutiny of the ballots, Bush's lead soon shrank to only 154. **It was clear that if the recount continued to find more votes for Gore, Bush would lose the Florida vote and with it the presidency.** In desperation, the Republican Party **asked the U.S. Supreme Court for an emergency meeting in hopes they would stop the recount. They told the Supreme Court justices that Bush would suffer "irreparable harm" if the recount was allowed to continue.**

The court's decision came quickly: **the Supreme Court voted five to four to stop the recount**.

To this day, that decision is still one of the most controversial in Supreme Court history. The decision, and more importantly, the close 5-4 vote, is often used as an example when people talk about the president's power to "stack" the Supreme Court. Many said you could have told in advance which of the judges were going to vote to stop the recount by simply knowing it had been a Republican president that had appointed them.

The four judges who had voted **against** stopping the recount were quite strident in their **opposition to the decision**. They denounced it as **a violation of both constitutional and democratic principles**. They said **the Florida Supreme Court had made a clear legal decision, under Florida state law, when they ordered the recount to continue**. They said it was not appropriate for the U.S. Supreme Court to step in and override the highest court in the state of Florida, something those five justices had never done before. **They asked how, in a democracy, carefully counting every vote could be a bad thing. They said the only danger of "irreparable harm" was**

> to the public and to the democracy, and that going against Florida law to stop a recount would "cast a cloud on the legitimacy of the election."
>
> Nevertheless, even though the Supreme Court had voted five to four along party-affiliation lines, it is the final law of the land. The recount was stopped. Katherine Harris certified the election in favor of Bush and there was nothing Gore or the Democrats could do abut it. **As a result, even though Al Gore had won the general election by more than half a million votes, Bush won in the Electoral College (by one vote), and therefore he became the president.**

Perhaps the most surprising outcome of the 2000 presidential election was the **lack of outrage by the public over the fact that the winner of the popular votes did not get to be president.**

In 1824, when Andrew Jackson won the nation's popular vote but didn't get to be president, the nation erupted in outrage. They said the people's wishes had been trampled. Many demanded that the election be overturned and that Jackson be put into his rightful place as president.

Jackson demanded an end to the outrageous Electoral College system of electing the president. He said it was ridiculous that the people didn't get to vote for the most important office in the country.

But when the same thing happened in 2000, Gore didn't complain, and the people didn't protest.

Many said it set the stage for the same thing to happen again in the future, and as we shall see, they were right.

Chapter Fifteen
Presidential Politics and the War on Terrorism

By the time **the 2004 presidential election** rolled around, Al Gore and the Electoral College debacle of 2000 had been forgotten because the nation was in an uproar over a terrorist event that had happened on **September 11, 2001**. On that date, young men from Egypt, the United Arab Emirates, Lebanon, and Saudi Arabia commandeered four airliners in order to crash them into important American buildings.

STORY

The events of September 11, 2001 were put into play many months before when a group of young Arab-looking men entered the U.S. on tourist, business, or student visas. They spoke little English, but in San Diego and in Florida, they began asking about pilot training. **They said they wanted to learn to fly big Boeing passenger jets**, but they were told they would have to learn to fly small airplanes first. They said **they were only interested in learning how to fly big passenger airliners**. The flying instructors testified later that they thought the young men just had big unrealistic dreams. The flight instructors told investigators that the students focused only on in-flight maneuvering and **had little interest in learning about takeoffs and landings**. The young Arab-looking men never actually got the chance to fly any large planes, but in the spring of 2011, in Arizona, they were able to get training on a Boeing 737 simulator. That triggered an alert, and the Arizona FBI was notified. **The Arizona branch of the FBI immediately alerted FBI headquarters in Washington D.C. that several Middle Easterners were training to fly large passenger jets.**

They recommended that other aviation schools nationwide be contacted to find out if other Arabs might be trying to learn how to fly large airplanes. It is not known if anybody in the FBI or in any other U.S. intelligence agency took note of the warning, but they must have been aware that airliner hijackings had long been a favorite way for militant groups to bring their causes to the public's attention. **Over the previous forty years, there had been several instances in which terrorists that had hijacked airliners said they were planning to crash them into important buildings.** It is not known how far up the line the Arizona FBI report went, but it is now known that at least two of the hijackers were already on an FBI watch list. But nothing was done.

On September 11, the hijackers bought tickets on four different flights. **They picked flights from Eastern cities with California destinations to make sure they would have heavy loads of fuel. Once on board, the terrorists used box cutters as weapons** and threatened that they had bombs. One group took control of American Airlines Flight 11 from Boston and **flew it into the North Tower of the World Trade Center.** A second group took control of American Airlines Flight 175 from Boston and **flew it into the south tower.** Another group took control of American Airlines Flight 77 from Washington D.C and **flew it into the Pentagon Building.** A fourth group took over United Airlines Flight 93 from Newark, but **reportedly, several of the passengers tried to overcome the hijackers,** and the plane crashed into the ground near Shanksville, Pennsylvania.

The nation watched in horror as every TV network showed the attack on the two World Trade Center towers. Unexpectedly, the south tower, the second tower to be hit, collapsed after burning for 56 minutes. Twenty one minutes later, the north tower also collapsed.

Later analysis determined that the collapse of both buildings was caused by the fire, not by the impact. The heat of burning jet fuel had melted important steel structural elements of the buildings. **According to the 9/11 commission report, the buildings would not have collapsed if the required fireproofing had been installed.**

By the end of that day, **2,606 people had died in the two towers and 125 had died at the Pentagon.** On the airliners, **246 passengers and crew had died**, along with the hijackers.

Bush went on TV to put the focus on one particular group of terrorists known as **al-Qaeda**, a group of Islamic militants led by a Saudi citizen named **Osama bin Laden** who was believed to be in Afghanistan. Many thought **al-Qaeda** was in league with the Taliban, an Islamist group that controlled Afghanistan.

The attacks on 9/11 brought about many changes in the United States. **In less than a month, U.S. military forces launched attacks in Afghanistan.** It was the first stage of President **Bush's new "war on terror."** He said from now on, it would be U.S. policy to go after terrorists anywhere in the world. He said the U.S. would not distinguish between terrorist organizations and governments that harbored them.

As U.S. forces, with support from Britain and Australia, approached Kabul, the capital city of Afghanistan, the Taliban retreated. By the middle of November, the allied forces were in control of the country. The war in Afghanistan was to become America's longest war, but over time, public interest in it faded, and it has not played a very important role in subsequent presidential elections.

By the spring of 2003, President Bush's war on terror had expanded to Iraq. Alleging that **Iraq was harboring al-Qaeda** and that **Iraqi President Saddam Hussein** was in the process of developing **weapons of mass destruction,** President Bush sought approval from Congress to invade Iraq. Although Congress did not approve a formal declaration of war against Iraq, they did pass a joint resolution **authorizing military action.** It was not an uncontested vote. **In the House, the Republicans were nearly unanimously in favor of it. The majority of the Democrats voted against it.** They pointed out that United Nations inspectors had done a complete search of Iraq and had found **no evidence of any weapons of mass destruction** development and **no evidence of an al-Qaeda presence in Iraq.** In fact, the United Nations experts said the brutal government of Iraq under Saddam Hussein had been making sure there was **no support for al-Qaeda in Iraq.**

In the Senate, the Republicans supported their Republican president and voted in favor of military action. Surprisingly, most Democratic senators also voted in favor of it. Essentially all of the senators from the conservative Southern and middle Western states voted in favor of military action in Iraq. It was a surprise to many that some senators from the more liberal Northern states also voted in favor of it. Senators like Kerry from Massachusetts, Clinton and Schumer from New York, Biden and Torricelli from New Jersey, Carper from Delaware, Feinstein from California, and Cantwell from Washington voted in favor of it. **Most of the Democrats later said they would have voted against the measure if they hadn't been lied to about what was going on there. That meant the measure would have failed and Bush would not have had the authority to send U.S. troops to Iraq.**

With congressional approval in hand, President Bush soon ordered air attacks on Iraq, and on March 20, 2003, the ground invasion of Iraq began. With the support of extensive air power, the U.S. forces moved quickly, and within a few weeks, they took the capital city of Baghdad.

> A month later, speaking from the deck of the U.S. aircraft carrier, USS Abraham Lincoln, President **Bush said the war in Iraq was over** and a new era in Iraq could begin. In reality, it took many more years and a new U.S. president before most (but not all) of the U.S. troops were withdrawn from Iraq.
>
> All told, **well over a million members of the U.S. military** served in Iraq, and despite the best medical care in any U.S. war, **4,484 American soldiers died** in Iraq, many of them from insurgent ambushes and from so-called **improvised explosive devices** (IEDs). **317 coalition forces** from countries other than the U.S. also died in combat. Estimates of the numbers of wounded American soldiers **vary widely from 100,000 to more than half a million**, depending on what type of injuries are counted.
>
> The number of deaths and injuries to Iraqi civilians is unknown but **estimates vary from 151,000 to over a million**.

The Presidential Election of 2004

In 2004, with two wars still going on, the Democrats thought they had a good chance of regaining the White House. The Democratic primaries saw 10 candidates come forward.

Howard Dean was the early favorite, but **John Kerry, a Vietnam war hero who had turned against the war in Vietnam,** pulled out a win in **New Hampshire**.

Then, in the **South Carolina** primary, **John Edwards** won.

In **Oklahoma**, **Wesley Clark** won, but **Edwards was a close second**.

Kerry then won primaries in Hawaii, Idaho, Maine, Michigan, Nevada, Tennessee, Washington, and Washington, D.C.

He went on to win at the Democratic national nominating convention. He selected North Carolina Senator **John Edwards** as his running mate.

> **STORY**
> From the beginning, it was clear that the presidential election of 2004 was going to be **a referendum on the war in Iraq**. Despite a flawed homeland security program that had allowed the 9/11 attacks to happen, **most people had not blamed the Bush administration**. After the 9/11 attacks, **Bush had quickly gotten the nation involved in two foreign wars, and presidents almost always gain popularity in a time of war**. When, in March of 2003, Bush proclaimed that the war in Iraq was all but over, he attained some of the highest presidential popularity ratings in history. However, it soon became clear that **no weapons of mass destruction had been found** in Iraq, and as time dragged on, it became clear that **the war *was not* over, and American soldiers were still dying there**. There was also widespread criticism of Bush's conduct of the war, especially after **evidence came out that U.S. personnel were torturing military prisoners**. Of special concern was the **Abu Ghraib prison in Iraq and the Guantanamo Bay detention camp in Cuba**, both of which were managed by the U.S. military.
>
> Nevertheless, despite Bush's steadily declining popularity ratings, no serious challengers appeared during the Republican primaries, and as a result, **Bush was nominated by the Republican party to run for reelection**. There were calls for him to dump his vice president, Dick Cheney, because he had been such a strong advocate of torturing prisoners of war (he referred to it as "**enhanced interrogation**"). Bush refused, and the Bush-Cheney ticket went forward.

The 2004 presidential campaign was, as predicted, mostly about Iraq and U.S. foreign policy. **Kerry attacked Bush's handling of the war in Iraq**, and he especially criticized **the treatment of prisoners in Guantanamo Bay** which he said were in violation of the Geneva Convention (a set of international laws that regulate the treatment of prisoners of war). Kerry said Bush had repeatedly acted without the support of the United Nations, and that his actions were hurting America's reputation abroad, even among America's allies.

Bush's campaign focused on the **worldwide terrorist threat**, which made it seem eerily similar to earlier Republican presidential campaigns during the Cold War that had focused on the **worldwide communist threat**.

During the campaign, Bush defended his approach to fighting terrorism. His ads suggested that Kerry's anti-war stance meant he would be weak on fighting terrorism.

STORY

During the presidential campaign of 2004, the Kerry campaign often compared **Kerry's record of service in Vietnam to Bush's lack of service**. They pointed out that **Kerry had voluntarily served in Vietnam and had won several service metals while Bush was "hiding out" in the Texas National Guard**. They said **Bush had used his father's political connections in Texas to get into easy (and safe) Texas National Guard assignments.** Even then, they said, Bush had rarely even bothered to perform his National Guard duties. A news investigation found evidence that showed Bush was actually out of the state when National Guard records showed he was in attendance at Texas National Guard meetings.

On the other hand, the Republicans **found some Vietnam veterans willing to say that Kerry's "dangerous" service in Vietnam was exaggerated. They even said he didn't deserve the medals he had won**. They pointed to the fact that upon his return to the United States, Kerry had joined the **veterans against the war in Vietnam**. They felt that was a betrayal of his former comrades.

> Meanwhile, Bush was focusing on his **"war on terror."** His campaign ads often focused on **"the Arab threat."** He also defended the harsh treatment of Arab prisoners, implying that it was a fitting response to the Americans who had died on 9/11.

Of course, Bush, being a Republican, won every Southern state, and he won many of the Midwestern and Western states.

Kerry won the West Coast, the upper Midwest, and the East.

While **the popular vote was relatively close**, 50.73 percent to 48.27 percent in favor of Bush, **the Electoral College vote was not as close. They voted 286 for Bush and 251 for Kerry.**

The Presidential Election of 2008

In 2008, President Bush's approval rating was very low, The American public was tired of hearing about continuing deaths of American servicemen in Iraq and Afghanistan. As a result, the Democrats were confident that they could take back the White House in 2008. Ten candidates came forward to compete in the Democratic primaries.

Many were surprised that Al Gore, the winner of the popular vote in 2000, wasn't among the candidates. At first he expressed interest, but eventually he decided against running again. The speculation was that he felt he was doing more good as an ambassador in **the fight against global warming**.

In the Iowa caucuses, the relatively unknown, but very eloquent, **first-term Senator Barack Obama** won. **John Edwards** came in second, and **Hillary Clinton, the senator from New York and wife of former president Bill Clinton,** came in third.

Clinton then won in New Hampshire, Michigan and Florida, but the Democratic National Committee disallowed those votes because they were held too early in the primary season. (Eventually, the Michigan and Florida votes were divided between

Clinton and Obama.) Next, **Obama won Nevada and South Carolina**, and from that point on, Obama and Clinton alternated wins.

As the Democratic national presidential nominating convention approached, many expected a contentious floor fight between Obama and Clinton. However, midway through the voting, **when it became clear that Obama was pulling into the lead, Clinton asked for Democratic unity and told her delegates to vote for Obama**. As a result, **Barack Obama** was nominated by unanimous acclamation. He was the first person of African-American heritage to be nominated by a major party (his mother was white, but she had married a Kenyan, Barack Hussein Obama Sr., while he was in the U.S going to college). Obama chose **Delaware Senator Joe Biden** as his running mate.

The Republicans knew they were going to have an uphill battle because of President Bush's very low approval ratings,. Eleven candidates came forward to compete in the Republican primaries.

Mike Huckabee won the Iowa caucuses, but then faded badly in New Hampshire. **Rudy Giuliani** and **Mitt Romney** also had disappointing finishes. **McCain** won New Hampshire.

After a third-place finish in Florida, Giuliani withdrew from the race and endorsed John McCain. **From then on, McCain won most of the primaries.** At the Republican national nominating convention in Minnesota, **McCain was nominated**. He surprised everyone by picking the outspoken conservative governor of Alaska, **Sarah Palin**, as his running mate.

STORY

While the 2004 presidential election had been about the wisdom of invading Iraq, the **Presidential Election of 2008** was clearly going to be a referendum on how well Bush had been handling the so-called war on terror. By the time the 2008 presidential election season began, national polls were indicating that Bush would leave office as **one of the most unpopular presidents in U.S. history**. Some polls showed he was even

> **more unpopular than Richard Nixon**, even though President Nixon had been forced to resign due to the Watergate scandal. It was quite **a contrast to Bush's 90 percent approval rating** when he stood on the deck of the aircraft carrier USS Abraham Lincoln and declared "mission accomplished" in Iraq. Paradoxically, when asked in 2008 why they disliked Bush's performance in office so much, most people mentioned the same thing that had formerly made him popular, the war in Iraq.
>
> Vice President Dick Cheney's ratings were even lower than Bush's, with only thirteen percent of Americans saying they approved of his performance in office.

As expected, **the 2008 election campaigns focused on the two ongoing wars in Afghanistan and Iraq.** Obama came out strongly against the Iraq war in particular, and **McCain, who had supported the two wars all along, was forced to defend them**.

Focusing on Bush's unpopularity, Obama reminded the voters that McCain had voted to support Bush 90 percent of the time.

McCain, as a long-time member of the U.S. Senate, focused on Obama's inexperience. He pointed out the fact that Obama was **a first-term senator**. Obama countered that charge by saying it was **time for a change**. He pointed out how the Republicans had turned Clinton's healthy economy and budget surplus into an unhealthy economy and a rapidly-growing budget deficit. He said he would enact universal health care, make America "green," and bring back respect for America abroad.

> ### COMMENT
> **By the time voters went to the polls in 2008, the country was in the midst of a financial crisis.** Only a few weeks before the general election, Lehman Brothers, one of the world's largest financial institutions was **forced to file for bankruptcy**

because of its exposure to newly-created risky and speculative financial instruments that were based on shaky subprime mortgages. Many other financial institutions around the world were also highly exposed to the new and very complicated financial instruments. As a result, the situation was **threatening to bring down America's entire financial system**. Bush's Secretary of the Treasury, Henry Paulson, the former head of the Goldman Sachs investment banking company, had gone before Congress to ask for hundreds of billions of dollars to bail out financial institutions. After much controversy, Congress finally authorized the money, and the crisis was averted. Nevertheless, investors in the stock market lost billions and the so-called "housing bubble" collapsed and many Americans found they owed much more on their homes than they were worth. With unemployment rising, many faced foreclosure.

As election day neared in 2008, the polls were showing it was **the economic crisis that was the most important issue,** more important even than the ongoing foreign wars. Although Americans were aware of Obama's inexperience, that seemed to be less important than the fact that people were hurting economically. They were ready for a change in Washington.

In the election, **the Republicans again held most of the South.** But McCain lost Florida, Virginia, and North Carolina by close votes.

Overall, Obama won the East, some of the Midwest, and the West Coast. McCain won 28 states, more than Obama's 22, but McCain's wins were all in states with smaller populations and fewer Electoral College votes. **Obama won all the larger population states *and* enough of the South and Midwest to secure the Electoral College vote, 365 to 173**.

The Presidential Election of 2012

The presidential election of 2012 **turned out to be closer than most would have predicted**. Although the war in Afghanistan was still going on, most assumed it would play only a minor role in the campaign because nobody expected the Republicans to be against it, even if it was now "President Obama's war."

It was said that if the states that had been voting Republican in the past went back to voting that way in 2012, Obama would have a hard time getting elected. It was even possible that the election would be a replay of 2000 when the Democratic candidate won the general election but lost in the Electoral College.

With President Obama assured of the Democratic nomination, all attention was on who the Republicans would nominate. The Republican primaries began, as usual, with the caucuses in Iowa and primary balloting in New Hampshire. And as usual, a great deal of attention was paid to those **first two primaries**; however, they **did little to predict which candidate would win the Republican nomination**. The outcome of the primary in Iowa was essentially a three-way tie between former **Pennsylvania Senator Rick Santorum, former Massachusetts governor Mitt Romney**, and **Texas Representative Ron Paul**. The following primaries saw the lead swing back and forth between those three candidates and **Newt Gingrich**. But then, Romney won Florida, and he won the most states on "Super Tuesday."

COMMENT

The primary elections of 2012 were the first presidential primary elections to be held after **a landmark Supreme Court five-to-four decision that had lifted the restrictions on corporate contributions to political campaigns**. As expected, the amounts spent on the candidates' campaigns broke all prior spending records.

At the Republican National Convention, Romney was nominated.

Early on, the polls consistently showed President Obama in the lead, but **the margin was never all that great.** Obama had withdrawn most of the U.S. troops from Iraq after the long war there, but the situation was still unstable. **What would happen to Iraq without a U.S. military presence was an open question.** And then there was the issue of the ongoing war in **Afghanistan, the longest war in U.S. history.** The Republicans revealed statistics that indicated Obama's war policies in Afghanistan were failing. They said **Afghanistan was a more dangerous place now than when he took office**.

During the 2008 campaign, Obama had been critical of President Bush's handling of the war in Afghanistan, but after taking office, he had **retained President Bush's Secretary of Defense, Robert Gates, and had approved the same "surge" approach** (increasing the number of troops and fighting resources) Bush had used in Iraq and Nixon had used in Vietnam.

No one really knew what Romney's position would be in Afghanistan. He would need to appear to be tough on terrorism, but was the country ready for another escalation of the conflict in Afghanistan? Obama had promised to get U.S. troops out "soon" and turn the defense of the country over to the Afghans. That was the approach he had used in Iraq, but it was still an open question as to whether it was going to work either there or in Afghanistan. There had been a sustained increase in violence in Iraq after the U.S. troops were pulled out. **Some people worried that Iraq would go the way of Vietnam.**

After the 9/11 attacks on the twin towers in New York City, President Bush had not only directed the military invasions of Iraq and Afghanistan but he had also created **a huge new division of government, the Department of Homeland Security**. Those moves had the approval of most Americans, but he had also instituted new policies that many said limited privacy.

Obama had kept all of those policies in place, and he had stepped up the "assassination by drone" program that Bush had initiated. That meant Obama had taken away one of the strongest Republican talking points.

The fact that Obama had ordered a successful CIA and Navy SEALs operation that went into Pakistan and **killed Osama bin Laden**, the supposed leader of the al-Qaeda terrorist organization, also played an important role in the election.

But the issue of **the country's ongoing economic problems was still a major campaign issue**. A sitting president must always run on his record, and from the outset, it was clear Mitt Romney would campaign against President Obama's handling of the economy. Although the financial crisis of the Bush administration had passed, **the unemployment rate had stayed stubbornly high throughout Obama's four-year term**.

Obama often pointed out that it was the previous Republican administration that had handed him an economy that was near collapse, and he had done his best to stabilize the situation through bailouts and government economic stimulus programs.

Nevertheless, many of the leaders of the nation's largest financial institutions were still in power, and none of them had been sent to prison.

Romney said the bailouts and the economic stimulus packages were the wrong approach. He laid out a five-point plan that had the blessing of many top economists. He said that as **an experienced businessman**, he could do a better job of getting the U.S. economy back on its feet.

In response, Obama portrayed Romney as a member of the group that had caused the country's economic problems.

In the spring of 2012, **the polls were indicating the race would be close.** Obama would not coast to the kind of easy victory he had enjoyed in 2008.

STORY
A turning point in the 2012 presidential election came when a video turned up of Romney's meeting with support-

ers at a dinner at the Boca Raton, Florida, home of Marc Leder, a financier. Unbeknownst to him, one of the catering staff was secretly making a video of Romney's comments at that dinner. The video was kept secret for some time, but on September 17th, Mother Jones magazine published an article titled, "SECRET VIDEO: Romney Tells Millionaire Donors What He REALLY Thinks of Obama Voters: When he doesn't know a camera's rolling, the GOP candidate shows his disdain for half of America." The article included a clip from the video in which Romney is heard to say " . . . **there are 47 percent who are with him [Obama], who are dependent on government, who believe they are victims, who believe the government has a responsibility to care for them . . . ."**

The national news media picked up the story, and for several weeks it was mentioned and the video was re-shown nearly every time Romney's name came up.

At first, Romney said his comments at that dinner were speculative and that they hadn't come out exactly the way he wanted them too. But later, he completely disavowed what he had said at the dinner, saying in no way did it reflect his true feelings. That did little to stop members of the media from using the video against him, and the Obama campaign also used it frequently.

Soon after the secret video came out, the polls began to show voters turning against Romney. Commentators on TV began to talk about an inevitable Obama victory.

As the election neared, someone in the U.S. put together a short, very **amateurish video that poked fun at the founders of the Muslim religion** and posted it on the YouTube internet site. Although few people had actually seen the short video clip, it set off a series of **anti-American demonstrations** in the Muslim world. From Egypt to Australia and in some European countries, there were protests and burnings of the U.S. flag. In countries like

Yemen and Tunesia, the protests turned violent.

After several U.S. embassies were attacked on September 11th, the anniversary of the 9/11 attacks in New York in 2001, government officials in Washington, and elsewhere, were closely watching the situation. However, **when reports starting coming in that the U.S. diplomatic mission in Benghazi, Libya was under attack, there was apparent confusion about what was going on there. The attack ended with four Americans dead, including U.S. Ambassador J. Christopher Stevens.**

Although al-Qaeda claimed responsibility for the attack, in the weeks that followed, representatives of the Obama administration were saying it was just another protest against the anti-Muslim video that had gotten out of control. In the middle of a closely contested presidential election, such an event was bound to come under close scrutiny, which **brought Obama's foreign policy (and the policies of his Secretary of State, Hillary Clinton) into question.**

When the video was released, showing that there were no demonstrations in that area of Benghazi and that the men who attacked the embassy were heavily armed, some people began to suspect that the Obama administration was trying play down the attack. They suggested the attack showed that anti-American extremists were well entrenched in Libya, despite the administration's support of the uprising there that had removed Libya's leader. President Obama strongly denied that accusation, but the attacks from Republicans continued. They included accusations that Ambassador Stevens and others had been worried about just such an attack, and that they had asked for more security. But the requests had been denied.

Eventually, the facts came out: **the attack was a well-coordinated mission, pre-planned to take place on the anniversary of the 9/11 attacks.** Reports surfaced that the attackers were militants related to al-Qaeda, and that the group included seasoned al-Qaeda fighters that had been brought in from Tunisia and Iraq.

President Obama announced that they were trying to track down the killers, and he said he was beefing up security at all U.S.

facilities in the region.

But that didn't end the controversy. Critics said the Obama administration had tried to cover up the true nature of the Benghazi attack because it might reflect badly on U.S. foreign policy in the region. Republican lawmakers started hearings on the matter.

President Obama, and other members of his administration, denied that there had been any sort of cover-up. They said they had not been given correct information about the true nature of the Benghazi attack from their intelligence sources. Nevertheless, the Benghazi attack and the aftermath continued to be a topic of dispute throughout the rest of the campaign.

In the three presidential debates, Romney was eager to talk about the economy. He mentioned the rapid rise in the deficit, and he described people who had come up to him with stories of lost jobs and difficult times.

But Obama said he had created five million jobs in the private sector, that the automobile industry had come roaring back, and housing sales had begun to rise. He attacked Romney for his unwillingness to raise taxes on the wealthy. He pointed out that it was the previous Republican administration that had created the economic problems and that Romney wanted to take the country back there by reducing taxes on the rich and by doing away regulation of Wall Street.

After the debates were over, **the polls indicated the race was still very close.**

COMMENT

Some of the very conservative Republican senatorial candidates were not helping Romney's attempts to sound more moderate. Republican **"tea party" candidates were taking a hard line on abortion and illegal immigration.** The Democrats used Romney's endorsement of those candidates against him.

The Green Party presidential candidate, Jill Stein, was getting some national attention by talking about U.S. wars and military adventures. She pointed out that President Obama had dramatically increased the frequency of deadly **"assassination by drone"** attacks by U.S. unmanned drones, and that he had also started to use drone attacks in Yemen and Somalia. She said the drone attacks resulted in 75 percent of Pakistani civilians believing the U.S was their chief enemy, not the Taliban or al-Qaeda.

> **COMMENT**
> **The changing demographics of the United States was to play an important role in the 2012 presidential election.** In the last two U.S. censuses, the number of people that identified themselves as of Hispanic origin had increased dramatically. In fact, Hispanics accounted for more than half of the nation's growth in the last decade. That hurt Romney's chances because only 20 percent of Hispanics polled said they were planning to vote for him.
>
> The 2010 census also showed that the segment of the population that identified themselves as black or African-American **had increased from twelve percent of the population in 2000 to over sixteen percent** in 2012, and nearly all of the polled African-American voters said they were planning to vote for President Obama.
>
> Because of the design of the Electoral College, even non-voters were to play a role in the 2012 presidential election. Since 1964, the number of electors has been fixed at 538. **States are assigned electors based on their total population, not the number of eligible voters.** Based on the most recent census, the number of electors assigned to a state are recalculated before every presidential election. States gain electors if their populations increase, which means electors have to be taken away from states whose populations have not increased. In 2012, it is notable that states like Arizona and Texas gained

electors. **Since the presidential election of 2000, Arizona has gained three electors, and Texas has gained six electors.** Those nine electors were taken away from other states that did not have such large increases in their populations. It is known that much of the increase in population in Arizona and Texas is due to the influx of undocumented people from south of the border.

Therefore, in 2012, we had the unusual situation that some states gained electors even though they did not gain voters.

As the election campaign entered its last few weeks, the polls were showing that **the race couldn't be closer.** It looked like **Romney would have to win Florida, Virginia, and Ohio, plus at least two of the other swing states to become president. Nevertheless, he said he was sure he would win.**

STORY

Historically, in some presidential elections, there have been last minute events that may have changed the outcome. Known as an "**October surprise**," events such as Henry Kissinger's statement just days before the 1972 election that "**peace is at hand**" in Vietnam helped assure Nixon's reelection despite the news that was coming out about the Watergate break-ins.

An October **non-surprise** took place in the presidential election of 1980. The Iran hostage crisis had dragged on for years and was hurting incumbent Jimmy Carter's chances of being reelected. Carter thought he had a last minute deal to free the hostages before the election, but the deal fell through. Later, the president of Iran said Reagan's campaign aides had **struck a deal with Iran to delay the release of the hostages until after the election. Reagan denied it, but the later arms-for-**

> hostages scheme in Iran carried out by members of Reagan's executive branch gave credence to the idea.
>
> As the 2012 presidential campaign neared its end, there was widespread discussion as to **the likelihood of an October surprise** in such a close and hard-fought election.
>
> **As it turned out, the only October surprise in 2012 was the weather.** An unusual Autumn hurricane hit the upper East Coast a week before the election. President Obama canceled his scheduled campaign appearances, and Romney said that out of respect for those who were suffering from the hurricane's impact, he would also cancel all of his campaign appearances.
>
> Although Obama didn't hold any official campaign events, as president, he got to be constantly in the news by holding many official press conferences about his administration's ongoing disaster relief efforts. It's an example of why it's so hard to beat an incumbent president.

Obama **squeaked out wins in the key swing states** of Colorado, Iowa, Virginia, Florida, and Ohio. **He lost two of the states he had won in 2008 (Indiana and North Carolina). Nevertheless, he held onto all the other swing states, even though his margins of victory in those states was much lower than in 2008. He won in the Electoral College, 332 to 206.**

Chapter Sixteen
TV Celebrity Versus Experienced Politician

The Presidential Election of 2016

With no incumbent president running for reelection, the field of potential candidates for the presidential election of 2016 was wide open. In fact, according to the Federal Election Commission, 1,817 candidates filed a Statement of Candidacy. Of course, only a handful of them would ever become well known.

The Democratic Debates

The way the voting public gets to know the candidates is through televised debates. Based on the early poll results, **five candidates were invited to participate in the initial Democratic debate: Lincoln Chafee**, former governor of Rhode Island, **Hillary Clinton,** former U.S. Senator from New York and U.S. Secretary of State, **Martin O'Malley**, former governor of Maryland, **Bernie Sanders**, an Independent U.S. Senator from Vermont, and **Jim Webb**, former U.S. Senator from Virginia. In addition, Vice President **Joe Biden** was invited to debate, but he declined. Most of the media focus was on Hillary Clinton (the media was just calling her "Hillary"). As a former Senator and wife of a former president, she was well known.

By the time the second Democratic debate came around, the field had been narrowed down to Clinton, Sanders, and O'Malley. With a terrorist attack in Paris having just occurred, the focus was on terrorism and foreign policy. Each of the candidates **described terrorism as a great threat to the world. Clinton reminded the audience of the depth of her experience in foreign affairs**.

Sanders focused more on domestic affairs. He hammered on one main theme, that **the country was being run (and ruined)**

by Wall Street and the big banks. O'Malley focused on both terrorism and U.S. economic problems.

In the debates that followed, **Clinton showed her experience** at debating, parrying any and all attacks while still managing to get her main points across. **She focused more on the Republicans** than on her Democratic debate opponents.

The early polls indicated Hillary Clinton was in the lead, but **the message of economic inequality that Sanders was focusing on was also getting a lot of attention**.

In the polls, O'Malley hardly registered. As a result, only Hillary and Bernie (as the news media had begun to refer to them) participated in the final few debates. Hillary continued to talk about her experience in foreign affairs. Bernie proposed a "Medicare for all" plan. The two candidates did agree that there needed to be more control over who could buy a gun, especially assault rifles. Both candidates also talked about the problems of racial discrimination, and **they also talked about immigration** because it was sure to be a leading topic from the Republican side.

The Republican Debates

Based on the early polls, ten candidates were invited to the initial televised Republican debate. Five other candidates were invited to a "second-level" debate. Several of the Republican candidates were well known. **Jeb Bush** was the former governor of Florida, the son of President George H. W. Bush, and the brother of President George W. Bush. Others had held high political offices: **Chris Christie,** Governor of New Jersey, **Ted Cruz**, U.S. Senator from Texas, **Mike Huckabee**, former Governor of Arkansas, **John Kasich**, Governor of Ohio, **Rand Paul**, U.S. Senator from Kentucky, **Marco Rubio**, U.S. Senator from Florida, and **Scott Walker**, Governor of Wisconsin. There were also two "outsiders" who had never held public office: **Ben Carson** was a retired neurosurgeon who had written several books and was well known in the African-American community, and **Donald Trump,** a well-known TV entertainer. He said he was one of America's wealthiest men, so he knew how to get things done. However, **Trump had filed for bankruptcy several times in the past, so his actual worth was not known**. He said he was going to fund his own campaign and would not take donations from anybody. However, he was already quietly accepting campaign donations.

The Republican debates were decidedly uncivil. In the very first Republican debate, the moderator asked if all the candidates would pledge support to the eventual nominee of the Republican party. Only **Trump refused**, and that encouraged the other candidates to immediately begin to attack him. Despite getting booed by the audience, Trump wouldn't back down.

After that odd beginning, attention turned to Jeb Bush who, although not leading in the early polls, was **still considered to be the favorite** because of name recognition and the amount of campaign donation money he was getting. When asked why the county needed another Bush in the Oval Office, he said that as governor of Florida, he had cut taxes and saved the state money by vetoing unneeded budget line items.

When the moderator asked Trump why he had **referred to women as "fat pigs, dogs, slobs, and disgusting animals**," he said he just liked to kid around. But when she pressed the issue with more examples, he said, "I think the big problem this country has is being **politically correct**."

The moment that refocused the debate was when **Trump turned to what would become his signature issue, illegal immigration from Mexico**. He said he alone had brought the immigration issue to the public's attention. He said he would send the estimated eleven million illegal immigrants back home, and **he would build a wall to keep them out**. Furthermore, he said **he would make Mexico pay for that wall**. He said the immigration problem existed "because our leaders are stupid." He said immigrants shouldn't be given citizenship just because they were born here. **He even criticized Bush for sometimes speaking Spanish.** Bush responded, saying **Trump was "not a real Republican." He pointed out that Trump had been a registered Democrat and had donated money to Planned Parenthood.**

When a moderator asked Trump about his business practices and his bankruptcies, Trump said he had just **"used the laws."** However, the other candidates were not willing to let that go. **Governor Walker said, "You took four major projects into bankruptcy. You can't take America into bankruptcy."**

After that, there were **numerous attacks on Trump, and he aggressively responded with counterattacks.** By then, **Trump was leading in the polls** and feeling more confident. He often interrupted the other candidates. **He said he thought he would "get along" with world leaders like Putin.**

Now that he was leading in the polls, **Trump refused to participate in the Iowa debate**. But he was back for the next one, and the rancorous attacks and counterattacks began again. **Trump was turning attacks on his fellow Republicans into something of an art form, constantly coming up with new and ever more degrading insults of every one of the other candidates.** He even continued the attacks outside of the debates by sending out insulting "tweets" using his online Twitter account. He went after Bush, tweeting, **"Low energy Jeb Bush just endorsed a man he truly hates, Lyin' Ted Cruz. Honestly, I can't blame Jeb in that I drove him into oblivion."**

After twelve debates, based on the polls, only Cruz, Rubio, and Trump remained. There was supposed to be one more debate in Salt Lake City, but Trump said he wasn't interested in attending. That led the other candidates to also back out, and that signaled the end of the Republican debates.

The Democratic Primaries

The first test of the Democratic candidates was in the **Iowa "caucuses."** The result was close between Hillary and Bernie.

In the **New Hampshire primary**, 28 Democratic candidates got votes (including perennial candidate, Vermin Supreme, whose promise to give every American a free pony garnered him 260 votes and placed him ahead of 24 other candidates).

Of the "serious" candidates, only **Bernie Sanders** and **Hillary**

Clinton got a significant number of votes. O'Malley got only a few votes and soon thereafter announced his withdrawal from the race. From that point on, most of the primaries were close contests between Hillary and Bernie. Hillary won 34 of the state primaries and Bernie won 23. The clincher turned out to be the largest state, California. Hillary won that state convincingly and was thereby assured the nomination at the Democratic National Convention. Nevertheless, **many of the passionate Sanders supporters refused to accept the results**, and they vowed to fight on.

The Republican Primaries

The Republican primaries were more wide open. **In Iowa, twelve candidates got votes**, led by Ted Cruz and Trump. **Most of the other candidates got less than 2% of the votes**, even though some of them should have been well known to the voters. Of special note was the fact that **Jeb Bush got less than three percent of the vote. After** that first primary, **Huckabee, Paul, and Santorum withdrew.**

The next primary, New Hampshire, was the first win for Trump; he got 35% of the vote. It was not a good primary for Ted Cruz; he only got 12% of the vote. The rest trailed far behind.

Trump also won the next significant primary, South Carolina, with 32.5% of the vote. This time, Rubio came in second with 22.5% of the vote, and Cruz was close behind with 22.3% of the vote. Jeb Bush only got 7.8%, and he withdrew from the race.

Next was "super" Tuesday. Trump won and became the presumptive nominee.

The 2016 Republican National Convention

At the Republican National Convention, **Trump** chose conservative anti-abortion Governor **Mike Pence** as his vice president.

The "Dump Trump" and the "Never Trump" movements within the Republican Party tried to disrupt the convention with innuendo and rumors about Trump's business and personal dealings.

Senator **Ted Cruz** of Texas spoke at the convention, but he still pointedly refused to endorse Trump. In response, **Trump heaped insults on him,** saying he didn't want Cruz's endorsement anyhow. It was clear that even after his resounding victory, **Trump was not willing to try to mend fences** with the other Republicans that had opposed him. In fact, he said he might try to raise money to orchestrate Cruz's defeat in his bid to be reelected to his Texas Senate seat. Trump also tried to link Cruz's father to the Kennedy assassination, referring to **a conspiracy theory fed by an old news photo that seemed to show Ted Cruz's father, Rafael Cruz, a one-time supporter of Fidel Castro, with Lee Harvey Oswald. Trump even attacked Ohio Governor John Kasich, despite the fact that he would need the governor's support** to help him win the crucial swing state of Ohio.

The convention got off to a rocky start with the delegates that were opposed to Trump's nomination demanding a roll-call vote to change the convention rules. When that motion was denied, there were accusations of secret manipulation of the process, and **the entire Colorado delegation got up and walked out.**

Nevertheless, Trump's supporters were still solidly behind him. His slogan of **"Make America Great Again"** appealed to those who were dissatisfied. It also appealed to those who worried that the country was gradually being taken over by an influx of nonwhites. Some began to say what Trump's slogan really meant was **"Make America White Again."** Trump's long and rambling acceptance speech **was described by most observers as "dark."** He said there was a dramatically increasing level of crime in the country and great danger of terrorist attacks by what he called **"Radical Islamic Terrorism."** He blamed President Obama for all kinds of things, and he also blamed Hillary Clinton, which prompted the crowd to chant, "Lock her up. Lock her up."

STORY

In 2016, the Republicans hoped authorities would find Hillary Clinton guilty of **some kind of criminal wrongdoing in how she handled her e-mail**. Trump said her use of private email was a crime "worse than Watergate." Although there was nothing wrong with government employees having private e-mail accounts in addition to their office government e-mail accounts (most did), a private e-mail account wasn't supposed to be used to send or receive confidential information. **Secretary Clinton said she was following the same e-mailing methods that had been established by all prior Secretaries of State** and by other government officials. That was true, but by the time she became Secretary of State, **the rules regarding private mail servers had been changed** for security reasons. Private mail servers could still be used, but not for classified information. Therefore, **the main issue was not over her use of the private server for personal e-mailing, but whether she had sent or received correspondence marked as secret or classified.** She repeatedly said she had never used her personal e-mail account for secret information.

Under pressure from Congressional Republicans, **the FBI investigated her e-mail in great detail** and found that text in few of her e-mails *had* been marked as classified, although **they lacked classified headers and were only marked with a small "c" in parentheses somewhere within the body of the text**. The director of the FBI stated that Hillary, and the Secretary of State office in general, had been **"extremely careless in the handling of very sensitive, highly classified information,"** but that it was possible **Ms. Clinton was not "technically sophisticated"** enough to understand what that small "c" symbol, in the middle of text meant. His recommendation to the Justice Department was that no charges were justified.

Trump accused the government of "covering up her crimes." He said they had **"saved her from facing justice for her terrible, terrible crimes." **Many were shocked that a presidential nominee from a major party would suggest that the government was involved in a cover-up in order to influence a presidential election**, but many of Trump's supporters said they believed it. **Trump said she had deleted "personal" e-mails "to hide something."** Her staff, who had done the erasing, said those e-mails were mostly about family matters. Nevertheless, as the campaign went on, Trump at first implied, and then later flat-out said, she had deleted all those e-mails because they would have incriminated her. He offered no proof of that accusation. He often called her a liar, and he **began calling her "crooked Hillary,"** but he never said what he thought she had done that was "crooked." However, his accusations were repeated so often, the press began referring to it as the e-mail **"scandal."** Some polls indicated that the constant Republican attacks on her related to the e-mail "scandal" *did* **have the desired effect of creating a feeling of mistrust about her.** Trump's supporters began holding up professionally-printed signs saying things like, "Lock her up" and "Hillary for Prison in 2016."

Presidential candidates always get a "bounce" in the polls after all the TV exposure their conventions give them. The data showed that **every single nominated candidate had gotten a two to forty-five percent increase in voter approval** after their national convention. But this time, after the Republican convention, the polls indicated **voters were *less* likely to vote for Trump.**

STORY
After Trump was chosen to be the Republican nominee for president, a lot more information came out about him. The people soon learned Donald Trump's story was not the

usual American politician's story. He was the first nominee of a major party in U.S. history to have **never played a role in elected politics**. Since he had no experience in government, he talked about his experience in business. He said that his skills in becoming rich would be applied to making the United States a better country. Right from the start, he made it clear he was running as an outsider, and that **only an outsider could "fix" the nation's many problems**.

Trump's father was a well-known real estate developer in New York. Donald was sent to a prestigious college-prep school, but he soon left that school (reportedly because of behavior problems) and was enrolled in the New York Military Academy where he later said he **"got more training militarily than a lot of the guys that go into the military."**

After military school, he went to the Wharton School of Finance and Commerce to major in real estate (**members of his family later said he had cheated his way into that college**).

After college, he was in danger of getting drafted and sent to Vietnam, but despite his frequent athletic activity, he got a medical deferment for unexplained "heel spurs."

Back in New York, **he joined his father's construction firm** that had expanded from building single-family homes in Queens, New York to building apartment buildings. The senior Trump had received some unwanted publicity when **Woody Guthrie**, the famous folksinger, became a tenant and **accused him of being a racist slum landlord**. In 1973, **the U.S. Justice Department filed a suit against the Trumps**, charging that they had systematically refused to rent to African-Americans. The Trumps hired a top lawyer, and after a lengthy court battle, the suit was settled in 1975 with a consent decree.

With a large amount of seed money from his father, Donald Trump began to make real estate deals on his own and soon got a reputation as a rough and tough, self-promoting deal maker who had mastered the art of "creative" financing.

However, after making a number of high-profile real estate investments in Manhattan, **he decided to go into the casino business in Atlantic City**. He formed a partnership with Harrah's and opened his first casino. It didn't do well, but that didn't slow him down; he bought a partially completed building that wasn't on the famous Atlantic City Boardwalk like all the other casinos, but instead, was in the nearby Marina District. He named it Trump Castle. He followed that up by buying another casino on the Atlantic City boardwalk. He named this new one the Taj Mahal.

Unfortunately, developing all those casinos put Trump heavily in debt, and as it turned out, the casinos could not earn enough money to service his many loans. One by one, **the casinos all filed for Chapter 11 bankruptcy**. But **Trump himself never went personally bankrupt because his creditors gave him time to sell off the casino properties before paying them back**. (He was later to say, "I do play with the bankruptcy laws. They're very good for me.")

After the Atlantic City casino fiascoes, Trump began developing hotels and golf courses, and **he got involved in creating beauty pageants**. He created **Trump University**, a for-profit company that used high-pressure sales tactics to get student to sign up for expensive classes in real estate. Eventually the "university" (it was not accredited) became the target of lawsuits and federal class actions. Trump settled for $25 million and the school was shut down,

Beginning in the 1980s, Trump **began to publish books** (using ghost writers) about how to get rich quick. His first, *Art of the Deal,* with co-writer Tony Schwartz, reached number one on the New York Times Best Seller list (Schwartz later claimed that Trump had never actually written any of it).

In 2003, **Trump was featured on an NBC reality show called "The Apprentice"** in which competitors battled for management jobs. One by one, the contestants were "fired" and eliminated (Trump has filed a trademark application for the phrase "You're fired"). For a while, the show was popular, and it helped Trump market his name as a "brand." Some real estate developers paid Trump a fee to let them name their buildings after him. **He also allowed merchandisers to put the Trump name on many other thing**s, including a board game, bottled water, clothing (made in Bangladesh), cologne, a luxury airline, steaks, vodka, a watch, a magazine, restaurants, and wine.

Trump also got involved in a large number of partnerships and foundations in nearly every country. The Trump name and the Trump empire is unbelievably complicated, so many wondered how he was going to manage all that while running for president. They asked **what would happen to all these business relationships, especially the foreign relationships, if he was elected president**.

Although Trump had no experience in politics or government service, he had often said he was thinking about running for president of the United States. In 1999, **he joined the Reform Party, and for three years, he ran a presidential exploratory committee**. But after that, **he joined the Democratic Party**. Then, in 2008, **he switched back to the Republican Party** and endorsed John McCain for President. But then, in 2011, **he switched to the Independent Party** and **became a voice in the "birther" movement** which questioned Barack Obama's citizenship. By 2013, he was **back in the Republican Party** where he again began to plan a run for the presidency.

The 2016 Democratic National Convention

By the time of the 2016 Democratic National Convention, **Hillary had already locked up the nomination**. She chose Virginia Senator, **Tim Kaine**, to be her running mate.

But the convention did have its **moments of dissent**. When internal **Democratic National Committee emails were leaked** (allegedly by Russian intelligence agency hackers) that seemed to favor Hillary over Sanders, apparently because he was a registered Independent, his supporters began to protest.

The Sanders supporters made such a fuss about there being bias within the party, the chairperson of the Democratic National Committee was forced to resign. From that point on, **most of the speakers (including Hillary) were careful to show their approval of Sanders.**

By bringing on numerous African-American speakers, gospel singers, and even rap artists, **the Democrats made it clear they were the multicultural party**. And they also made it clear that they strongly disagreed with Trump's "Make America Great Again" slogan by repeating over and over again that **America *already was* the greatest country on Earth**. Several of the speakers criticized Trump's negative view of America.

All three of the living Democratic presidents addressed the convention in support of Hillary. That was in marked contrast with the Republican convention where **the two living Republican presidents were noticeably absent and were not willing to endorse Trump.**

STORY

A highlight of the Democratic convention was the appearance of **the father of a U.S. soldier, Humayun Khan**, an American Muslim who had been a captain in the U.S. Army who had been killed in Iraq while protecting his men. Appearing on the stage along with his wife, Mr. Khan said, "If it was up to Donald Trump, my son never would have been in America." He said Trump consistently smeared the character of Muslims, and he disrespects other minorities and women. **He then pulled out a pocket-sized version of the U.S. Constitution and waved it in the air, saying "I will gladly lend you my copy. In this document, look for the words 'liberty' and 'equal protection of law.'**"

> Trump's reaction was quick, and as was typical of him, he responded with a counterattack. He questioned Mr. Khan's honesty, saying, "Who wrote that? **Did Hillary's script writers write it?**" He also questioned why the man's wife didn't speak, saying "Wasn't she allowed to speak?" (Mrs. Khan later said she had been too overcome with grief to speak.)

Hillary started her acceptance speech by calling attention to the fact that this moment was a historic milestone, **the first time in our nation's history that a woman would be a major party's nominee** for president of the United States.

The focus of her speech was Trump. She said he was "**temperamentally unfit**" to be president and commander-in-chief. She said he was not just trying to build a wall between America and Mexico, he was **trying to wall off Americans from each other.** She said his "Make America Great Again" slogan was code for talking **America backwards**, back to a time when opportunity and dignity were reserved for the few. She pointed out that **Trump had said a distinguished judge born in Indiana couldn't do his job properly because of his Mexican heritage.** She said he had mocked a reporter with disabilities, and he had called women "pigs." She said **"Bridges are better than walls**." She said "We are stronger together," which was to become her main campaign slogan.

After her relatively short speech at the convention, many in the news media commented on **how upbeat her speech was as compared to that of Donald Trump**.

> **STORY**
>
> After Hillary was chosen to be the Democrat's nominee for president, a lot more information came out about her. The people soon learned Hillary Rodham Clinton's story was not your usual American politician's story.

Growing up in a conservative family in a conservative suburb of Chicago, she was a standout in high school where she was a National Merit finalist and voted "most likely to succeed." She went on to **major in political science at Wellesley College**, a private women's liberal-arts college in Massachusetts that was well-known as a breeding ground for women who were destined to go on to "big things." As a freshman, she already stood out and was soon to become **president of the Wellesley Young Republicans**. But **the Vietnam War and the Civil Rights Movement eventually convinced her to switch her allegiance to the Democratic Party**.

In 1968, **she was elected president of the Wellesley College Government Association, and was described as not only a leader of her group, but as the de facto leader of the entire student body**. Despite the school's tradition of not allowing students to speak at commencement, the other students forced the school's administration to let her speak. She gave an inspirational speech that fired up the students. **Some of them said she might go on to be the nation's first female president**.

Hillary then attended **Yale Law School** where she served on the editorial board of the Yale Review of Law and Social Action. She also volunteered at New Haven Legal Services to provide free legal advice for the poor.

At Yale, **she met fellow student, Bill Clinton, who soon asked her to marry him**. She said no, but they did move in together, and in 1972, they campaigned together for Democratic presidential candidate George McGovern.

She did **postgraduate work as a staff attorney for the Children's Defense Fund** in Cambridge, Massachusetts, and she then **became a member of the House of Representative's Watergate inquiry staff**.

People saw a bright future for Hillary in politics, but she decided to "follow her heart," and she went with Bill Clinton back to his home state of Arkansas. There, she became only the second **female faculty member at the University of Arkansas School of Law**, and she became the first director of the school's new legal aid clinic.

In 1975, she finally **agreed to marry Bill, but chose to keep her own last name, Rodham**. That didn't go over well in conservative Arkansas, especially after Bill was elected Arkansas Attorney General. Hillary continued her own career, joining a prestigious law firm, and she also **continued to provide free legal aid to the poor**.

In 1978, **Bill was elected Governor of Arkansas, and Hillary soon became known as a most unusual first-lady** of Arkansas by maintaining her own law career. In 1980, Bill was defeated in his bid for reelection, and some said it was because of his "uppity" wife. That same year, their daughter Chelsea was born. In 1982, Bill again ran for governor, and this time he was successful. Back in her position as Arkansas's First Lady, she **changed her name to Hillary Rodham Clinton**, but she continued to practice law.

In 1992, Bill ran for president. In the middle of the election campaign, **a potential scandal arose when a woman came forward to say she had been having an affair with Bill. Hillary stood by him,** and nothing was ever proved.

Bill was elected president, and as the nation's first-lady, Hillary was not content to merely host diplomatic dinners. **She had her own office in the West Wing** near the president's office **and took an active role in presidential affairs**. Most notably, she **chaired a task force designed to reform health care** in the United States. However, the Republicans in Congress called it **"Hillarycare"** and were able to stop any type of new health program from being put in place. She did manage to help create the **Office on Violence Against Women** at the Department of Justice, and she **initiated the Adoption and Safe Families Act**.

> When the House impeached her husband for the Monica Lewinsky affair, she again stood by him.
>
> After leaving the White House, in 2000, **Hillary ran for the open Senate seat in New York**. She won easily.
>
> **In 2008, Hillary decided to run for president**, but Obama beat her in the primaries. **After Obama was elected president, he appointed Hillary as his Secretary of State.**

"Third-Party" Candidates

As I pointed out earlier, if someone wants to run for president of the United States, all they have to do is file a Statement of Candidacy with the Federal Election Commission. In 2016, thousands did so. The next step is to **get enough signatures to appear on a state ballot**, and a few also did that. However, few of those candidates had the money or the connections to publicize their candidacy. Nevertheless, a few of the "third-party" candidates were able to garner some attention, and therefore, some votes.

As the nation's attention was focused on the extensive TV coverage of the Republican and Democratic national conventions, **other political parties were also holding national conventions**.

> **COMMENT**
>
> The **Libertarian Party** candidates got on the ballot in all 50 states, and the **Green Party** candidates got on the ballot in 40 states. Thirty other **"third-party" candidates for president were "ballot qualified" in at least one state**. The **Constitution Party, a conservative party with the goal of restoring American jurisprudence to its Christian Biblical foundations** and limiting the federal government was ballot qualified in 15 states, and the **Socialist Party that opposed oppression, including capitalism and authoritarian forms of communism,** got ballot qualified in a few states. The **Peace and Free-**

dom Party, which had been around since the sixties, got ballot qualified in several states. None of the so-called "third parties" were able to get any electoral votes, but in a few states **they may have taken enough votes away from Hillary to cost her the election.**

The 2016 Presidential Campaigns

After national conventions had determined who the candidates would be, the "real" campaign began. Hillary started touring the swing states, at first by bus, but then later in her own campaign jet. She was energetic and upbeat, refusing to hook into the non-stop attacks from Trump.

> **COMMENT**
> Ever wonder where the terms "**red state**" and "**blue state**" came from? Apparently, the terms originated from the large map NBC News displayed on TV during the very close 2000 presidential election. To clarify which way states were leaning, they showed the Republican-leaning states in red and the Democratic-leaning states in blue. That kind of visual representation of where the states stood became the standard way to represent them, and the two terms "red state" and "blue state" eventually also caught on.

Trump was also hitting many different states in his campaign jet, which he said was bigger than the president's Air Force One (it wasn't). **His campaign speeches were mostly about what bad shape the country was in.** He emphasized how bad the economy was, insisting that **Obama and Hillary had hurt the livelihoods of working-class people by making trade deals** that sent American jobs out of the country. Hillary countered that **President Bush had handed Obama a very challenging economic** situation after the worst recession since the great depression, and President Obama had been successful in bringing it back.

As Republican politicians had been doing for many years, Trump talked a lot about **law and order**. He said **Obama and Hillary had made America a dangerous place to live**. He said police needed to have more power, and that useful policies like "stop and frisk" had been taken away from them (the stop-and-frisk policy had been declared unconstitutional because it had been found to unfairly target people of color.)

Hillary said Trump was creating a divisive climate with his negativity about America and his never-ending claim that he was going to "build a great wall" and deport all illegal aliens. Her slogan of "Stronger Together" was designed to point out Trump's saying he would ban Muslim from coming into the country, and he would deport Mexicans who he called "rapists and killers."

COMMENT

When the polls showed Trump was losing badly among African-Americans and Hispanics, **Trump began to talk about how terrible conditions were in "the African-American community."** He said things were so bad, few African-Americans had jobs, their schools were a disaster, and **they were afraid to go out in the street lest they get shot**. He said **things had never been worse in the African-American community, and it was Hillary's fault.** He began saying, "What do you have to lose?" Even after Hillary supporters disputed his grim statistics and pointed out that schools in America were no longer separated by race, he kept on saying, "What do you have to lose?" **When polling among African-Americans indicated that his "What do you have to lose" strategy was not working, he abandoned it and went back to mostly appealing to his base, non-college educated white men and white Evangelicals.** To deal with his lack of support among Hispanics, his campaign staff announced that **he was going to "moderate" his harsh plan to immediately deport all illegal immigrants. **He made a trip to Mexico to meet with the Mexican president**, followed by a nationally televised speech in Arizona in which he tried to walk a fine line between insisting he was going to "build a wall" (with Mexico paying for it) and a supposedly more moderate policy of first deporting illegal immigrants that had been convicted of crimes. **He said he would "deal with"** all the other illegal immigrants later, but he still emphasized that **"we are a country of laws,"** and that meant illegal immigrants had to be deported.

He then **brought a series of people up onto the stage with him who said their loved ones had been killed by illegal immigrants**. The message was clear: **illegal immigrants were killers**. From that point on, there was no more talk from the Trump campaign about moderating his hard stance on immigration policy. In fact, **he began suggesting that Hillary wanted an "open border" policy**. He said that would mean "**we no longer have a country.**"

As the campaign went on, **Trump and his supporters kept up their attacks on Hillary with regard to how she had handled her e-mail**. At the same time, Republicans in Congress continued to press the FBI for more information about their investigation of the matter. **The Democrats in Congress said the Republican efforts were "purely political."**

Out on the campaign trail, Trump was insisting that Hillary had "lied" to the FBI (the FBI never said that). Congressional Republicans began to insist that the Justice Department should undertake a whole new investigation of Hillary, **suggesting that she had lied to Congress about how she handled her e-mail**. The FBI continued to say they had found nothing criminal in her actions or in what she had said to the FBI. Trump also began to talk about **the relationship between the State Department and the Clinton Foundation** during Hillary's tenure, suggesting that the Clinton's had somehow personally profited from the non-profit foundation and that donors to the foundation might have been given special access to the State Department. However, Hillary denied it and Trump never produced any evidence.

Trump's campaign staff wanted him to stick to issues like that, but **Trump preferred to talk off-the-cuff**, sometimes saying things he would later have to take back. During the campaign, **Trump fired some of the leading members of his campaign staff and replaced them with more aggressive anti-establishment muckrakers** who were more in tune with his desired image of being an "outsider" (he even wanted to be seen as outside of the Republican mainstream). He said, "I am who I am," and promised his followers he wasn't going to change.

Trump often talked about the atrocities that had been perpetrated in the name of "radical Islam. In typical Trumpian style, he blamed President Obama and Hillary not only for the rise of ISIS, but also for other trouble in the Middle East. **He said the violence of "radical Islamic" terrorism all over the world only started after the election of President Obama** (he never mentioned the role President Bush's invasion of Iraq had played). After Hillary said the fight was not against Islam but against terrorism, Trump said Hillary was unwilling to use the phrase, "radical Islamic terrorism." **He said if he was elected president he would stop ISIS, even if it took "vicious" methods**. He said we "have to play the game at **a much tougher level**." He suggested that tougher approach should include **killing the families of the terrorists**. When it was pointed out to him that killing the families of suspects was against international law, he backed off a bit, claiming he had only said he would "go after" them." **He said he would keep open the prison at Guantanamo Bay and that he was in total support of waterboarding**. He said we should do "whatever it takes." **He also said he would cut off the terrorists' access to the internet all over the world**. Throughout the campaign, Trump often made reference to "**political correctness**," and said it was keeping the U.S. from effectively fighting illegal immigration and terrorism. He said if he was elected president, he would give the immigration authorities permission to engage in "**extreme vetting**" to make sure no bad actors got into our country. He even talked about **teaming up with Russia to fight ISIS**. Soon, it was revealed that his campaign chief had a business relationship with the Russians.

> **STORY**
> At one point in the campaign, **Trump called Hillary "a bigot."** Hillary immediately responded in a speech that **suggested the real bigots, white supremacists and KKK-related figures, were strongly supporting Trump**.
> Later, in another speech, she said, **"To just be grossly generalistic, you can put half of Trump supporters into what I call the basket of deplorables. Right? Racist, sexist, homophobic, xenophobic, Islamaphobic, you name it. The other basket of people are people who feel that government has let them down, the economy has let them down, nobody cares about them, nobody worries about what happens to their lives and their futures. They are just desperate for change. Those are people who we have to understand and empathize with as well."**
> It seemed to be a well-thought out statement designed to attract some of Trump's less radical supporters, the ones who felt the government and the economy had "let them down," and the ones who just wanted things to change. But she failed to think through how the Trump campaign and the news media would pick and chose which of her words to report on. **They grabbed onto the words "deplorables, racist, sexist, homophobic, xenophobic, and Islamaphobic, and ignored the rest of her statement**. She quickly came out with an apology, saying she shouldn't have used the word "**half**." She said she only meant that "some" of Trump's supporters were like that. Nevertheless, Trump continued to attack her on it, **saying what she really meant was that "all" of his supporters were "deplorable."**

> His forces quickly created an anti-Hillary TV commercial that suggested she thought anyone who might think about voting for Trump was "deplorable." It didn't seem to hurt Hillary much in the polls, but it was a hard lesson for her to learn about how words can be taken out of context.

While Hillary frequently pointed out her extensive knowledge of foreign affairs, Trump's ventures into that subject sometimes got him into trouble. In interviews, he often praised Russian President Vladimir Putin, describing him as a leader who had high favorable ratings in Russia. Previously, Putin had praised Trump, describing him as "bright and talented" and the "absolute leader of the presidential race" in the U.S.

When asked about Putin's alleged killing of journalists and political opponents, Trump dismissed it, saying we have a lot of killing in this country too. **Regarding Putin, Trump said, "At least he's a leader, unlike what we have in this country."**

Earlier, in the GOP debates, **Trump had bragged that he knew Putin personally. He said, "I got to know him very well because we were both on 60 Minutes. We were stablemates, and we did very well that night."** (Actually, they couldn't have met because Trump was interviewed for the program in the United States and Putin was interviewed in Russia.)

Trump had also stated that he and Putin had spoken directly at a National Press Club luncheon in Moscow, and he said, President Putin "could not have been nicer." (Later, Trump said he had never met Putin.) Trump began saying Russia and the U.S. ought to be on better terms, and **maybe the U.S. ought to back out of its commitments to NATO. Trump's comments sounded like he was approving Putin's methods and policies**, and that brought him a lot of criticism, even from members of his own party.

Many expected Trump to bring up Benghazi often—just as Romney had done in the presidential election of 2012—and at first he did. During the primary season, **he said Hillary's decisions as Secretary of State "spread death, destruction and terrorism everywhere she touched."** He said that Benghazi and the death of Ambassador Chris Stevens was one of her biggest failures, and he accused her of **"sleeping through"** the Benghazi attack. He said, "I mean what she did with him was absolutely horrible. **He was left helpless to die as Hillary Clinton soundly slept in her bed.** That's right. When the phone rang at three in the morning, **Hillary Clinton was sleeping.**" (Actually, the Benghazi attack took place at about 3:30 in the afternoon, Washington D.C. time, and Hillary was in her State Department office monitoring the situation in Benghazi.)

COMMENT

In the 57 prior U.S. presidential elections, there had never been a female candidate nominated by either the Republicans or the Democrats. When Hillary was nominated by the Democrats in 2016, many said she would have an uphill battle. That turned out to be true. Despite the fact that she had twice been elected a U.S. Senator and had served as the U.S. Secretary of State, many voters said they didn't trust her. Few ever said why that was, but **some came right out and said it was because she was a woman. They said they didn't think a woman would have "the strength" to be a president. Others said they "wanted a man in charge."** In the campaign, **Trump was quick to jump on that idea, but he couched it in vague terms.** He said Hillary didn't have "the presidential look," and **he often referred to her as weak and lacking stamina.** Sometimes, on stage at his rallies, he would parody her by pretending to walk in a very feeble way. He said she was so weak, she was often "barely able to make it back to her car." In fact, late in the campaign, he said "she should be drug tested," **implying that she was so weak she must be using performance-enhancing drugs to keep going.** And then, in the middle of the campaign, **Hillary was videotaped looking tired and weak on her way to her car** after she had attended a public event on a hot day. It was discovered that **she was suffering from pneumonia**, and on doctor's orders she had to take a few days off of campaigning. **Trump made fun of her need to "rest" all the time.**

However, **a few days later, despite suffering from pneumonia, Hillary was back on the campaign trail**, and when Trump mentioned her lack of "stamina" in one of the debates, she replied, **"As soon as he travels to 112 countries and negotiates a peace deal, a cease fire, a release of dissidents, an opening of new opportunities in nations around the world, or even spends 11 hours testifying in front of a congressional committee he can talk to me about stamina."**

Nevertheless, during the campaign, even though **Hillary held a huge polling advantage over Trump with women**, many men and some women still didn't feel comfortable about electing a woman as president. There was **a religious divide among voters**, with some quoting **passages from the Bible that suggested a woman should not try to lead men**. Earlier, a Republican campaign e-mail asked, "Is it God's highest desire, that is, his Biblically expressed will, … to have a woman rule the institutions of the family, the church, and the state?"

Some pointed out that the Bible says **Eve's origin was subordinate to Adam.** They pointed to a Bible passage that seemed to say it was **"shameful" when a woman has to step up and lead when male leaders falter**. Others mentioned another Bible verse that said, "The husband is the head of the wife as Christ is the head of the church."

A number of Republican-led congressional investigations into Benghazi were launched, but **despite bringing Hillary before Republican-led Congressional committees with many very long sessions that featured seemingly endless attacks on her by**

Republicans, they were unable to shake Hillary or prove that she was in any way responsible for what happened in Benghazi. The Democrat's claim that the "investigations" were "purely political" was soon given credence when it was revealed that some Republicans were **congratulating themselves for how their congressional investigations had managed to drive down Hillary's poll numbers**.

During the campaign, Russian intelligence agencies hacked computers belonging to the Democratic National Committee. They released damaging DNC e-mails through the Wikileaks organization in order to try to influence the U.S. elections in Trump's favor.

Also, there were hacks of Hillary's staff e-mails that U.S. government intelligence agencies said were being done by the Russian government in an attempt to help Trump.

In a campaign speech, Trump said, "Russia, if you're listening, I hope you're able to find the 30,000 e-mails that are missing." Inviting a foreign power to get involved in the U.S. presidential election by hacking U.S. computers outraged a lot of people. Some went so far as to describe it as **treasonous**.

Years before, when Trump was a Democrat, he had been a supporter of the Planned Parenthood organization. But now that he was a candidate for president on the Republican ticket, he said he was against abortion. In an interview, he even said if he was successful in making abortion illegal in the United States, **he would punish a woman for having an abortion**.

That unleashed a firestorm of criticism, and he backed off, saying he would only punish the doctor that had performed the abortion.

After a number of such controversial statements, even his supporters began to say they wished he would just stick to attacking Hillary.

And for a short time, he did that, but soon he was back to making his usual outrageous statements. Trump said that's just the way he was, and he wasn't about to change.

STORY

As has become common in modern presidential elections, the candidates tried to keep themselves in the media spotlight as much as possible. Buying TV time in placed ads is very expensive, so the **candidates try to get free "air time" by making** news. It didn't take long for Trump, the experienced entertainer, to show that he was good at that. **His outlandish statements (and frequent retractions) were sure to grab the news headlines. Trump seemed to be going for the "any publicity is good publicity" approach.**

News outlets took varying approaches to reporting on the presidential campaign, but some seemed to favor one or the other of the candidates. If reporters reported news Trump felt was not favorable to him, he banned them from his press conferences, and branded them as evil. He frequently attacked the biggest TV news media outlets (except for Fox News).

Hillary **didn't have Trump's news-grabbing ability**. But as **long as she maintained her lead in the polls, she seemed willing to let Trump grab all the headlines.**

Throughout the 2016 presidential campaign, Trump got into the habit of making what became known as Trump's "outrageous statement of the day."

Here is a partial list of what might be called "outrageous Trumpisms":

- **"I will be the greatest jobs president God ever created."**
- **"When Mexico sends its people, they're not sending their best. They're sending people that have lots of problems. They're bringing drugs. They're bringing crime. They're rapists."**
- **"I will build a great wall – and nobody builds walls better than me, believe me – and I'll build them very inexpensively. I will build a great, great wall on our southern bor-**

der, and I will make Mexico pay for that wall. Mark my words."

• "Hey, I watched when the World Trade Center came tumbling down. And I watched in Jersey City, New Jersey, where thousands and thousands of people were cheering as that building was coming down. Thousands of people were cheering." (Trump made it clear he was describing Arab-looking people cheering the fall of the Trade Tower buildings, but no television network reported broadcasting such a thing. If it would have happened, they said, it would have been a major news event.)

• "The concept of global warming was created by and for the Chinese in order to make U.S. manufacturing non-competitive."

• "There is no drought in California. They're sending the water out to the ocean to protect a certain kind of three-inch fish." (At the time he made this statement, 80% of California was in the fifth year of devastating drought.)

• "John McCain is not a war hero. He's a war hero 'cause he was captured. I like people that weren't captured, OK?" (McCain was a Navy pilot that was shot down and captured and tortured during the Vietnam War. He spent more than five years as a prisoner of war in North Vietnam.)

• "Hillary wants to abolish, essentially abolish the Second Amendment. By the way, and if she gets to pick — if she gets to pick her judges, nothing you can do, folks. Although the Second Amendment people, maybe there is, I don't know." (This was widely seen as a suggestion that maybe the only way to stop Hillary from taking away everybody's guns was with a gun. After nearly universal outrage, Trump said he was only suggesting Second Amendment people should vote against her.)

- "I know more about ISIS than the generals."
- "**Mr. Putin is very much of a leader, far more than our president.**" Many quickly pointed out that Trump's statement ignored the fact that Putin is a dictator who suppresses any and all dissent, has driven his country's economy into the ground and created a state-sponsored doping program that got many of Russia's greatest athletes banned from the Olympics.
- "**Look, we're led by a man that either is not tough, not smart, or he's got something else in mind. And the something else in mind — you know, people can't believe it. People cannot, they cannot believe that President Obama is acting the way he acts and can't even mention the words 'radical Islamic terrorism.' There's something going on. It's inconceivable.**"

But perhaps the best example of Trump's strategy of getting media attention with outrageous statements was a claim he made after he started to fall behind in the polls: he said, "**Obama is the founder of ISIS.**" (It is unknown whether or not Trump was aware of it, but it was a replication of the anti-American propaganda Russian state media was pushing.) Trump's supporters quickly scrambled to try to say it was only a metaphor, but Trump wouldn't go along with that: he said it was no metaphor, "**Obama really is the founder of ISIS, and Hillary helped.**"

But then, the next day, he got himself a brand new set of headlines by saying it was "**only sarcasm.**" For a presidential candidate to employ that kind of say-it-and-then-retract-it approach to getting in the news might seem like a silly thing to do, but his supporters seemed to be going for it. Although his radically new attack-oriented approach to campaigning seemed to be hurting him among moderates, his support in the solidly-Republican states never faltered.

When his handlers and other top Republicans tried to convince him to get back on track and quit making such outlandish statements, he said he was just going to keep on doing the same thing all the way to the end. **"It's either going to work or I'm going to have a very, very nice, long vacation."**

That got people talking too, suggesting that maybe he was preparing for new enterprises after the election, and **there was a rumor that he was already preparing to launch his own post-election TV show, or maybe even an anti-establishment TV network.**

In the last few weeks of the campaign, Trump began making even more outrageous statements, such as "**The election of Hillary Clinton would lead to the destruction of our country**" and "**Hillary Clinton is the most corrupt politician ever to seek the office of the presidency**," and "**Hillary Clinton's corruption is on a scale we have never seen before. We must not let her take her criminal scheme to the Oval Office.**" No prior presidential candidate had ever made such unfounded outrageous accusations against an opponent, but by then, everybody was used to his outlandish statements.

As the two campaigns moved into the fall, the polls were making it clear to everybody (except for the die-hard Trump supporters) that **if Trump didn't change his approach to campaigning, he had little chance of being elected president**. He did overhaul his campaign staff, but not to moderate his approach. In August, he got rid of some professional campaigners and hired people that were described as "ultra-conservative" or "Alt-Right," people that were known to favor aggressive attacks on anyone who didn't agree with them, even attacks against other Republicans that were seen as "**not conservative enough**."

As fall approached, Trump **refocused his campaign to do even more attacks on Hillary and Obama. That strategy *did* strengthen his support in the "red" states**, but the national polls continued to indicate that as long as nothing changed by election day, Hillary would win. Meanwhile, in speech after speech,

Hillary's message was clear: she had the experience; her opponent did not. She often suggested that **Trump didn't have the temperament to be president,** and **she used Trump's own words against him.**

STORY

In the heated 2016 presidential race, TV ads were even more significant than in prior elections. However, **unless you lived in one of the so-called "swing states," you probably didn't see any of them**. TV ads are very expensive, and the candidates were not about to waste money on the states they figured they were not going to win anyhow. **Many of the TV ads did not appear until mid-October**, the period when the candidates believed undecided voters where making up their minds.

The trend toward more negative ads continued in 2016, with **"attack ads" that often featured the candidate's own words.**

One of Hillary's ads that was aired on TV all over the nation showed young girls looking into a mirrors while Trump's words were spoken saying, **"I'd look her right in that fat, ugly face of hers . . . She's a slob . . . A person who's flat-chested is very hard to be a ten."** The words, **"Is this the president we want for our daughters?"** was displayed.

Other Hillary ads used Trumps' words about how he treated women, including his words in **the Hollywood Access audio tape about how he could get away with "grabbing women by the pussy"** because he was a star.

Trump's ads often used fear and demagoguery. One of them that aired in New Hampshire, North Carolina, Ohio, and Pennsylvania, featured a weeping mother describing how an illegal immigrant had murdered her child and set him on fire. The ad finished with her saying the words, **"Hillary Clinton's border policy is going to allow people into the country just like the one that murdered my son."**

Hillary's ads were often optimistic as she talked about education, jobs, and equal opportunity. She aired ads that talked about child care and quality education. **Many of her ads were described as "uplifting."** In one, she said, "We are going to lift each other up. I want us to heal our country and bring it together . . . This is the America that I know and love. If we set those goals and we go together, there's nothing that America can't do." Those kinds of upbeat ads aired repeatedly in all the swing states.

In another Hillary ad, aired in all the swing states, Khizr Khan, father of the slain Muslim soldier, Captain **Humayun Khan,** is featured asking, "Mr. Trump, would my son have a place in your America?"

The National Rifle Association paid $6.5 million to air an ad in Ohio, Nevada, North Carolina, Pennsylvania and Virginia that featured a woman who says a man with a knife tried to rob her, but he failed because "I carry a pistol." (She shot him twice.) She says, "Don't let politicians take away your right to own a gun."

Other Trump ads tried to foster suspicion about Hillary and the Clinton charitable foundation. In one, he asked, "How did Hillary end up filthy rich?" He answered his own question with, "Pay to play politics. . . Hillary Clinton only cares about power, money, and herself."

At many of Trump's speeches and in **some of his ads, he proclaimed that the FBI had said she lied to the FBI about her e-mails.** The director of the FBI, James Comey contradicted that. In sworn testimony before Congress, when pressed by a Republican Congressman about whether Hillary had lied, he said, **"We have no basis to conclude she lied to the FBI." Nevertheless, the ad continued to play on TV**. Late in the campaign, some of Trump's ads claimed Hillary was "under investigation." That was not true. What *was* being investigated were some e-mails found on the laptop of her assistant.

> **Some of Hillary's ads focused on Trump's business ties with Russia**; others referred to the fact that many of his products were made in places like Bangladesh even though comparable products were available from American manufacturers.

On the campaign trail, Hillary talked about **Trump's refusal to release copies of his income tax statements,** suggesting he had "something to hide." She released copies of her IRS tax filings and challenged Trump to do the same. She described herself as the daughter of a small business owner (silk screening fabrics) and the granddaughter of a factory worker. **It was a clear attempt to point out the contrast between her modest family history and the wealthy family of Donald Trump who had given him his start in business.** She said she couldn't imagine how average Americans would possibly support billionaire Trump.

> **COMMENT**
> **The issue of releasing copies of IRS tax filings** was constantly in the news throughout the campaign. **Hillary released copies of her and husband Bill's tax filings,** which showed that they had made a lot of money from writing books and from giving speeches The tax forms showed that they had paid a very high tax rate in 2014 and 2015, despite giving almost 10% of their income to charity. (Some said the 35.7% rate they had paid was abnormally high and suggested that maybe they should get a better tax accountant.) Hillary then demanded to know what kind of tax rate Trump had paid on his supposedly very high income.
> Early in his run for the presidency, **Trump promised to release copies of his tax returns, just as every presidential candidate had done for the past forty years**. But once the

campaign had actually begun, when news reporters asked Trump about that, he said it was none of their business.

The Democratic vice presidential nominee, **Tim Kaine, also released copies of his tax filing documents** and pointed out that every presidential candidate since Lyndon Johnson had released their tax statements to the public. **He said even Nixon had released his tax statements, so why couldn't Trump?**

Trump's only response was that he couldn't do it because he was undergoing "a routine audit" by the IRS. (The IRS said there was no restriction on him releasing his tax filings just because he was undergoing an audit.)

Hillary's supporters said that he should at least release his earlier tax statements that were not under audit. Trump also refused to do that. Hillary asked him to at least state what tax rate he had paid, but **Trump again said it was nobody's business**.

After that, **Hillary started asking if the real reason Trump wouldn't release copies of this present or prior taxes was because he "had something to hide."** She also suggested that **maybe Trump, after claiming bankruptcy multiple times and "stiffing" his employees, wasn't as rich and successful as he claimed**. In mid-campaign, even Trump's running mate, **Mike Pence released copies of his tax filing documents**. Many thought that would embarrass Trump into releasing his taxes, but he still refused to do it.

Late in the campaign, a story came out showing that in 1995, **Trump had declared a 916 million dollar loss on his income tax returns**. Tax experts said that meant **he might not have paid any personal income taxes** for as many as 18 years after that. **Trump's response was that he had simply taken advantage of the tax laws.**

Meanwhile, Trump, on the campaign trail, was saying the U.S. was in terrible shape. **He said we were becoming a third-world country.** He said he would "get tough" on our trading partners, especially China, and he would impose tariffs. **He also said he would repeal the Affordable Care Act (known as Obamacare).**

In an interview on ABC television, **he said the Putin "is** not going into Ukraine, OK, just so you understand. He's not going to go into Ukraine, all right? You can mark it down." When **the interviewer pointed out that the Russians had already moved into Ukraine**, seizing the country's Crimean Peninsula, Trump said, "OK, well, he's there in a certain way. . . Frankly, that whole part of the world is a mess under Obama."

In his speeches, about foreign affairs, **Trump mostly focused on the issue of terrorism**. He said he was sure he could take care of ISIS. In fact, **he said he knew more about ISIS than the generals. He said he was "the only one" who could deal with ISIS.** In some speeches, he said the U.S. military was in terrible shape and needed to be dramatically rebuilt. These kinds of statements did not endear him to military leaders and foreign policy experts, and a number of them came forward to publicly denounce Trump's foreign policy ideas. Also, **an anti-Trump letter was signed by 50 foreign affairs and defense specialists that had served in Republican administrations.** The letter stated:

"From a foreign policy perspective, Donald Trump is not qualified to be President and Commander-in-Chief. Indeed, we are convinced that he would be a dangerous President and would put at risk our country's national security and well-being.

"Mr. Trump lacks the character, values, and experience to be President. He weakens U.S. moral authority as the leader of the free world. He appears to lack basic knowledge about and belief in the U.S. Constitution, U.S. laws, and U.S. institutions, including religious tolerance, freedom of the press, and an independent judiciary.

"In addition, Mr. Trump has demonstrated repeatedly that he has little understanding of America's vital national interests, its complex diplomatic challenges, its indispensable alliances, and the democratic values on which U.S. foreign policy must be based. At the same time, he persistently compliments our adversaries and threatens our allies and friends. Unlike previous Presi-

dents who had limited experience in foreign affairs, Mr. Trump has shown no interest in educating himself. He continues to display an alarming ignorance of basic facts of contemporary international politics."

Trump dismissed them all as "the dangerous Washington elite." Nevertheless, the fact that 50 such high ranking defense experts would make such inflammatory statements about the Republican nominee got everybody's attention, and it clearly hurt Trump in the polls that came out soon thereafter.

> **COMMENT**
>
> The 50 foreign affairs experts who had served in Republican administrations were not going to be the first or the last Republicans to turn against Trump. **One after another, prominent Republicans were starting to come out against him**. The New York Times reported that more than 160 Republican leaders were not supporting Trump. This degree of lack of support of the nominee of your own party was something unheard of in any modern presidential elections. Trump brushed them all off, saying he didn't want their support anyhow.
>
> In fact, many other well-known Republicans had already come out against Trump, and he either ignored them or began to verbally attack them. Below are only a few of the many well-known Republicans who came out publicly against Trump early in the 2016 presidential campaign.
>
> **Barbara Bush**, wife of former Republican President George H. W. Bush. (Her husband and two sons, Jeb and the former president, George, refused to support Trump but didn't say how they would vote; they all pointedly stayed away from the Republican National Convention).
>
> **Michael Bloomberg**, former Republican Mayor of New York City not only disavowed any support for Trump, he also spoke on behalf of Hillary Clinton at the Democratic National Convention.

Colin Powell, a retired U.S. general who had served as Secretary of State under President George W. Bush said he was going to vote for Hillary.

Susan Collins, a Republican Senator from Maine said Trump would slash and burn and trample anything and anyone he perceived as being in his way or an easy scapegoat.

Bob Dole, Republican Congressman from Illinois said "Whether it be Mr. Trump's comments about women, his comments about Muslims, his comments about Latinos, for me it was very personal his comments about POWs." He said he might write in a name.)

Lindsey Graham, a Republican Senator from South Carolina. After Trump's attacks on Judge Gonzalo Curiel, Graham said his fellow Republicans should all withdraw their endorsements. He added "This is the most un-American thing from a politician since Joe McCarthy."

Richard Hanna, a Republican Congressman from New York, said he would vote for Hillary, adding, "For me, it is not enough to simply denounce Trump. He is unfit to serve our party and cannot lead this country."

Gordon Humphrey, former Republican Senator from New Hampshire called Trump "a sociopath without a conscience or feelings of guilt, shame or remorse."

Larry Pressler, former three-term Republican senator from South Dakota said he wouldn't vote for Trump, he endorsed Hillary Clinton.

Hank Paulson, former Secretary of the Treasury under George W. Bush said he was going to vote for Hillary "with the hope that she can bring Americans together to do the things necessary to strengthen our economy, our environment and our place in the world."

Sally Bradshaw, an aide to Republican Jeb Bush, said she "could not abide the hateful rhetoric of Donald Trump and his complete lack of principles."

Marc Racicot, chair of the Republican National Committee from 2001 to 2003 said "Trump has demonstrated neither the aforementioned qualities of principled leadership, nor offered any substantive or serious conservative policy proposals consistent with historical Republican Party platform positions."

Vin Weber, a former Minnesota Republican congressman, said he would not remain a Republican if Trump won.

George Will, conservative columnist said he had left the Republican Party because of Trump's nomination.

Mitt Romney, the 2012 Republican nominee for President, said, "I wanted my grand-kids to see that I simply couldn't ignore what Mr. Trump was saying and doing. I reveals a character and temperament unfit for the leader of the free world."

In addition to the Republicans listed above, **seventy-five former ambassadors, including 57 that had been appointed by Republican presidents**, released a letter endorsing Hillary Clinton and saying Donald Trump is "entirely unqualified."

Although no prior candidate had ever failed to receive the support of so many well-known officials in his own party, Trump brushed it off, describing all of them as "just jealous," and described them as Washington establishment people. He said, "Look at the terrible job they've done."

A number of terrorist events in the U.S. and around the world happened during the 2016 presidential campaign. They all became fodder for Trump's campaign. He said immigration from areas of the world where there is known terrorism should be prevented.

COMMENT

At one of his boisterous campaign rallies, Trump said that the "Second Amendment people" (gun rights people) should do something to stop Hillary. It was part of a warning that if she wasn't stopped, she would get to pick the next Supreme Court justice. Underlying Trump's words was a widespread belief that Supreme Court justices were not objective about the law. There was plenty of evidence to support that belief. Justice Scalia had consistently voted on cases in a way that most Republicans would approve of. In fact, you can often predict how Supreme Court justices will vote simply by knowing which president appointed them, Republican or Democratic.

But how can that be? Aren't judges who are at the very highest level of jurisprudence supposed to be making their decisions based on the law, not on personal preferences? The problem turns out to be what psychologists call cognitive dissonance reduction. That is, once a person begins to look at something in a certain way, data that competes with that point of view tends to make that person psychologically uncomfortable. It will cause cognitive dissonance. Humans (even judges) will therefore strive to reduce that dissonance by interpreting incoming data in a way that fits their established world view. As a result, if a president wants to "stack" the Supreme Court, all they have to do is analyze a judge's long history of decisions and find one that consistently votes in a certain way. Trump said he would do that if he was elected president, and he assumed Hillary would do the same thing.

After Justice Scalia died, President Obama did what the Constitution specified and quickly named a replacement. As was typical of President Obama, to be accommodating with both sides, **he picked a moderate judge**, Merrick Garland, the chief judge for the U.S. Court of Appeals for the D.C. Circuit.

According to the Constitution, the judge chosen by the president then must go before the Senate to be confirmed.

However, **the Republican leadership in the Senate did something unprecedented: they refused to do their Constitutional duty of voting on the new judge. In fact, they refused to even hold the required hearings**. They said it would

> not be appropriate to do so in an election year (even though six Supreme court justices had previously been confirmed in a presidential election year). **A few Republican Senators did apparently approve of President Obama's moderate pick.** They wanted to start the confirmation hearings on Judge Garland, but they were overruled by the Republican leadership.
>
> The Democrats were outraged. They said it was a violation of their Constitutional duty. And it was. But it showed that in the modern era, power politics (when in power, do whatever it takes to win) was the dominant rule in the Republican Party.

As the November election drew closer, Trump fell even farther behind in the national polls, but Trump continued to say the polls were wrong. He said the size of the crowds at his rallies proved it. It was true that Trump was still drawing large crowds to his rallies, and the crowds were as boisterous as ever. Whenever Hillary's name was mentioned, someone would yell "Hillary is a whore!" or "Kill the Bitch!" They often broke into the "Lock her up!" chant, and Trump egged them on.

> ### COMMENT
> **In presidential elections, there has always been propaganda.** What varies is the amount and viciousness of it. The Trump campaign established new levels of it. **Propaganda is defined as biased derogatory information used to promote a particular political point of view.** In its simplest form, propaganda can be just name-calling, but propaganda can also be used to associate your opponent with something unsavory or illegal. Early on in the 2016 presidential race, **Trump began calling Hillary Clinton, "crooked Hillary,"** an unsavory name that **implied that she had been convicted of something illegal**. When he failed to specify what made her "crooked," it showed

he had decided to enter the world of political propaganda. Soon thereafter, **he escalated the name-calling** by saying she was "a liar," often referring to her as "lying Hillary," adding that she was **a "dangerous liar."** In a speech early in the summer, he called her **"a world-class liar,"** adding that she was the "most corrupt person to ever run for president." Again, he offered no proof of that, and in fact, he didn't even say what he was referring to. Some speculated that he might be referring to how she handled her e-mail when she was the U.S. Secretary of State, but few could see how that made her **"the most corrupt person to ever run for president."**

Next, he said her full name, Hillary Rodham Clinton, sounded a lot like "Hillary Rotten Clinton." **It was a sneaky, if childish, way to say she was "rotten,"** but if asked, he could say it was just how her name sounded to him.

A few weeks later, he said Bernie Sanders had "made a deal with the devil," adding, **"She's the devil."**

Later in the campaign, probably **in response to some psychologists getting themselves into the news by suggesting that *he* had mental problems**, Trump began saying *she* was "unhinged," and that she was an "unbalanced person."

For the next stage of the propaganda campaign, a group of people paid by the Trump organization, began hitting the TV and radio talk shows, all of them referring to Hillary as "a liar." Once the propaganda campaign was fully operational, they began to self-referentially remind people of that by saying she was **a "well-known liar."**

Members of Trump's election staff also furthered Trump's unsubstantiated accusations of corruption by appearing on as many TV and radio shows as possible to call Hillary "corrupt." They eventually upped the level of their propaganda tactic by starting to call her "*totally* corrupt," and "*completely* untrustworthy." Instead of talking about policy and Trump's vision for the country, portraying Hillary as corrupt and as a liar eventually became the central tactic of his campaign.

But **does propaganda work?** It does, and many psychologists and social scientists have tried to figure out why. They say **the most effective propaganda works by associating a person or an idea with something unsavory or unpleasant, something people already have negative feelings about.** But it only works if it gets repeated often enough, and the 24-hour availability of news radio, online news, and cable TV are the perfect venue for such repetitions.

But **did it work this time?** Was repeatedly associating Hillary's name with negative connotations like "crooked" or "corrupt," or "untrustworthy" able to change people's opinion about her even though she was so well known?

The polls provided the answer. Before the election campaign began, **only 26% of those questioned nationwide rated Hillary unfavorably**. But by the fall of 2016, after a year of non-stop negative propaganda from Trump and his supporters about her honesty, **more than 50% of those polled rated her unfavorably.** Polls that focused specifically on the propaganda words Trump was using showed that trend even more clearly: **by the fall of 2016, polls were indicating that 67% were now rating her as "untrustworthy."**

Hillary mostly ignored it. When asked about Trump's insults, she said she was not going to engage in "the kind of insult fest that he seems to thrive on." She added, "**It is beneath the character of the kind of dialogue we should have**, because we have serious problems to solve." Her running mate, Tim Kaine added, "**Most of us stopped the name-calling thing about fifth grade.**"

However, Trump eventually pushed the propaganda too far: he said, "Hillary Clinton is a Bigot." That was like a trial lawyer bringing a topic into a case that should have been kept out of the jury members' minds. **Hillary reacted.** She said,

> "**From the start, Donald Trump has built his campaign on prejudice and paranoia.** He's taking hate groups mainstream and helping a radical fringe take over one of America's two major political parties." **She pointed out that Trump had launched his campaign for president with racist lies about Mexican immigrants, portraying them as rapists and criminals.** In fact, she said, **his whole campaign was based on a steady stream of bigotry,** including banning people from entering the United States based on their religion. She reminded voters that Trump's campaign operation was headed by those that had been in charge of the right-wing web sites that appealed to the Alt-Right, a fringe group of ultra-conservative Republicans that opposed multiculturalism and had long been associated with white supremacist groups.
>
> Hillary began to parody Trump's "Make America great again" slogan, saying his real goal was to **"Make America hate again."** Hillary's strong response to Trump's "She's a bigot" accusation may not have completely undone the effect Trump's negative propaganda was having, but the polls showed **Trump's "likability" numbers stated to drop.**
>
> But all the negative propaganda was having an effect on both of them: people began to talk about the 2016 presidential campaign being **a race between two unlikable candidates.**

As the first nationally televised debate approached, some were saying Trump had better get his act together or he was sure to lose the election. Most agreed that Hillary had far more experience at dealing with the debate format.

As Hillary retreated from the campaign trail to prepare for the debate, Trump continued to hold huge rallies so he could bask in the glory of his adoring fans. In fact, he made fun of Hillary's taking time out to prepare for the first debate, saying she wasn't actually preparing, but only resting. **He said he didn't need to prepare. He guaranteed that he would easily win the debates.**

The 2016 Presidential Debates

The televised presidential debates of 2016 began with the two candidates debating about job creation. Hillary outlined her economic program. She talked about trade deals and cutting taxes on businesses. Hillary said Trump's plan was trickle-down economics designed to help the rich. She called it "trumped-up" trickle-down. She reminded the audience that eight years ago the country was in the middle of the worst financial crisis since the 1930s, due, in large part, to tax policies that slashed taxes on the wealthy.

Trump interrupted to say, "That's called business, by the way."

Hillary went on to point out that nine million people had lost their jobs, and five million people had lost their homes. She wanted to talk about investing in clean energy, but Trump kept on interrupting by asking why she hadn't done anything in thirty years. He said her husband had approved NAFTA, the single worst trade deal ever approved in this country.

Hillary said creating green energy was good for the economy, and added "Donald thinks that climate change is a hoax perpetrated by the Chinese."

Trump said Hillary was going to drive businesses out of the country by increasing regulations "all over the place."

It was clear that throughout the debates, Hillary was going to talk facts and figures, and Trump was mainly going to interrupt.

The moderators often tried to get the debate back on track, but Trump wouldn't stop interrupting. He said "She's going to raise taxes $1.3 trillion. . . She tells you how to fight ISIS, but I don't think General Douglas MacArthur would like that too much. . . You're telling the enemy everything you want to do."

When a moderator asked Trump why he hadn't released his tax returns like all previous candidates had, Trump gave his usual response about being under audit, and added that he would release his taxes as soon as Hillary released her 33,000 lost e-mails.

When Hillary suggested that maybe he hadn't been paying any federal taxes," Trump interrupted with, "That makes me smart."

When a moderator asked Hillary about her use of a private e-mail server, she said, "If I had to do it over again, I would, obviously, do it differently. But I'm not going to make any excuses. It was a mistake, and I take responsibility for that."

Regarding crime, Trump defended the outlawed "stop and frisk" policy. Referring to the black communities, he said, "You walk down the street, you get shot."

Hillary described the vibrancy of the black church and black businesses, and she pointed out that violent crime was one-half of what it was in 1991.

When a moderator asked Trump about his false claim that the nation's first president to have a black father was not a natural-born citizen, Trump, oddly, said Hillary had started it.

Hillary mentioned the troubling cyber attacks from Russia and Trump's praise of Putin. She said she was shocked when Donald publicly invited Putin to hack into American systems, and she said it was one of the reasons why 50 national security officials who served in Republican administrations said Trump was unfit.

Trump said he had been endorsed by over 200 admirals and generals and by ICE, and he added that Hillary didn't know for sure if it was the Russians. He said, "It could also be China. It could also be lots of other people. It also could be somebody sitting on their bed that weighs 400 pounds."

When a moderator asked about acts of terror on American soil, Trump said President Obama and Secretary Clinton had created a vacuum for ISIS by the way they got out of Iraq.

Hillary pointed out that Trump had supported the Iraq war.

Trump said, "We have the greatest mess anyone's ever seen. You look at the Middle East, it's a total mess under your direction. He then went on to talk about "the Iran deal, another beauty."

When a moderator repeated Hillary's claim that Trump was on record as supporting the invasion of Iraq, Trump said, "That is mainstream media nonsense put out by her. I think the best person in her campaign is mainstream media."

He went on to say he had told Sean Hannity of Fox News that he was against the war, but nobody will check with Hannity.

Hillary reminded Trump that he had said if Iranian sailors taunted American sailors, he'd blow them out of the water.

Trump said the U.S. was falling behind in nuclear weapons.

The moderators often tried to rein Trump in, but it wasn't easy. Oddly, he sometimes left his podium to lurk behind Hillary, and he frequently used his time to attack her. He said, "She's got no business ability. **She doesn't have the look** and the stamina." When the moderator asked Hillary to respond to that, she repeated her statement that, "Well, as soon as he travels to 112 countries and negotiates a peace deal, a cease-fire, a release of dissidents, an opening of new opportunities in nations around the world, or even spends 11 hours testifying in front of a congressional committee, he can talk to me about stamina."

When Hillary said Trump wanted to get rid of the Affordable Care Act, which would leave 20 million people without health insurance, Trump responded with "Obamacare is a disaster. You know it. We all know it." He said he would replace it with a health program that was "the finest health care plan there is." A moderator asked Trump for more specifics, but Trump just went back to criticizing Obamacare.

When Hillary suggested that is was good that someone with the temperament of Donald Trump is not in charge of the law in our country, Trump interrupted with, "**Because you'd be in jail**."

Trump spent a lot of his debate time talking about the need for "a wall." He said giving citizenship to those who had entered the country illegally was unfair to those who were waiting to enter legally. He accused Hillary of wanting open borders, and in response to Hillary's mention of Russia, Trump he was willing to talk to Putin. He said Putin had said "some nice things about me. If we got along well, that would be good."

Hillary said Putin favored Trump because "He'd like to have a puppet as president of the United States."

For some reason, Trump replied, "You're the puppet."

Hillary ignored that and went on to say that it was unprecedented to have a foreign government interfering in our elections."

Trump said "She has no idea whether it's Russia, China, or anybody else."

Hillary said, Seventeen intelligence agencies said so."

After the debates, the polls indicated that Hillary had won all of them convincingly.

Nevertheless, Trump insisted that he had won.

Most of the news commentators had predicted that Trump would come to the debate prepared to be calm and acting "presidential," but he didn't. He was loud and aggressive throughout the debates. He seemed nervous and agitated, and he was doing a lot of sniffing. His supporters were quick to say it was only seasonal allergies, but Trump denied that. He also denied having a cold.

Much of the post debate discussion was about Trump's refusal to say he would accept the outcome of the election. Many elected officials, including a number of Republicans, came forward to condemn that as being against the very concept of democracy. Nevertheless, back on the campaign trail, Trump continued to say the only reason he could lose would be because of voter fraud.

After the debates, even more women came out to accuse Trump of sexually molesting them, and Hillary made sure people didn't forget about that.

Trump said the women's claims "had largely been debunked," but in fact, just the opposite was true: after the debate, friends and acquaintances of the women began coming forward to back up the accusations.

Trump and his supporters repeatedly put forward the story that the women were all lying, they had been "put up to it" by Hillary.

After the release of the Access Hollywood audio tape in which Trump bragged about sexually assaulting women, Trump brought out three women that he had paid to come to the debate in order to accuse Bill Clinton of sexual abuse. Some called Trump's event a "stunt" that used women whose stories had long been known and previously disproved. Everyone agreed that it was a desperate attempt to divert attention away from the Access Hollywood audio tape before it was brought up in the debates.

STORY

One of the most explosive events of the 2016 presidential campaign happened not long after the first presidential debate. It was **the release of an audio tape that had been made in preparation for a Trump appearance on the Access Hollywood TV show. The tape had been made when Trump was 59-years old**. In the tape, Trump can be heard using vulgar language to **brag about how he could get away with sexually accosting women. He said he could even get away with "grabbing their pussy" because he was a star.** Hearing what Trump had said on that audio tape set off a media firestorm. The tape was heard on every radio and TV station, and it was reproduced in every newspaper and news-oriented web site.

After the release of the Access Hollywood audio tape, Trump dismissed it, saying it was only **"locker-room banter."** He said Bill Clinton had said far worse things on the golf course. But he added, "I apologize if anyone was offended."

Most agreed that it wasn't a sincere apology, and the Democrats were not willing to dismiss it so easily. Neither were a lot of Republicans. **Not wanting their own careers to be tied to a presidential candidate bragging about sexual assault, a large number of elected Republicans withdrew their support from Trump**. Others just refused to talk about it. House Speaker, Paul Ryan, avoided withdrawing his endorsement of Trump merely saying **he was no longer going to campaign for Trump**. But then it got worse for Trump: dozens of elected Republicans actually called for him to withdraw his name from the ticket, despite the fact that it was the late stages of the campaign. That set off a series of Twitter tweets from Trump accusing them of disloyalty. **He called Ryan "Our very weak and ineffective leader."**

In addition, **hundreds of newspapers across the country immediately endorsed Hillary. Only a few newspapers were now willing to go on the record as supporting Trump**. Even the newspapers that had formerly always endorsed Republicans, refused to endorse Trump. For example, **the Phoenix Arizona Republic (which was founded in 1890 and was originally named "The Arizona Republican") endorsed Hillary.** It was the first time in the newspaper's history that they had ever endorsed a Democrat. (It resulted in outrage from local Trump supporters and even some **death threats to the newspaper staff**.) However, most politicians from the so-called "red states" continued to support Trump. Some of Trump's paid staff appeared on TV and radio news programs and talk shows to reiterate his claim that it was "only locker room talk." They said they had frequently heard men talk like that. However, many well-known athletes came forward to say they had never heard such talk in any locker room.

Soon the polls were indicating Trump might even lose traditionally Republican states like Utah, Arizona, and Georgia.

Surprisingly, many **Christian Evangelist leaders came forward to say they would continue to support Trump.** But that was **not true in Mormon Utah**. Although the state had long been voting Republican, **most of the state's Republican leaders immediately withdrew their support for Trump and said they would not vote for him. However, after many Republican voters criticized them, they quickly reversed course and tried to walk a neutral line**. Nevertheless, Utah's newspapers withdrew their support for Trump, including the Deseret News, a newspaper owned by the Mormon Church that had long supported Republicans.

Discussion of the Debates

The post-debate polls indicated that Hillary had won all of the debates convincingly. Nevertheless, Trump was quick to dispute that: he said he won the debates "in a landslide," and that every poll proved it (he didn't provide any poll results).

There was much post-debate talk about Trump's assertion that

Hillary had "**hate in her heart.**" Many also commented about his stalking of her around the stage. Of special note was his statement **that if he was elected, he would try to have Hillary put in jail**.

At about the same time, **WikiLeaks,** an organization that publishes information from anonymous sources, released on its web site what they said were hacked e-mails from members of Hillary's campaign staff. Trump made much of the hacked e-mails, implying that they proved Washington "insiders" like Hillary **said one thing in public and then said something quite different in their private e-mails**. Hillary's campaign staff said they could not verify the accuracy of the information in the supposedly hacked e-mails and said the **U.S. intelligence officials had said they believed the e-mail hacking had been done by the Russian state in an attempt to help Trump get elected.**

After the debates, **women soon began to come forward to describe Trump's behavior toward them, behavior that matched what he had bragged about in the audio tape.**

Trump was again put on the defensive, no longer just being accused of inappropriate "locker room" talk, but now being accused of actual sexual assault. As more and more women came forward, people began to talk about a "pattern of behavior" that was going to be hard for Trump to deny.

But Trump did deny it, every bit of it. He said all of the women were liars. He said they were being directed by Hillary's forces as part of a vast conspiracy against him. He said all you had to do was "look at the women" to see that he wouldn't have made advances on them.

When the news media continued to file stories about Trump's relationships with women, his poll numbers continued to drop. **Trump started saying the election was "rigged."**

STORY

In 2016, there was more **voter polling** than ever. If polls were important in prior presidential elections, they were now seen as crucial. That's because **the polling data from all the prior elections was now available to the analysts for comparison**, and those comparisons were providing some valuable information. For one thing, the analysts now knew that the early polling data was not all that significant in terms of predicting who would win. In 1980, early on, the incumbent president, Jimmy Carter was way ahead in the polls, but eventually lost to Ronald Reagan. But in all the elections that followed, the data clearly showed that such a reversal was not likely; it would take significant world or national events (like the Iran hostages situation) to change people's minds once they had stated their preference in a poll.

The analysts had also learned that when voters read about poll results, it can influence their behavior. When polled, people are more likely to say they are going to vote for the candidate that seems to be winning.

Nearing the end of the campaign, the polls showed Hillary leading nationally and in most of the swing states.

Nevertheless, Trump continued to claim he was leading in the polls. He continued to talk **about how the election might be stolen from him**. He didn't elaborate on how that could be done when elections were conducted by local people in tens of thousands of different polling places. He talked about the need for stricter voter identification requirements (a common Republican talking point). He said that without strict voter identification rules, people could walk in and vote for Hillary 15 times. He didn't explain how that could be done or why he was sure the voting cheaters would all vote for Hillary, but he did say **he might not accept the outcome of the race**.

Democrats said the Republican push for strict voter ID rules was a ploy to intimidate minority voters, especially Hispanics. The Republicans had good reason to push for voter identification rules that might keep Hispanics from voting. The polls were indicating that support for Trump among Hispanics was at historic lows. Undoubtedly, it was due to Trump's demeaning of Hispanic immigrants.

The polls were also indicating that Trumps' support among African-Americans were also startlingly low. Although most African-Americans usually voted Democratic, the pollsters were finding far fewer voters than usual in that subgroup willing to say they would vote for Trump.

Another startling result came out of the polling of young people. One survey that polled those under 35 found Hillary trouncing Trump 56% to 20%. That was a historic low for a Republican candidate, lower even than the few young people who had supported Nixon.

The polls indicated that Hillary had a lead among white voters who were college educated (a group that had supported Romney in the previous election). But Trump held a solid lead among white voters who had not gone to college, and he had strong support from white evangelicals.

Pollsters often asked people about the issue of restrictions on guns. Although the majority of Americans polled said they would favor more restrictions on gun ownership, those who said they were against gun restrictions strongly favored Trump.

The news media seemed mostly interested in the national polls. They seemed to have forgotten the past elections in which a candidate won the vote, but lost in the Electoral College. Nevertheless, as Hillary moved farther and farther into the polling lead, it seemed as if she was destined to be the next president. **Trump disputed the polls. He said the huge crowds he was drawing proved the polls were wrong.**

Despite her lead in the polls, on the campaign trail, Hillary continued to campaign in the same way had all along. She mostly focused on her experience. Whenever she did mention Trump, it was only to say that his words and his behavior proved he was **"not fit to be president of the United States."**

STORY

Every four years, as the presidential campaign season is winding down, many are waiting for an "**October surprise**," **some last minute bit of information that has the potential to change the outcome of the election**. Only eleven days before the election, an announcement from the director of the FBI, James Comey, looked like it might be that October surprise.

Comey went on TV to announce that he had sent a letter to key members of Congress saying **new e-mails had been found** that might have relevance to the prior investigation of Hillary's use of a private e-mail server. Because Comey didn't say what was in those e-mails or why he was notifying Congress about it, many said it must mean there was something explosive in them. Otherwise, why would he publicly announce it, and why was he notifying Congress about it?

Trump, of course, made it out to be a *very* big deal, saying **the new emails would prove what he had been saying** all along, that Hillary was "totally corrupt," so corrupt that she "**should never have been allowed to run for president**." He immediately put out a new TV ad saying **Hillary's e-mail had been found on the laptop of "a pervert."** The ad said Hillary was under FBI investigation, and that "**Decades of lies, cover-ups, and scandal had finally caught up with her**."

For over a week, Trump talked about little else, saying that with the "reopening" of the e-mail "scandal," we were "finally going to learn the truth about Hillary's "crooked" email usage. He was clearly excited by the news. He made a sudden and dramatic change of course—instead of constantly castigating the FBI as corrupt, as he had been doing for months, he started saying the FBI was doing a good thing in "going after" Hillary. At his rallies, his **very mention of the FBI brought excited cheers from the boisterous audience**, and many went back to the anti-Hillary chants of "Lock her up," or "Hang the Bitch."

Trump responded to their excitement, saying, "**Clinton's corruption is on a scale we have never seen before ... We must not let her take her criminal scheme into the Oval Office.**"

When the news media grabbed onto the issue, Hillary was upset that Comey had made that kind of vague announcement so close to the election. It soon came out that the head of the Justice Department (Comey's boss) had been against him doing it, but Comey went ahead and did it anyhow. Some said Comey's suggestion that the new FBI investigation of Hillary's email was a violation of the Hatch Act, a law that forbids employees in the executive branch of the federal government from engaging in political activity.

Democrats criticized the timing of the Comey's announcement, pointing out that the FBI had also been investigating connections between the Trump campaign and Russian hacking, but they had not released any information about *that* investigation because they knew it could influence the election.

The renewed "investigation" about Hillary's emails didn't turn up anything, but the damage had been done, and Hillary started to drop in the polls.

The 2016 Popular Election Versus the Electoral College

Election night was a nail biter. At first Hillary and then Trump seemed to be in the lead. It soon became obvious the election was going to be a lot closer than anybody thought. Still, most of the analysts continued to believe Hillary would win because **Trump would have to win *all* the swing states** in order to win in the Electoral College, and he was losing in the key swing states of Virginia, Colorado, and Nevada. Even when it looked like Trump was going to squeak out wins in Florida, North Carolina, and Ohio, **most assumed Hillary would win all the states that traditionally voted Democratic**. But **the analysts hadn't count on Trump's appeal in the so-called "rust belt" states of Pennsylvania, Michigan, and Wisconsin**. Trump won all three of those states, but by the tiniest of margins. While Hillary was racking up large numbers of votes in the big cities, Trump was managing to win the rural counties. Even though **Hillary ended up easily winning the popular vote by almost three million votes, just as the polls had predicted,** the final vote tallies in those three historically Democratic states gave Trump enough votes to win in the Electoral College, making it **the fifth time in U.S. History that the winner of the general election did not get to be president.**

> **COMMENT**
>
> After the election of 2016 was over, there was **a lot of analysis** of what had caused such a monumental upset in the Electoral College. Some blamed the low turnout of African-Americans as compared to the two previous elections when Obama was on the ballot. Others blamed the low turnout of young voters. Many of them said they were "turned off" by the tenor of the attack-oriented campaign.
>
> **Hillary won the non-white women's vote, but not the vote of white women.** Many of them said they just didn't want a woman to be their leader. **Hillary won among white college-educated voters, but not the votes of the white voters who had not been to college.**
>
> After Trump's many negative comments about Mexicans and illegal immigrants, many had expected a huge turnout of Hispanic voters who would vote for Hillary. Although there was an increase in their numbers, and she did win their vote, there was not enough of them to make a difference.

There was a lot of analysis about **campaign strategy**. Most analysts had seen **Hillary's two-pronged approach** of staying upbeat and talking about togetherness, mixed in with comments about Trump's character, often using his own words against him, as a winning strategy. **Trump's campaign strategy** on the other hand, was harder to define. **He mostly ran an attack-oriented** campaign, and he liked to shoot from the hip and make seemingly outrageous off-the-cuff statements and Twitter tweets that often got him into trouble. **A great deal of his campaign was based on trying to associate his opponent with negative concepts like "crooked" and "corrupt."** Without any supporting evidence, he often called Hillary "a liar" or "a world-class liar." **He called her "the most corrupt candidate in history."** Most of the political analysts, including those in the news media, got so used to hearing outlandish statements from Trump they stopped paying much attention. But **in a few keys states, some people were listening, and apparently, believing**. From the start, Trump seemed to have adopted an entertainer's **all-news-is-good-news** approach, and his extreme statements and outrageous Twitter tweets did manage to keep him in the news. Despite all the focus on Trump's seemingly off-kilter statements, what undoubtedly got him a lot of votes was **his description of himself as "an outsider"** who was going to go to Washington to "fix things" ("drain the swamp"). **Even though the national polls were right and Hillary did win overwhelmingly, that voting doesn't count; the only thing that does count is the vote in the Electoral College**, and as we have seen, the votes gained in a few key states can be enough to make the vote in the Electoral College disagree with the popular vote. **Even though Trump lost the election by almost three million votes, enough people voted for him in a few of the swing states to secure his election in the Electoral College**. Many said the **voters in the swing states were not ready to vote for a woman**, and **they didn't care that Trump had lost every debate**. And they didn't seem to be bothered by the fact that so many top Republicans had come out against him, and that the still-living past Republican presidents refused to back him. Most significantly, the voters were willing to overlook the many accusations of Trump accosting women, and even his bragging about grabbing women by the genitals. Voters interviewed later said they **they just wanted a change from the usual politicians.** Apparently they thought electing a TV celebrity would accomplish that. As we shall see in the next chapter, if that was what they wanted, they got it.

Chapter Seventeen
Impeachment, Racial Strife, and Pandemic

The Presidential Election of 2020

The surprise election of a TV celebrity as president in 2016 not by the people but by the Electoral College took many by surprise. The fact that he lost the popular election by almost three million votes meant there would be an unrelenting effort by the Democrats to make Trump a one-tern president.

As soon as he was elected, there were **nationwide protests against the new president**, some of them attracting over half a million people. **There hadn't been such huge demonstrations in the United States since the Vietnam War**, but Trump downplayed both their size and their importance.

After he took office in January of 2017, many wondered if finding himself in the position of being the President of the United States would temper Trump enough to stop his outrageous statements and begin to act more "presidential." They didn't have to wait long to find out: **Trump continued to let his erratic feelings be known, often using his Twitter internet account to post late-night "tweets."** Some U.S. Citizens liked having the President of the United States constantly broadcasting his personal thoughts, because **they revealed who the man really was**. The late-night tweets were very unlike the usual presidential statements that are carefully prepared by presidential staff. On the other hand, **his supporters disliked his late-night tweets**, and they were always trying to get him to stop. But it was to no avail: Trump continued to issue the tweets whenever he felt like it. Soon, he even began to deliver official government policy by tweet, including his frequent firing of government employees that he imagined were being "disloyal" to him. He watched TV constantly, and many of his tweets were **attacks on the American news media. He called them "the corrupt media," "the lying media," and "the lamestream media" He said they were "the enemy of the people."** He specifically called out the Washington Post, the New York Times, NBC, ABC, CBS, and CNN. He said they were purveyors of "fake news." Even Republicans were startled by the ferocity of this attacks on the news media, some of them suggesting that **such behavior was like "banana republic dictators" who try to suppress the free press**.

Despite their constant criticism of him, it was clear the news media was fixated on Trump. They often brought light to bear on what they called **Trump's Tsunami of lies**. It was suggested that **by his third year in office he had already made more than 20,000 false or misleading public statement**s. Many of his statements could easily be verified as lies, but Trump didn't seem to care; he apparently felt his "base" would accept anything he said. Apparently there was some truth to that because despite the reports that **the White House was constantly in chaos**, the polls indicated that support from Trump's "base" never wavered. Even as Trump appointed new advisers and then abruptly fired them, and cabinet members were appointed and then let go (often by late-night tweet), the polls showed he still had a low, but steady, approval rating of around 40%. Apparently, Trump had unleashed in that part of the electorate a willingness to tolerate seemingly unhinged presidential behavior. For example, even when women came forward to accuse Trump of molesting them, or even raping them, the polls indicated he still had the support of evangelical Christians, a subgroup that had helped secure his 2016 Electoral College win in 2016. White-supremacists, a group that rarely got interested in national politics, also strongly supported Trump. The White House taxpayer-paid press spokespersons tried their best to explain away Trump's often off-kilter actions, but Trump kept on replacing them until he found one who would act simply as his personal PR agent. That was a shock to seasoned White House reporters who, having reported on prior presidents, were used to a

White House press spokesperson who would give them accurate daily information about presidential policies.

Not long after he was elected, **Trump began to make strange statements**. For example, with no evidence, **he said Obama had "bugged" his phones.** He called Obama "a bad sick guy."

Even though he made many extended trips out of the White House, for some unexplained reason, one day Trump announced, **"I haven't actually left the White House in months."** And he often bragged about supposed accomplishments. He said, **"I won every debate. I won everything I did, and I won easily. I ran a campaign that now they say was better than Andrew Jackson's campaign."** And he often seemed to think the Democrats were "out to get him." After reporters questioned his steadiness going down a ramp, he said, **"I have to tell you, that runway is like an ice-skating rink. And the first step, I said, you know this sucker is slippery. I think it was put in by the Democrats."** When he was criticized by the press, he often blamed the Democrats, calling them criminals: **"The crime was by the Democrats, folks. They've committed many crimes."** He tried to get the U.S. Justice department to investigate supposed crimes against his 2016 campaign by the Democrats: **"They were spying on our campaign.** I'll tell you what, if that ever happened to the other side this thing would have been over two years ago, and you know it would have been treason. **They would have called it treason, and that's what it is."**

Trump seemed to have a fondness for odd **conspiracy theories.** He suggested that Hillary and Bill Clinton **might have arranged the death of his multi-millionaire friend Jeffrey Epstein**, a convicted sex offender. He copied **a Twitter post that proposed an unfounded conspiracy theory that Obama's military operation that killed Osama bin Laden had been faked.** As a result, **some of his supporters began posted astounding conspiracies such as one that said prominent Democrats were being controlled by the devil and were engaging in evil acts.**

In response to Trump behavior that was seeming more and more unhinged, a group of 70 psychologists, psychiatrists, and

mental health professionals sent a letter to the White House physician, imploring him to evaluate Trump's neurological health. Their request was ignored.

Meanwhile, there were reports of the Trump family making lots of money off of the Trump presidency, especially off of Trump properties. For example, **the very expensive Trump Hotel, only a few blocks from the White House, was said to be *the* place for those wanting to get close to the Trump circle of influence**. After one of his very expensive Florida golf courses became his official weekend golfing hideaway, there was a sudden surge in membership applications, so they immediately doubled the club's already high membership fee.

Trump installed members of his family into important government positions. This clearly conflicted with his pre-election pledge to offload his business interests to them, and it often appeared as if Trump and his family members were making decisions specifically to enhance those businesses. Even new tax cuts he implemented, that obviously favored the rich and the large corporations, also favored the Trump businesses.

There were also numerous accusations that members of his family and other White House staff member were in violation of the Hatch Act, the law that forbids executive branch employees from engaging in partisan political activities. Trump ignored those accusations, and his still-undisclosed tax filings became an even bigger issue. Although a number of civil and criminal cases were filed against him demanding to see those taxes, Trump's large contingent of lawyers managed to keep them a secret for most of his presidency. **Only in his last year in office did a New York Times report come out saying they had learned that Trump had only paid $750 in taxes in the preceding two years.** It reported that in many years, **he had paid no taxes at all**. Trump denied it, but the Democrats immediately began comparing the $750 Trump had reportedly paid in taxes to how much more teachers and ordinary workers paid in taxes.

Despite all that, the polls reported that Trump was still holding onto his 35 to 40% "base" of supporters. That base held solid even when a woman was murdered at a rally of his supporters in Charlottesville, Virginia. The rally had included neo-Nazis and white supremacists. Trump refused to condemn the violence, saying there were "**good people on both sides.**"

Meanwhile, **U.S. government intelligence agencies were reporting that they had conclusive evidence that Russia had interfered in the presidential election, specifically to try to get Trump elected president**. Trump said he didn't believe it, and told the press that the Russian leader, Vladimir Putin, had assured him that Russia hadn't done any such thing. Trump suggested that he believed Putin over his own intelligence agencies, and he fired **James Comey**, the head of the FBI, specifically, he said, to stop any FBI investigation of Russian interference in the election.

Nevertheless, **a special prosecutor was appointed** to investigate the matter more fully. **Robert Mueller**, a highly-respected investigator who had served as FBI director under George Bush, was appointed to head it. **Trump refused to cooperate**, and either refused to answer questions from the Mueller investigation team, or said he didn't remember. Also, Republicans in Congress blocked anything that might help the investigation. When Mueller began to look into **possible links between Trump's associates and the Russians, Trump wanted Mueller fired**. However, by then, Jeff Sessions, Trump's hand-picked Attorney General, had been forced to recuse himself because he had been a member of Trump's election team. The recusal angered Trump, and he fired Sessions for doing it. (Trump never forgave Sessions for his recusal. In fact, he actively worked against Sessions from then on, helping to get him defeated in his bid to return to the Senate.)

After the Sessions recusal, oversight of the Russia investigation fell to Deputy Attorney General **Rod Rosenstein**, and **he was not willing to fire Mueller**. Trump therefore went looking for a new Attorney General who would be more willing to protect him. He soon found his man, **William Barr**, an attorney who had served as Attorney General during the George H.W. Bush administration.

Mueller and the multiple legal teams that worked under him found **significant Russian involvement in the U.S. election**, much of it intended to help Trump get elected. They also found links between several Trump associates and Russian officials. In the end, **Mueller indicted 34 people, seven U.S. nationals, 26 Russian nationals, and one Dutch national. Charges were filed against five members of the Trump campaign team.** However, before Mueller's report could be released to Congress and the public, Trump's new, much more loyal, Attorney General, Bill **Barr, tried to "spin" what the report was going to say.** Barr's version basically **suggested that the investigation had exonerated Trump**. But Mueller soon came forward to say Barr's "spin" version did not match what the actual report said. He said Justice Department policy prevented him from charging the Trump with a crime. However, he said, "**While this report does not conclude that the President committed a crime, it also does not exonerate him.**" Trump and his supporters preferred Barr's version.

From then on, **despite several members of Trump's team eventually being found guilty of various crimes, the Republicans continued to act as if Mueller's Russia investigation had found nothing of consequence**. And when the Democrats tried to introduce a bill in Congress to protect future elections from foreign influence, the Republicans quickly killed it.

COMMENT

Throughout Trump's presidency, books were being published about him. Of course, there were the usual books that were supportive of Trump the president, but the public mostly wanted to read "inside stories" about him. Many of the books that provided that type of information became instant bestsellers.

Many of the books about the inner workings of Trump's White House were very critical of Trump. Trump and his loyal Attorney General William Barr tried to stop their publication, but in each case, they failed. Whenever Trump got rid of one of his government employees, there was the danger that they might reveal **the chaos that was going on inside the Trump** administration. One of the most consequential books was **written by Trump's former national security adviser, John Bolton.** His book, *The Room Where it Happened* got a lot of attention because when Bolton had joined Trump's team, he was a strong supporter of both Trump and the Republican agenda. However, in the book, Bolton said he had come to believe Trump was **incompetent and not fit for office**. He wrote that **Trump probably should have been impeached and removed from office**. He said Trump practiced obstruction of justice as his normal way of doing business. He also confirmed what other had been saying, that Trump's top staff often mocked him behind his back. Bolton wrote that Trump made most of his decisions based on how they would reflect on himself, and that he seemed to have **a particular affinity for dictators**. He said Trump often talked about serving more than two terms, hoping to find a way to repeal the two-term constitutional limit.

One of the most dramatic books to come out while Trump was still in office was *Disloyal* by Michael Cohen, Trump's self-described "fixer" lawyer. Cohen had already become well-known when it was revealed that he was the lawyer who had been **the go-between arranging payoffs to buy the silences of adult film star Stormy Daniels and Playboy model Karen McDougal**. Both of them had claimed to have had **sexual affairs with Trump even though he was married**. Cohen called Trump **a fraud, a bully, a racist, a predator, and a con man**.

Trump's niece, **Mary Trump**, a PhD psychologist, wrote a book about him titled *Too Much and Never Enough: How My Family Created the World's Most Dangerous Man*. In the book, she claimed **Trump had been psychologically damaged by an abusive father, and had therefore become driven to always succeed**, even if it meant cheating. **She said he had even hired someone to take his college entrance exams**.

There were many other notable books written about Trump.

True Crimes and Misdemeanors: The Investigation of Donald Trump, written by CNN legal analyst Jeffrey Toobin, is a condensation of evidence against Trump, presented in much like a prosecutor would present evidence to a jury.

Donald Trump v. The United States: Inside the Struggle to Stop a President, written by Pulitzer-prize winning New York Times reporter Michael Schmidt, is an analysis of attempts to curb Trump. He writes that Trump views the rule of law as something for others, and he believes his political adversaries deserve to go to prison. He reminds readers that Trump got his son-in-law Jared Kushner a top secret security clearance despite objections from the intelligence community.

A Very Stable Genius: Donald J. Trump's Testing of America by Philip Rucker and Carol Leonnig, uses as its title Trump's infamous quote **proclaiming himself to be "a very stable genius."** Those two Pulitzer-winning Washington Post reporters described internal battles in the White House where Trump was running the government like a family business wherein everything is personal to him.

Bob Woodward, author of books about nine different presidents, also wrote one about Trump. Of all the writers, Woodward had the most access to Trump. After interviewing Trump 17 times, he dryly summarized Trump by saying he was "the wrong man for the job. In those interviews, Trump often revealed to Woodward how he honestly felt, and it was often quite different from what he was telling the citizens of the country.

For example, even as Trump was publicly playing down the urgency of the emerging coronavirus, describing it as nothing to worry about because it would soon go away, **he was telling Woodward the virus was easily transmittable and deadly**. Later, when asked about his statements to Woodward, Trump said he was only trying to avoid creating a panic.

Meanwhile, Trump was taking action with regard to foreign relations. **He denounced many long-term relationships the U.S. had with allies.** He said such agreements did not favor the United States. He launched into a aggressive trade war with China that most experts eventually concluded had accomplished little. Nevertheless, **Trump bragged about it often, saying trade wars are "easy to win."** He claimed that the trade war had brought the U.S. a lot of money, when it was actually costing U.S. consumers a lot of money. When China retaliated by refusing to buy products from U.S. farmers, Trump tried to make up for it by giving farmers money from the U.S. Treasury.

Trump withdrew from the Paris Agreement, an agreement related to the United Nations Framework Convention on Climate Change. **He also refused to sign the Trans-Pacific Partnership,** a trade agreement with Australia, Brunei, Canada, Chile, Japan, Malaysia, Mexico, New Zealand, Peru, Singapore, and Vietnam.

On the home front, **Trump was reversing many of the policies put in place by Obama and prior administrations.** He allowed **oil drilling** in areas that formerly been protected. He **cut back many of the regulations** on big business that had been passed after the Great Recession of 2008, and he worked with the Republican-controlled Congress to pass **new tax rules that favored the rich and the largest corporations.** His federal budget cut assistance programs for seniors and low-income families, and he reduced the food stamp assistance program. He **got rid of many of the Community Services Block Grants** that were designed to alleviate the causes and conditions of poverty in poor communities. He also got rid of Obama's transportation-enhancement program and Obama's programs that helped rural areas obtain reliable drinking water and sewage disposal systems. He **cut many Environmental Protection Agency programs.** He cut the Housing and Urban Development Department budget, including grants to state and local governments for infrastructure, housing, and other public services. He eliminated many of the Obama programs that were designed to enhance the effectiveness of the nation's education systems, including **the Effective Instruction**

State Grants Program which provided funding to state and local education agencies. He eliminated Obama's **Global Climate Change Initiative**, and he worked with the Republican-controlled Congress to **try to get rid of the Affordable Care Act,** known as Obamacare. **Trump promised to throw out the "terrible" Obamacare program** and replace it with something much better. However, despite the Republicans having control of both houses of Congress, all they did was eliminate parts of Obamacare, and **they never did come up with any replacement health care program**. Reporters kept on asking Trump about a healthcare program, but he just kept on saying **it would be ready "soon."** When asked who was working on it, he simply said "lots of people."

The one campaign promise he did carry out was to divert money from other programs to build at least some of "**his wall**" at the southern border. And he did manage to impose **much more restrictive immigration policies**, especially from Muslim countries, and he **withdrew from the Iran nuclear arms agreement**. Even though the other countries that had participated in the Iran agreement stood by it. With the U.S. out, Iran soon announced they they were renewing their nuclear program.

As that was going on, **North Korea was rapidly developing their nuclear capability**. They had been trying to develop it since the 1980s, and in 2006 they had successfully conducted an underground test of a small nuclear bomb. Now they claimed to have much bigger nuclear bombs, and **Kim Jong-un, North Korea's young dictator, announced that they had developed a missile with the capability to reach the United States**. That prompted Trump to engage in a war of words with him, **calling him "little rocket man**," while bragging about how much bigger the United States nuclear bombs were. (Many in the Trump White House later admitted they were very frightened that **a nuclear war might result from Trump's actions**.)

But then **Trump switched gears and arranged a meeting with Kim Jong-un**. After the meeting, Trump said he had developed a good relationshp with the North Korean dictator. He told the press, "**I just received a beautiful letter from Kim Jong

Un. I can't show you the letter, obviously, but it was a very personal, very warm, very nice letter." He began to imply that he would be soon able to convince North Korea to dismantle their entire nuclear weapons program and their missle program. That never happened, and after other meetings between them made no progress, Kim Jong-un went back to his prior beligerant attitude toward the U.S. As a result of this foreign policy failure, Trump didn't like to talk about it.

Even as he was engaging in personal diplomacy with Russia and North Korea, Trump was increasing the national defense budget. **He proposed a $54 billion increase in defense spending.** Much of the increase was needed, he said, to fight what he called a **war against the Islamic State**.

At the same time, Trump was often criticizing the top military commanders at the Pentagon. He felt they weren't supportive enough of his foreign-policy wishes. And behind the scenes, he was reportedly mocking American soldiers that had been killed in action, **calling them "losers" and "suckers."** It reminded many of his criticism of Senator and prior Republican presidential candidate John McCain simply because he had been captured during the Vietnam War.

Later, after Trump had made many speeches attacking what he called "Islam terrorism," he oversaw a military operation that resulted in the **death of Abu Bakr al-Baghdadi,** a self-proclaimed Islamic terrorist leader. Also, without any input from the State Department, Trump ordered military operations into Yemen. None of these military actions drew much attention from the public until he ordered a drone strike into Iraq to assassinate **Qasem Soleimani**, an Iranian major general. Soleimani and the nine people who happened to be in the car with him were killed.

Iran immediately protested, and many in the international community questioned the legal authority of an assassination of a foreign military commander, along with nine apparently innocent people. Trump said the attack was warranted because Soleimani was "planning" attacks on American soldiers. He didn't mention the nine innocent people who had also been killed.

Soon thereafter, in revenge for the Soleimani assassination, Iran launched ballistic missiles at an airbase in Iraq where American personnel were located. A number of U.S. personnel were seriously injured in the attack, but Trump played it down, saying some soldiers had "headaches and a couple of other things."

STORY

Throughout Trump's tenure, there were a number of scandals, but perhaps the most damning was the scandal referred to as **"kids in cages."** As part of Trump's continuing plan to drastically limit the number of immigrants coming into the United States from south of the border, it was decided to punish immigrant parents by taking their kids away from them. It was part of a **"zero tolerance" policy** that involved prosecuting every person caught crossing the border illegally. Designed as a way to deter illegal immigration, they began taking children of all ages away from their parents. Later, someone smuggled out a photo of a large number of unaccompanied children locked in metal cages. When the children said they were given little to eat and had not had a clean change of clothing or a bath for weeks, it suddenly became front-page news. Further investigation by civil rights groups revealed that more than a thousand children had been taken away from their parents, and that some of the children had been sent away from the area of the border. Their current location was unknown, and there was a fear that the government might be planning on putting them up for adoption elsewhere in the U.S. **At first, Trump said there was nothing he could do about it, but eventually the public pressure became so great he had to relent. He ended the program by executive order.** However, for the entire remainder of Trump's tenure in office, there were news stories published saying more children were still being taken away from their immigrant parents, and often those parents were summarily deported, forcing them to leave their children behind.

During the 2016 presidential campaign, Trump had made it clear he would pursue an "America first" policy. He was true to his word; he cast doubt on renewing America's long-term strategic alliances and he modified the country's economic relationships with foreign countries using tariff-wars against them.

Also, he worked hard to limit immigration of all kinds. At his rallies, he often described immigrants as rapists and killers. Such tactics met with the approval of extremist groups like the neo-Nazis and the white supremacists who began having rallies of their own, often showing banners supporting Trump.

All this resulted in **the country becoming more polarized than it had been since the Vietnam War**. After several incidents in which black people were shot by police, anti-police demonstrations, some of them violent, started up across the nation. Trump responded by making speeches disparaging the demonstrators. He called them "thugs," or "sick and deranged anarchists." Like Nixon, he began calling himself the "law-and-order" candidate. Also like Nixon, he often raged against "enemies" that he believed were against him. He encouraged his loyal Attorney General William Barr to go after the criminals" of the hidden "deep state," government employees that he imagined were against him. However, despite Trump claiming to be the law-and-order candidate. even after several mass murders by men using high-powered semi-automatic weapons, **he and the Republicans in Congress steadfastly refused to support any anti-gun legislation.** Some of the mass murderers claimed to have been inspired by Trump.

In the fall of 2019, it was learned that **an official whistleblower complaint had been filed accusing Trump of using the power of his office to try to coerce a foreign leader into helping him in his upcoming reelection campaign.**

STORY

The potential for a presidential **impeachment of Trump** began when a whistleblower reported that there was much talk in government circles about a supposed phone call that Trump had made to the newly-elected President of Ukraine, Volodymyr Zelensky. At the time, Ukraine was under attack from Russia, and the U.S. Congress had voted to give them military aid. **In the phone call, Trump had supposedly said he would withhold that military aid unless Ukraine helped him get reelected. It was said he had asked Zelensky to find "dirt" on Joe Biden's son Hunter** who had previously done legal work in Ukraine. At first, not much could be found out about the phone call because **the record of the call had been hidden on one of the government's most secure servers, a server normally reserved only for top secrets**. However, investigators eventually learned that **the phone call actually had been made, and that it did contain a political request from Trump tied to the threat of withholding military aid.**

A number of Democrats in the house began to suggest that the only way to stop such illegal presidential behavior was to begin the impeachment process as spelled out in the U.S. Constitution. For some time, the House leaders resisted those demands, but eventually six House committees begin formal impeachment inquiries. **Trump refused to cooperate**, and he threatened any government employ who would dare to cooperate with the Congressional investigation in any way. The committee hearings were televised, so it soon became of interest to the public to see which government employees would defy Trump and respond to the Congressional subpoenas. Some did, and their testimony supported the whistleblower's allegation. Through their testimonies, it was also learned that Trump's personal attorney, Rudy Giuliani, and others had been involved in pressuring Ukraine to help Trump get reelected, and that **Trump himself had suggested that Zelensky should work with Giuliani and Attorney General Barr to help them find something that could be used against Joe Biden, his expected opponent**. After it all came out, Trump said there was nothing wrong with his phone call to Zelensky. He did admit that he had talked to Zelensky about Biden, but he said there was nothing wrong with doing so. **He said it was an "absolutely perfect" phone call.**

A number of witnesses were called before the House Judiciary Committee and each member of the Committee was given the opportunity to ask questions. **A group of psychiatrists wanted to testify as to Trump capability to continue serving as president, but their request was turned down.**

The Democratic members of the committee mostly asked questions designed to get to the bottom of what Trump and his associates had done. The Republican members of the committee mostly complained about the process.

In the end, **the Judiciary Committee voted along party lines and passed two articles of impeachment, abuse of power, and obstruction of Congress. The Democrats had more votes, so Trump was impeached and the two article of impeachment went forward to the Senate.**

In **the Senate impeachment trial, Trump again refused to cooperate** in any way. However, some of the Senate Republicans did try to defend him. They did not deny the facts of the case; instead, **they said the House had not adequately made their case for impeachment.** When it came time to vote, it became clear that the required two-thirds majority was not going to happen in the Republican-controlled Senate. **The final vote was again along party lines except for the Republican senator from Utah, Mitt Romney,** who voted to convict Trump on one of the counts. That made him the first senator in history to vote for the impeachment of a president from his own party. In the end, 48 Senators voted guilty, and 52 Senators voted not guilty. Therefore, Trump was not removed from office. That prompted Trump to proclaim his innocence, calling the whole thing **a Democratic witch hunt, and he quickly began firing or demoting anybody he felt had not fully supported him.**

Most thought the fact that Trump had been impeached would hurt his chances for reelection, and the early polls did indicate that. However, in January of 2020, there was talk about something that could potentially be even more significant in the next election. It was a new coronavirus coming out of China that was reportedly more deadly than the seasonal flu virus that kills between 12,000 and 60,000 Americans every year. At that time, few knew what an impact it was going to have on the country and on the upcoming election.

STORY

The new coronavirus virus, which became known as COVID-19, was said to have come from Wuhan, Hubei, China. There was an attempt to close down that part of China, but some who were infected left China and the new virus soon spread throughout the world. In the United State, by the end of March, cases had been been confirmed in all fifty states. In many states, it was suggested that people should stay indoors as much as possible, and if they did have to go out, they should wear a mask and maintain "social distance" from each other. Businesses deemed "non-essential" were forced to close down. By doing that, some states had limited success in controlling the spread of the virus. However, **there was no consistent set of guidelines coming from Washington. Trump himself refused to wear a mask and played down the danger of the virus.** As a result, the wearing or not wearing of a mask and taking precautions soon became a contentious issue. **Many followed Trump's lead and combatively refused to wear a mask, saying it was an attack on their personal liberty.**

To help people affected by the forced closing of businesses, **Congress authorized money to be sent to every citizen. Trump made sure his name and signature appeared on every check (the first time in history a president's name had ever appeared on an IRS check).**

Businesses got even more money, and unemployment benefits were temporarily increased. At the same time, the Fed began propping up the stock market.

However, **there was still no national mandate** regarding how to safely avoid the virus. It soon became clear that while other countries were establishing national policies to combat what was becoming an international pandemic, the U.S. was quickly becoming the prime example of how not to do it. While other countries were steadily reducing the number of COVID cases, in the United States, the problem was only getting worse.

Trump's response to the situation was bizarre. Instead of doing what the scientists were recommending and establishing a national mask-wearing mandate and providing every citizen with a high quality N-95 mask, he said there was little to worry about because there were very few cases in the United States. **He said the number of cases in the U.S. would soon drop to zero. He said, "We have it totally under control.** Looks like by April, you know, in theory, when it gets a little warmer, it miraculously goes away."

When the Democratic candidates began to criticize his lack of response to the outbreak, **he began saying the whole thing was a Democratic "hoax"** designed to hurt his chances of being reelected. He said the virus was only like the flu, nothing that we really need to worry much about. He added that it was "the Democrat policy of open borders that brought the virus into the United States in the first place." **He began calling it "the China virus," and he blamed China for allowing it to infect the whole world.** He also blamed Obama and the World Health Organization for not being prepared for it.

His dismissive attitude about the virus and the resulting growing death count made it a huge campaign issue. Most had believed Trump's impeachment would be the overriding issue of the 2020 presidential campaign, but suddenly, **his lack**

of response to what was becoming a worldwide pandemic became *the* issue.

Despite the fact that the polls were indicating that people were unhappy with his response to the crisis, Trump would not stop tossing out odd statements about it. **He said, "I like this stuff. I really get it. People are surprised that I understand it. Every one of these doctors said, 'How do you know so much about this?' Maybe I have a natural ability. Maybe I should have done that instead of running for president." He then suggested that drinking or injecting liquid disinfectants might help, and he started promoting an anti-malaria drug, hydroxychloroquine, as a "game-changer."** He said he was taking it as a virus preventative, and "many doctors" were also taking it. However, follow-up studies of the drug showed it was of little or no value in treating COVID-19. Worse, the research indicated that users of the drug were more likely to suffer heart problems that could lead to death.

Trump put together a "coronavirus team." It was mostly made up of scientists that were specialists in infectious diseases, but it was led by vice president Pence. Pence began holding daily press briefings in the White House to update the country on what was being done to combat the virus. The briefings were covered by most of the TV networks, and that led Trump to take over the daily televised briefings. The scientists were sidelined, and Trump did most of the talking. Actually, he didn't talk all that much about the virus, preferring instead to talk about himself and what a great job he was doing. The daily briefings began to look more like one of Trump's campaign rallies, so most of the TV networks stopped covering them. Trump loved the limelight, and he wanted to take advantage of a situation that was getting him daily free TV time just as he was getting ready for a reelection campaign. Unfortunately for him, the reporters that were in attendance at the briefings kept asking troublesome questions. He soon solved that by inviting "friendly" reporters and only calling on them. But even that didn't work; his ratings continued to drop. Trump seemed to think the main reason his popularity was dropping was because of what the virus had done to the economy, so he began to demand that the country should "open up." He said Republican governors should "liberate" their citizens and allow businesses to reopen. Many of them did that, but that only caused new cases of the virus. In Michigan, after Governor Gretchen Whitmer ordered certain businesses to stay closed, a group of heavily-armed militants took Trump's words seriously and came up with a plan to abduct her and "put her on trial." Luckily, the FBI found out about it and arrested them before they could put their plan into action. Trump wasn't willing to denounce them, and at his next Michigan rally, he lashed out at her, triggering the crowd to start doing the old "lock her up" chant.

In response to disturbing news about a surge in new coronavirus cases and the resulting deaths, government epidemiology experts suggested that certain types of "super-spreader" businesses should stay closed until a vaccine could be developed. Trump sidelined those experts. He preferred the advice of non-experts who were proposing "herd immunity," the discredited concept that if you allow enough people to get the virus (and perhaps die), the society would gradually gain immunity to the virus. Because many schools had been closed, and much of the learning was taking place "virtually" online, Trump demanded that they reopen. Some states that were led by Republicans tried that, but unfortunately, that immediately caused a spike in COVID cases among young people.

It soon became apparent that while most of the world's other countries were starting to get a handle on dealing with the virus, the situation in the United States was continuing to get worse. Despite having only 4% of the world's population, the United States had 25% of the world's COVID cases. And instead of improving, the number of new cases kept rising. In some other countries, the number of new virus cases had been rapidly dropping, so they were able to go back to life more or less as normal. In the United States, the virus hadn't magically gone away as Trump had promised, and with his reelection campaign coming up, the Democrats didn't let him forget it.

Even after Trump himself contracted the virus, along with many others he had been in contact with in the White House, he continued to insist that the virus was no big deal. Even though more than 220,000 U.S. citizens had by then died from the virus, he said it was nothing the U.S. needed to be overly concerned about. Although he had been rushed to the Walter Reed National Military Medical Center, one of the best hospitals in the world, **he claimed the virus had not made him very sick**. The White House doctor refused to release any information about how ill Trump had been, and people at the hospital were asked to sign non-disclosure documents. Nevertheless, it was known that while in the hospital he had been treated with a variety of drugs usually only given to the most serious coronavirus cases. Some of the drugs he was given were experimental and not available to ordinary citizens.

Once he had recovered enough to go back on the campaign trail, **he inexplicably described his infection by the virus as "a blessing from God."** He went right back to saying the virus was no big deal, and that encouraged his supporters to stop wearing masks. The number of new COVID-19 cases soon skyrocketed, setting new all-time daily records. Trump told the people not to worry about all those new cases and resulting deaths because **a vaccine against the virus would soon be available, probably before the election**. Like so many of his promises regarding the coronavirus crisis, that didn't happen. Nevertheless, on the rally circuit, Trump continued to say the states run by Democrats "were bad" and should be "liberated."

The 2020 Presidential Campaign

Democratic debates were scheduled for the summer of 2019. Twenty-nine well-known Democratic candidates were were eager to take on Trump. Although each of them had a specific vision of what they could do for the country as president, the one thing they all had in common was a sense of urgency to get Trump out of office before, they said, "he could do any more damage to the country." They all spoke about Trump's bigotry, his constant lying, his alienation of foreign allies, and his fawning relationships with foreign dictators. But mostly they talked about his "failed response" to formulate a policy to deal with the cornavirus crisis.

It was decided that with so many candidates, **polling numbers and campaign donations would determine which candidates would be invited to the Democratic debates**.

At the debates, because **Joe Biden**, the former vice president under Obama had been leading in the polls, some of the other Democratic candidates chose to use their debate time to attack him. However, as the debates were being conducted, primary elections were already taking place, and the voting soon began to indicate it was going to be a two-horse race between former vice president Joe Biden and Senator Bernie Sanders. Sanders had made a good run against Hillary Clinton in the 2016 election, and in some polls he was doing well.

But when the coronavirus epidemic hit the country hard, Biden began to focus on Trump's failed response to it, and the remaining Democratic debates were canceled.

The 2020 Primaries

Although it was assumed that Trump would be the presumptive nominee on **the Republican ticket**, a few other Republicans did come forward to challenge him. **Bill Weld**, the former governor of Massachusetts, announced his intention to run against Trump, as did **Mark Sanford**, the former governor of South Carolina. However, their campaigns never gained much momentum, and by March, Trump had secured enough pledged delegates to be the presumptive Republican presidential nominee.

The first few **Democratic primaries** showed unexpected results. The first primary, in Iowa, was actually a series of local "caucuses." Sanders won the most delegates. However, South Bend, Indiana Mayor Pete Buttigieg, a former navy officer who had served in the Afghanistan war also did well. To many that result was **a surprise because Buttigieg was an openly gay candidate. Another surprise was that Biden had not done as well as expected**. That unexpected result seemed to be confirmed when those same two candidates again got the most votes in the second primary, in New Hampshire.

Because Biden had not done well in the first two primaries, many in the media counted him out. However, **old hands in politics were pointing to the fact that neither Iowa nor New Hampshire were at all representative of the Democratic electorate**. They said Biden would come back in the more representative states. Sure enough, **Biden won the South Carolina primary, claiming nearly fifty per cent of popular vote**. And then he won again in the multiple primaries of "Super Tuesday." It meant that **despite his late start, Biden had ended up with just about as many delegates as Sanders**.

With Biden and Sanders pulling into the lead, most of the other Democratic candidates began to drop out of the race. And as Biden won more primaries, most of them began endorsing him. By the time the Democratic primaries were winding down, it was becoming clear that Biden would win the most delegates. At first, Sanders refused to drop out of the race, but as Biden racked up more and more wins, Sanders dropped out and endorsed Biden.

COMMENT

It seems likely that the voters liked Biden because he was a "normal candidate," a known commodity, in contrast to the very unnormal president he was running against.

Biden was raised in small-towns in Pennsylvania and Delaware. He was the oldest child in a financially-strapped Catholic family. In high school, he was a standout on the school's football team. Although not a standout student academically, after overcoming a childhood stutter, he became very popular and was elected class president in his junior and senior years.

He studied at the University of Delaware, and then went on to earn a law degree from Syracuse University. He did not serve in the military, receiving student draft deferments and a medical deferment due to his asthma.

He clerked at a law firm headed by a prominent Republican, but he registered as an independent because he didn't like Richard Nixon. In 1972, after serving on the Wilmington county council, he was elected to the Senate as a Democrat, defeating the Republican incumbent to become one of the youngest senators ever. Unfortunately, before being sworn in as Delaware's new senator, his wife and their one-year-old daughter were killed in a car accident. His two sons were also seriously injured in the accident. He strongly considered resigning from the Senate, but was talked out of it. He continued to struggle with the two deaths, but continued to serve in the Senate. Eventually, he married Jill Stevenson, a school teacher. Biden now credits Jill with a renewal of his interest in politics and life. Biden was reelected to the Senate six times until 2008 when he resigned to be President Obama's vice president. He considered running for president in 1987, and he was one of the leading candidates, but he was accused of using the speeches of prior politicians without attributions. It led to so much negative press, he dropped out of the race. In 2016, he was again said to have a good chance to win the nomination, but he declined to run because his son Beau had recently died of brain cancer.

Again in 2019, many were pressuring him to run again, and he finally agreed, citing a "sense of duty" to oppose Trump.

The National Nominating Conventions

By summer, despite the ongoing pandemic, the two major parties needed to hold their national nominating conventions for the 2020 presidential election.

By the time the **Democratic National Nominating Convention** started, Biden had secured enough delegate votes to be the presumptive nominee. He chose Kamala Harris, a Senator from California who was of African and Indian descent, to be his vice presidential running mate. The convention was a four day event, mostly done "virtually." The speakers, for the most part, appeared remotely, many of them using video that was being broadcast from their own homes. Biden and his running mate made their televised speeches from a convention center in Wilmington, Delaware in front of very small audiences. Joe Biden's wife, Dr. Jill Biden spoke remotely from the classroom she used to teach in.

No delegates were in attendance at the convention. Instead, the delegates appeared via remote video broadcast from their home states. That gave the delegates the opportunity to not only report the number of votes each candidate had received in their state primaries, but also to promote the virtues of their states to the huge TV audience (more that 24 million viewers tuned in).

The Democratic Convention was clearly meant to be a multicultural event, with speakers and entertainers designed to show inclusion, that the Democratic Party was the party of everyone.

The selection of **speakers included former president Bill Clinton and his wife, Hillary, the prior presidential candidate. Former president Obama and his wife Michelle both gave powerful speeches** (in fact, it was rumored that Biden had considered Michelle as his vice president nominee). Bernie Sanders, House Speaker Nancy Pelosi and Senator Elizabeth Warren also spoke. **Several notable Republicans also spoke** at the Democratic convention, including former Ohio Governor John Kasich. They said they were not renouncing their membership in the Republican Party, but were renouncing Trump.

Some of the speakers advocated gun control, and many speakers decried Trump's failure to directly address the worldwide pandemic that other countries were starting to get under control. There was one woman speaker who said her husband had died from the COVID-19 virus simply because he had trusted Trump's advice not to worry about getting the virus.

The **Republican National Nominating Convention was dramatically different.** Trump originally wanted to hold it in Charlotte, North Carolina. However, local safety regulations forbid such large gatherings because of the pandemic, so Trump angrily abandoned Charlotte and went looking for another venue. Florida Governor Ron DeSantis and Jacksonville Mayor Lenny Curry lobbied in favor of Florida, Trump's new home state, and eventually Trump announced that he was moving the convention to Jacksonville, Florida. However, there was limited hotel space in Jacksonville, so for a while, there was talk of bringing in cruise ships to use as hotel rooms. However local safety regulations there also ruled that site out. Finally, **Trump decided to hold the convention in Washington D.C. using government buildings, including the White House. The use of government property for a political reelection event had never been tried before, and many said it would be illegal**. But that didn't stop Trump. The plan to hold the Republican convention events in Washington, D.C. went forward.

The Republican nominating convention was clearly meant to be different from that of the Democrats. The convention began with pro-gun statements from a well-off couple who had been indicted for coming out of their house to point their guns at peaceful demonstrators who had been passing by on the street. Other speakers also spoke **against any kind of gun control**.

The convention events defied the safety concerns local governments were putting in place due to the ongoing pandemic. In fact, Trump's acceptance speech was an extravaganza with fireworks and opera held in front of a large **masks-optional, no-social-distancing crowd on the steps of the White House**. (Legal scholars are still debating whether it was illegal to hold a political reelection event on government property, especially one that used the White House as a venue and prop.)

The speakers at the Republican convention were the usual line-up of Republican politicians, with the addition of members of Trump's family. Most of the speakers used their time to warn against electing Joe Biden. Some of them tried to tie him to the ongoing Black Lives Matter street demonstrations. Oddly, some speakers, including Trump himself, warned voters who lived in the suburbs that if Biden was elected, those kinds of riots would soon come to their neighborhoods. They made the unfounded claim that Biden wanted to defund the police. Some even suggested that Biden was being controlled by a secret cabal of "cosmopolitan elites" who were trying to control everyone's thoughts and actions. Other such **conspiracy theories** were put forward, suggesting to some that the 2020 Republican National Convention ought to be called **the "conspiracy convention**.

One dramatic difference from the Democratic convention was that none of the living former presidents showed up to support Trump. In fact, not one of the former Republican presidential nominees showed up to support Trump, and one of them, **Mitt Romney, went so far as to state publicly that he would not be voting for Trump**. With reference to the ongoing COVID-19 pandemic, some speakers made the very strange suggestion that Trump had all but defeated the virus (actually, it was getting much worse). Others referred to Trump's desire to "open up" the country, saying the Democrats wanted to keep everyone locked up until they become totally dependent on the central government. They implied that Biden and the Democrats were socialists, and not like the successful socialists of the Scandinavian countries, but more like the Communists of "Red" China and Cuba.

COMMENT

Money has become a huge issue in modern political campaigns. A presidential candidate has three main needs for money: 1) to pay campaign staff, 2) to pay political advertising specialists and political advertising companies, and 3) to pay for the advertising itself. The latter has become the largest campaign expense, especially TV advertising. Social media advertising was also becoming important.

Although there is some public financing of elections, contributions from individual citizens has long been the main source of a candidate's campaign funding.

However, the Federal Election Commission and individual states set limits on how much an individual can give. Nevertheless, candidates and political parties have found many creative ways to get around the limits. One solution is to create a **political action committee (PAC)**, an organization that pools campaign contributions. Also, in 2010, the Supreme Court ruled, in a case that became known as the **Citizens United** case, that the free speech clause of the U.S. Constitution prohibits the government from restricting how much corporations can finance political campaigns.

In the 2020 presidential election, huge amounts of money poured into the coffers of both candidates. However, early on, it was becoming clear that Joe Biden was getting a lot more money in campaign contributions than a challenger usually gets. Trump's campaign funds soon began running low.

Remembering the deciding role the Electoral College had played in the prior presidential election, Biden spent a lot of his massive campaign war chest in the so-called "swing states." In fact, he spent most of his advertising money in just six states, Arizona, Florida, North Carolina, Michigan, Pennsylvania, and Wisconsin. Hillary Clinton had been accused of ignoring the so-called "Blue Wall" states of Michigan, Pennsylvania, and Wisconsin. It had resulted in Trump narrowly winning them. Biden was determined not to make that mistake, and he far outspent Trump in those states.

Despite the ongoing pandemic, and even after he had become infected with the coronavirus, **Trump's campaign strategy was the same as in 2016,** hold **large indoor and outdoor rallies with people crowded together**. And because Trump had repeatedly played down the need for masks, many who attended his rallies defied local ordinances by refusing to wear them.

Biden on the other hand held fewer rallies, and they were smaller. He always modeled the wearing of a mask and insisted that those who attended his events should do the same.

Of course, Trump made fun of him for that. He tried to portray Biden as being cowardly, afraid of getting sick. He even made fun of people in his rally audiences for wearing masks, saying they mus want to be "politically correct."

STORY

Late in September, **Ruth Bader Ginsburg, a revered member of the Supreme Court, died.** It was only 47 days before the election, so most thought there would not be enough time for Trump to get a replacement through the nominating and install process. Up until then, the average time it took to confirm a Supreme Court judge had been 70 days.

Besides, **in 2016, the Republican leadership of the Senate had refused to do their Constitutional duty of voting on the new Supreme Court judge that had been selected by President Obama.** Back then, they'd said it would not be appropriate to do so in an election year, even though there were many months before the election and many Supreme Court vacancies had been filled in prior election years. Many of them said it didn't matter if it was a Democratic president; if it was a Republican president, they would still refuse to put a nominee on the court in an election year.

Justice Ginsburg, knowing she was very ill, specified that if she died, she did not want her seat on the court to be filled until after the election. Nevertheless, very soon after

Ginsburg's death was announced, Trump and the Senate Republican leadership shocked everyone by announcing that they would immediately pick and install a replacement judge on the court, even if they had to break all the Senate rules to do it.

Biden and many others cried hypocrisy. They pointed out that in 2016, the Republicans had said they would never confirm a Supreme Court nominee in an election year, let alone do so at such a late date when people were already voting.

Nevertheless, Trump went ahead and nominated **Amy Coney Barrett**, an appeals court judge who had been recommended to him as being very conservative, one who was likely to vote to get rid of Obamacare, something Trump had been trying to do for years. She had formerly been a law clerk to **Antonin Scalia**, a conservative Supreme Court judge, and it was said she might very well vote to ban a woman's right to an abortion.

The Republican leadership in the Senate went to work trying to rush her nomination through, even though the pre-election polls were indicating that it was quite possible that by the time she took her seat on the court, Trump would no longer be the president and the Republicans who voted to confirm her would no longer be in charge of the Senate.

Nevertheless, only one Republican voted no, meaning the new justice would be confirmed and quickly sworn in with only a week to go before the election. It meant **five of the nine current Supreme Court justices were appointed by Republican presidents that had not won the popular vote.**

The First 2020 Presidential Debate

The first presidential debate of 2020 was chaotic because Trump wouldn't debate. He ignored the moderator, constantly interrupted Biden, and wouldn't stop talking even when it was not his turn. He interrupted Biden more that 100 times, and he argued every point Biden made, often just saying Biden was wrong without addressing the issues brought up. For example,. when Biden tried to bring up the report that Trump had only paid $750 in taxes, Trump just interrupted again, saying, "That's wrong," and then he began talking again. The moderator tried to get him to stop, but he wouldn't. Finally, the moderator said Trump had to stop talking and let Vice President Biden talk. That only worked briefly before Trump began interrupting again.

On the topic of the rushed nomination of a new Supreme Court justice, **Trump said he won the presidency** so he had the right.

Biden said people were already voting, so they should wait until after the election. He added that the nominee they had picked was intended to be the deciding vote that would get rid of "Obamacare" (the Patient Protection and Affordable Care Act) which would eliminate health coverage for those with preexisting conditions and strip 20 million people from having health insurance. Biden also said Trump's nominee would likely vote to cut women's health care rights.

To that, Trump said "Well, **you're certainly going to socialist**." When Biden said that was not true, Trump said, "Your party wants to go socialist medicine and socialist healthcare."

Biden reminded Trump that more than 200,000 people had died and seven million people had contracted COVID on his watch. He said, "What does it mean for them going forward if you strike down the Affordable Care Act?"

Trump began talking about how the virus was China's fault.

The moderator again tried to get Trump to stop talking, but he wouldn't. Finally, the moderator changed the subject, saying to Trump, "Over the last four years, you have promised to repeal and replace Obamacare, but you have never in these four years come up with a plan, a comprehensive plan, to replace Obamacare."

Trump said "Of course, I have. The individual mandate." The moderator tried to get him to stop talking, saying when I finish I'm going to give you an opportunity. But Trump wouldn't stop talking. He said, "Excuse me. I got rid of the individual mandate, which was a big chunk of Obamacare." The moderator said "That's not a comprehensive plan." Trump said "That is absolutely a big thing. That was the worst part of Obamacare." The moderator said, "You're debating him not me. Let me ask my question." But Trump still wouldn't stop. Finally, the moderator said, "Mr. President, I'm the moderator of this debate and I would like you to let me ask my question and then you can answer." And then he again asked Trump what his comprehensive health plan was. Trump responded with, "I guess I'm debating you, not him."

After a lot of pointless back and forth arguing, Trump finally said, "Obamacare is no good. We want to get rid of that and give something that's cheaper and better."

When Biden tried to talk about his plan for dealing with the coronavirus, Trump constantly interrupted with "Wrong. Wrong," and no matter how many times the moderator tried to get Trump to stop interrupting, he wouldn't. Trump said even the top scientists were wrong about masks and when a vaccine would be ready.

Biden reminded Trump that he had said the virus would be gone by Easter, and that he had claimed it would be gone as soon as it got warm, even though he knew that wasn't true. Biden then turned to the TV camera and said, "Do you believe for a moment what he's telling you in light of all the lies he's told you about the whole issue relating to COVID? He still hasn't even acknowledged that he knew this was happening, knew how dangerous it was going to be back in February, and he didn't even tell you. He's on record as saying it. A lot of people died, and a lot more are going to die unless he gets a lot smarter, a lot quicker."

Trump responded to that by saying, "Did you use the word smart? So you said you went to Delaware State. You graduated either the lowest or almost the lowest in your class. Don't ever use the word smart with me."

After more back and forth, with the moderator constantly trying to regain control, Trump went into a long accusation, saying Biden wanted to shut down the country and more people are hurt by shutting it down. Biden tried twice to respond to that, but Trump just made fun of how often Biden wore a mask.

The moderator asked Biden his opinion of masks. Biden said "Masks make a big difference." He pointed out that Trump's own head of the CDC had said if everybody wore a mask and social distanced between now and January, we'd probably save up to 100,000 lives." Trump interrupted with, "And they've also said the opposite." The moderator then asked Trump why he holds rallies with people crowded together and not wearing masks. Trump said he was just doing his job as president. He said only the reason Biden wasn't holding big rallies is because nobody shows up.

When **the debate turned to the next topic, the economy**, Trump bragged about how fast the economy was coming back from the shutdown, but Biden said it was only rich people like Trump that were doing well. Biden again looked into the TV camera to ask, "You folks at home, you folks living in Scranton and Claymont and all the small towns and working class towns in America, how well are you doing? This guy paid a total of $750 in taxes." Trump interrupted, saying "That's wrong," and he tried to go on but the moderator stopped him, saying "You've agreed to the two minutes, so please let him have it." Biden went on to point out that Trump wanted to open up the country even as COVID infections and deaths were increasing. He said, "You can't fix the economy until you fix the COVID crisis."

Trump tried to respond to that, but the moderator said he had already used up his two minutes. Trump ignored the moderator and said, "People want the economy to open up. . . I'm the one that brought back football. It was me."

The moderator then brought up the report that Trump had paid only 750 dollars in taxes. When Trump denied it and said he had paid millions of dollars in taxes. Biden said "Show us your tax returns." As Trump continued to claim he had paid millions in taxes, the moderator repeatedly asked him if it was true that he had only paid 750 dollars in taxes. Trump just said he had taken advantage of the tax codes. Biden said, "Those tax codes put him in a position that he pays less tax than a school teacher. That's why I'm going to eliminate the Trump tax cuts and make sure that we invest in the people who in fact need the help."

Trump argued until finally, the moderator addressed Trump directly, saying, "I think that the country would be better served, if we allowed both people to speak with fewer interruptions."

After temporarily regaining control, the moderator opened up **the topic of race relations**. Biden was asked to go first, and he reminded Trump that in response to a march by white supremacists and neo-Nazis in which a young woman was killed, he had said "There were very fine people on both sides." He went on to remind Trump that when Mr. Floyd was killed, and there was a peaceful protest in front of the White House, Trump "came out of his bunker" and had the military use tear gas on them so he could walk across to a church and hold up a Bible. He said the Bishop of that very church said that it was a disgrace, and the general who was with Trump said all Trump ever wants to do is divide people.

Trump responded with, "You did a crime bill, 1994, where you call them super predators. African-Americans are super predators and they've never forgotten it. . . and as far as the church is concerned and as far as the generals are concerned, we just got the support of 250 military leaders and generals" He went on to claim he had the support of every law enforcement group, adding, "You can't even say the word law enforcement because if you say those words, you're going to lose all of your radical left supporters."

Biden said, "There's systemic injustice in this country, in education and work and in law enforcement and the way in which it's enforced." He added that the vast majority of police officers are good, decent, honorable men and women. Trump responded with, "During the Obama-Biden administration, there was tremendous division. There was hatred. You look at Ferguson, you look at many places, look at Oakland. Look what happened in Oakland. Look what happened in Baltimore. Look what happened. Frankly, it was more violent than what I'm even seeing now."

After a lot of back and forth arguing about law and order, the moderator mentioned the many wildfires currently burning and asked Trump if he believed in global warming. Trump was not willing to answer that question directly, saying only that the fires were caused by poor forest management. To that, Biden began criticizing Trump's record of eliminating pollution controls that were contributing to the problem. Trump said Biden's plan would cost too much. After a lot of back and forth arguing, the moderator finally got to the last issue to be discussed, election integrity. Biden said, "The fact is that there are going to be millions of people because of COVID that are going to be voting by mail-in ballots like he does, by the way." He said Trump was trying to dissuade people from voting, trying to scare people into thinking it's not going to be legitimate. He looked into the camera and said, "Show up and vote. You will determine the outcome of this election." He added that when the votes are counted, he would accept the outcome, adding that Trump was not willing to say that.

After the debate, the general consensus was that Biden had made some good points and had won the debate, despite Trump's attempt to create a chaotic atmosphere. **Those in charge of organizing the next debate said Trump's behavior was going to force a change in the rules**. There was talk about shutting off Trump's microphone to keep him from constantly interrupting, but others reminded them that Trump would still be standing right next to Biden and could still constantly interrupt to try to distract Biden and keep him from making his points.

After the debate, **Biden maintained his lead in the polls, both nationally and in the swing sates.** Perhaps more importantly, donations to Biden's campaign fund dramatically increased, and **91 newspapers came forward to publicly endorse Biden**. Only three newspapers were willing to endorse the incumbent president.

The Vice-Presidential Debate

The debate between Trump's vice president Mike Pence and Kamala Harris took place a week after the first presidential debate. Harris immediately put the focus on how the Trump administration had mishandled **the coronavirus crisis**. She called it **"the greatest failure of any presidential administration in the history of our country."** She also accused them of covering up information about the virus, and she said the Trump administration still didn't have a plan to combat the disease.

Pence tried to defend the steps they had taken, but even though he was the leader of the White House task force on the coronavirus, he preferred to talk about the economy. Harris ignored that and kept on bringing the discussion back to the pandemic.

After the debate, it seemed as though the press thought the most newsworthy aspect of their debate was what Trump thought of it. He defended Pence's performance and called Harris a "monster" and a "communist."

The Second 2020 Presidential Debate

Because Trump was still getting over being sick with the coronavirus, **the second 2020 presidential debate** was supposed to be held via teleconference. But Trump refused to participate in that type of debate, and it was canceled. Many speculated that the reason Trump refused to participate in that type of debate was because it did not fit his style of aggressive intimidation.

As a result, on that date, **Biden scheduled a televised "town hall" meeting in which citizens could ask him questions**.

Trump quickly scheduled his own televised town hall meeting on the same date.

Biden's town hall meeting went well because he was obviously very well prepared.

At his town hall meeting, **Trump was energetic and enthusiastic, but he ran into trouble when he seemed unprepared** for questions about why he had not condemned white supremacists and violent anti-government militia groups. He also struggled to answer questions about why **he had re-tweeted radical conspiracy theories from fringe groups**. Also, a lot of the questions from the audience were about the one subject he would have preferred not to discuss, why the U.S. was leading the world in active coronavirus cases and deaths.

After the two opposing town hall meetings, Biden increased his lead in the polls.

The Third 2020 Presidential Debate

Many felt the final presidential debate would be Trump's last chance to overcome Biden's lead in the polls. The rules of the debate had been changed because of Trump's uncontrollable behavior in the first debate; now, each candidate would be given two minutes to address each topic, with the microphone of his opponent turned off. Trump said those **rules proved the debate was rigged against him**, but this time he agreed to participate.

The two candidates were **required to be tested for the coronavirus**. In the first debate, the candidates were required to have been tested for the virus, but the committee didn't require proof, and it was later learned that Trump had not been tested.

Later, many speculated that he may have already been infected at then. This time the debate commission required proof.

Also, for this final debate, everyone in the audience was required to have been tested, and they had to wear masks. In the first debate, Melania Trump had refused to wear a mask, and it was later learned that she too was infected with the virus.

The debate began with the moderator asking the candidates about **the coronavirus crisis**.

Trump quoted some statistics about how much worse the pandemic could have been, but he spent most of his two minutes playing it down. He blamed China, and he said he had done a good thing by blocking people from China from coming into the U.S. He blamed "Democratic cities" like New York for most of the problems. He talked about his personal experience with having contracted the virus, trying to play it down. He said the virus was "going away."

Biden spent his two minutes talking about how bad the pandemic actually was. He said it was not going away, it was actually getting worse. He mentioned the 220,000 Americans that were already dead and the fact that a thousand Americans were still dying from the virus every day. He accused Trump of being xenophobic and pointed out the fact that Trump had not blocked people from China until 40 other countries had done so. And after the virus did come to the United States, he blamed Trump for playing it down and not doing enough to control it even though he knew how dangerous this new virus was. Biden said he had a comprehensive plan for dealing with the virus, and after all this time, Trump still did not. Trump responded with "We're learning to live with it. We can't lock ourselves up in a basement like Joe does."

On the topic of **security of elections**, Biden said he would make sure no foreign country could interfere with our elections. He said Trump had not even spoken to Putin about their interference in the last presidential election. He said Trump's own National Security Adviser told him about his buddy Rudy Giuliani being used as a Russian pawn. He said Trump is unwilling to take on Putin even though Russia is paying bounties to kill American soldiers in Afghanistan.

Trump responded that he had sold tank busters to Ukraine while Biden was only selling them pillows and sheets. He also said Biden had been getting a lot of money from Russia.

Biden responded that he had not taken a single penny from any foreign source. He pointed out that Trump didn't pay taxes in the United States, but he did pay taxes in China, and in fact, he still had a bank account over there. Biden also reminded the TV audience that he had already released all of his tax filings and Trump still hadn't.

Trump responded that he had paid millions in U.S. taxes, but he still wasn't willing to release them because the IRS was treating him badly. He added that "they" spied on my campaign, and that Mueller and 18 angry Democrats had gone over my tax returns and found nothing wrong. He then **launched into an attack on Biden's family, saying they had made millions from foreign sources, that they were getting rich, "sucking up money like a vacuum cleaner**." Biden said all of those things had been extensively investigated, and they found nothing wrong.

Next, the moderator said they should talk about North Korea, but Trump continued attacking Biden's family. It took a lot of time for the moderator to get back in control and again push them to talk about North Korea. **Trump said he had a good relationship with North Korea**, and added that "Having a good relationship with leaders of other countries is a good thing."

Biden responded with, "**We had a good relationship with Hitler before he invaded Europe**." He said the reason President

Obama wouldn't meet with the North Korean leaders was because he didn't want to legitimize them.

Trump wanted to talk more about that, but the moderator insisted it was time to talk about American families and **how important healthcare was** to them. She said Trump was trying to get rid of the Affordable Care Act, meaning 20 million Americans could lose their health insurance.

Trump said "I terminated the individual mandate. That is the worst part of Obamacare, as we call it." He said he was going to "come up with a better healthcare." He said Biden's healthcare plan would mean 180 million families would lose their private insurance healthcare. "It would be socialized medicine."

Biden denied that he wanted to eliminate private insurance healthcare. He said he differed from other Democrats in that he wanted a public healthcare option, but only as a voluntary option. He then pointed out that **Trump had been promising to come up with a better healthcare plan for years**, constantly saying it was coming, but it never did.

Trump responded that "they" had tried it in his state. "His governor was a very liberal governor."

Biden reminded Trump that he was running against him, not those other people. He reminded the TV audience that Trump's plan to withhold the tax on Social Security would bankrupt that system. Trump wanted to continue arguing that point, adding that if he was reelected, the stock market would boom, and if Biden was elected, the stock market would crash. In response, Biden disputed the idea that the stock market was the only measure of the economy. He said Scranton, where he came from, "people don't live off of the stock market." He then reminded the TV audience that in Trump's economy, only the billionaires were doing well. He said, "What happens to the ordinary people out there?"

The moderator tried to move on, but Trump kept talking about the economy. He claimed people's stocks were "going through the roof."

The moderator finally managed to get control again, saying "As of tonight, more than 12 million people are out of work. They see Washington fighting over a relief bill. **Mr. President, why haven't you been able to get them the help they need?**"

Trump blamed the Speaker of the House, Nancy Pelosi, but the moderator said, "You're the president" Trump ignored that and continued to blame Pelosi, adding "That's why we're going to take over the House." Biden said he'd been pushing for a stimulus bill, and one what been passed by the House, but the Republicans in the Senate hadn't want to agree to it. Trump responded "The bill that was passed in the House was a bailout of badly run, high crime, Democrat, all run by Democrat cities and states." Biden responded to that, saying "If I get elected, I'm going to be an American president. I don't see red states and blue states."

When the moderator asked both candidates about the minimum wage, Biden said we should raise it. Trump didn't seem to want to answer that question and said that would have to be a state option.

The moderator then introduced the subject of immigration, saying, "Mr. President, **your administration separated children from their parents at the border**, at least 4,000 kids. You've since reversed your zero tolerance policy, but the United States can't locate the parents of more than 500 children. So how will these families ever be reunited?"

Trump didn't answer that question. Instead, he said "Children are brought here by coyotes and lots of bad people, cartels. They're brought here and they used to use them to get into our country. We now have as strong a border as we've ever had. We're over 400 miles of brand new wall."

The moderator wouldn't let the question lie. She said, "But how will you reunite these kids with their families, Mr. President?"

Trump said, "Yes, we're working on it. But a lot of these kids come out without the parents. They come over through cartels and through coyotes and through gangs."

When it was Biden's turn, he said, "Those 500-plus kids came with their parents. They separated them at the border to make it a disincentive to come. Coyotes didn't bring them over. Their parents were with them. They got separated from their parents."

Trump jumped in with, "Who built the cages, Joe?" and Biden responded with "Let's talk about what we're talking about." He went on to say "Within a 100 days, I'm going to send to the United States Congress a pathway to citizenship for over 11 million undocumented people. And all of those so-called dreamers, those DACA kids, they're going to be immediately certified again to be able to stay in this country and put on a path to citizenship."

After a lot of back and forth talk, the moderator wanted to move to the next topic, race in America. **She asked if the candidates understood why black parents have to warn their children about how to deal with the police.**

Biden went first, telling the audience that he understood because his daughter is a social worker who works in an African-American district. He said that unlike black families, he would never have to warn his own white daughter to be careful when dealing with the police.

Trump's response was to say Biden had never done anything to help the black community. He said the 1994 crime bill had been bad, and added that **nobody had done more for the black community than he had, "with the possible exception of Lincoln."**

Biden defended his role both in fighting crime and for trying to get non-violent criminals out of jail. He said he wanted to eliminate minimum mandatories, and he wanted to set up drug courts so no one would go to jail because they have a drug problem. He said, "They should be going to rehabilitation, not to jail." Biden looked into the TV camera and said, "You know who I am. You know who he is. You know his character. You know my character. You know our reputations for honor and telling the truth. Our character's on the ballot. Look at us closely."

Trump responded with, "If this stuff is true about Russia, Ukraine, China, other countries, Iraq. If this is true, then he's a corrupt politician. So don't give me the stuff about how you're this innocent baby."

The moderator wanted them to get back to the issue of race in America, but Trump said, "They're calling it the laptop from hell." Biden responded with, "There are 50 former national intelligence folks who said that what he's accusing me of is a Russian plant. Five former heads of the CIA, both parties, say what he's saying is a bunch of garbage. Nobody believes it except him and his good friend, Rudy Giuliani."

Trump tried to argue about what Biden was saying, but the moderator wanted to get back to the race issue. She said, "**Mr. President you've described the Black Lives Matter movement as a symbol of hate**. You've shared a video of a man chanting white power to millions of your supporters. You've said that black professional athletes exercising their First Amendment rights should be fired. What do you say to Americans who say that kind of language from a president is contributing to a climate of hate and racial strife?" Trump responded with "Well, you have to understand the first time I ever heard of Black Lives Matter, they were chanting, "Pigs in a blanket," talking about police, pigs, pigs, talking about our police. 'Pigs in a blanket, fry them like bacon.' I thought it was a terrible thing. As far as my relationships with all people, I think I have great relationships with all people. **I am the least racist person in this room**."

The moderator tried hard to get them to stop talking, and finally she insisted that it was time to move on to the next topic, climate change. Trump went first, saying he loved the environment. He said, "We have the best lowest number in carbon emissions, which is a big standard that I noticed Obama goes with all the time. I haven't heard Joe use the term because I'm not sure he knows what it represents or means." He reminded the audience that he took the U.S. Out of the Paris climate accord because it would have cost too much money. Biden responded with, "**Climate change, global warming is an existential threat to humanity**. We have a moral obligation to deal with it." He went on to say his climate plan would create millions of new good paying jobs. He said his plan had been endorsed by every major environmental group and every labor group, labor, because they know where the future lies. Trump jumped in to say Biden's plan would cost jobs. He said "They want to take buildings down because they want to make bigger windows into smaller windows. As far as they're concerned, if you had no window, it would be a lovely thing. It is crazy. You'll destroy our country." He said Biden's plan was a pipe dream that would kill the economy. He said Biden was against fracking. Biden denied that, but Trump went on to accuse Biden of wanting to get rid of the oil industry.

The moderator then asked the final question which was about **people of color being forced to live near oil refineries and chemical plants**. She asked why Trump was rolling back regulations that would have helped such people. Trump responded that those people are making more money than they've ever made.

Biden's response to the same question was that he used to live near oil refineries and when his mother drove him to school in the morning there'd be an oil slick on the windshield. He said it was why so many people in his state were dying of cancer. He said there had to be restrictions on pollution.

Trump asked if that meant he would close down the oil industry, and Biden responded that we had to transition from the old industry and replace it, by 2050, with renewable energy.

Trump then said, "He's going to destroy the oil industry. Will you remember that Texas? Will you remember that Pennsylvania, Oklahoma?" The moderator tried to move to the next question, but Trump kept on asking "Is he going to get China to do it?"

When it was time for their final statements, **Trump said he would "make our country totally successful, as it was prior to the plague coming in from China."**

Biden's final statement was that he would be an American President to "represent all of you, whether you voted for me or against me." He said we would move to choose science over fiction, choose hope over fear, move forward with enormous opportunities, enormous opportunities to make things better. He said he would grow the economy with clean energy and deal with the systemic racism. He said, **"What is on the ballot here is the character of this country. Decency, honor, respect. Treating people with dignity, making sure that everyone has an even chance. And I'm going to make sure you get that. You haven't been getting it the last four year**s."

The **after-debate analysis** by the news organizations all agreed that the more restrictive rules of the debate (that Trump had complained about) **actually helped him because they forced him to be more restrained**. And his lack of restraint in the first debate is what got him the most criticism.

Polls taken immediately after the debate indicted that Biden had won. But those polls also indicated that the debate hadn't changed the minds of most voters; **Biden still led the polls nationally and in most of the swing states**.

As usual, the news media put their **fact checkers** to work analyzing the debate. The one thing they all agreed on was how wrong Trump's statement was that "we are rounding the corner" on dealing with virus and that he had implied that it was going away. In fact, on the very day he made that statement, there was a new all-time U.S. record of new COVID-19 infections. Also, **Trump's claim that he had saved two million lives was deemed false**. They also focused on Trump's statement that "We cannot lock ourselves in a basement like Joe does." **Biden was almost as active as Trump on the campaign trail**, but he did rallies with smaller audience with masks and social distancing required. They also pointed to Trump's statement that Dr. Anthony Fauci was a Democrat. Dr. Fauci, the director of the National Institute of Allergy and Infectious Diseases, is not affiliated with any political party, and he hasn't endorsed any political party or candidate. However, he has often criticized Trump for not listening to the advice of scientists when dealing with the coronavirus. They also pointed to Trump's statement in the debate that "**There was a spike in Florida. That is gone. There was a spike in Texas. That is gone. There was a spike in Arizona. It is gone.**" None of that was true. Like most U.S. states, at the time of the debate, the number of coronavirus cases was spiking in those states.

Regarding healthcare, **Trump had said that under Biden's plan, 180 million people would lose their health insurance**. There is absolutely no evidence that under Biden's health care proposal anybody would be removed from their insurance plans.

Trump's statement that "Joe got 3.5 million dollars from Russia" was judged untrue. Biden's son Hunter did earn money from foreign countries, but there is no evidence that Joe Biden had anything to do with it.

Trump had claimed he had closed his bank account in China before he ran for president, but his lawyer previously told the press that Trump's China bank account was still open.

Biden had said "**Trump has caused the deficit with China to go up, not down.**" The fact checkers said that only points to the broadest measurement of the balance of trade.

Trump had said Biden called Black Americans "**superpredators**." There is no evidence for that. Biden did once mention superpredator criminals, but he didn't mention Blacks.

Trump had falsely claimed that the Mueller investigation had gone over his taxes, and that "they" had spied on his campaign. There is no evidence of that, and his claim of Obama wiretapping him had been dismissed by everybody.

The fact checkers said one of the most obvious lies in the debate was Trump saying "Not since Abraham Lincoln has anybody done what I've done for the Black community." Many prior presidents have enacted policies that have helped people of color. Trump has not.

After the debates, the two candidates went **back on the campaign trail**, mostly hitting the so called "battleground states."

Trump had won traditionally Democratic states like Michigan, Wisconsin, and Pennsylvania in 2016, but in 2020, the polls were indicating a Biden lead. Even states that traditionally voted Republican, like Iowa, North Carolina, Georgia, and Arizona also seemed to be in play, and that meant control of the Senate might also flip from Republican to Democrat. History has shown that a vote for a Democrat president often also means a vote for the senatorial candidate from that same party because of the "coattails" effect. Nevertheless, as in the 2016 election, Trump said the size of the crowds at his rallies proved he was ahead. It was true that Trump was still drawing large crowds to his rallies, and the crowds were as boisterous as ever.

During the final days of campaigning, the messages of the two presidential candidates grew more intense. While Trump conintued to play down the pandemic, still saying over and over again that the virus was gong to "go away," even as the pandemic got worse every day with new csaes of the virus continuing to set new all-time daily records. Biden continued to press home the concept that Trump had failed to protect the nation from the pandemic. He presented specific plans on how he was going to deal with the pandemic, and he propsoed new plans for healthcare, the economy, foreign policy, race relations, and the environment. Biden was often joined by former president Obama who said, "What's at stake right now is our democracy."

Trump mostly avoided talking about the pandemic and his record as the incumbant. He preferred to attack Biden. He was still calling Biden "a socialist," saying Biden wanted to "lock down the country" and make everyone dependant on the federal government. **He said Biden would dismantle all the police departments** and "take away your guns." He said, "**Biden will take away your electricity.**" He said "Biden will "bury you in regulations," and the economy will sink into a depression. **He said Biden would terminate religious liberty**. Trying to scare suburban voters into voting for him, Trump said Biden would "**destroy your suburbs.**"

COMMENT

Nearing the election and falling behind in the polls, in desperation, Trump started **making more and more outrageous statements about the pandemic**. It was obvious that **he believed the virus was the only reason people people might vote against him.** As a result, in the fall, as the numbers of new coronavirus cases began to set all-time records, he not only continued to say we had "rounded the corner" on the virus, but he said it was soon going to go away. At a rally in Ohio, he declared the virus "affects virtually nobody."

Even after he was infected by the virus, he told the people not to be so worried about the virus. He said, "**Don't be afraid of COVID. Don't let it dominate your life.**" Even after more than 235,000 lives had been lost to the virus, he continued to play it down. **He claimed it was no worse than the ordinary seasonal flu. He continued to claim that the numbers were faked.** He went so far as to say **the coronavirus numbers were being faked by doctors who were inflating the numbers in order to make money** off of it. That was too much for the conservative American Medical Association (AMA), the nationwide organization of doctors that usually stayed out of politics. They immediately issued a formal statement, saying, "The suggestion that doctors—in the midst of a public health crisis—are overcounting COVID-19 patients or lying to line their pockets is a malicious, outrageous, and completely misguided charge."

The 2020 Presidential Vote

In 2020, because of the pandemic, many voters chose to mail in their ballots. Also, early voting was allowed. It turned out that in some states, more people voted by mail or early than had voted in total in a prior election. Nevertheless, both candidates kept on campaigning right up to the last minute. Trump maintained a frantic pace of electioneering, landing the huge Air Force One airplane at airports large and small to hold rallies using the plane as a magnificent backdrop. Few among the crowded-together people that showed up wore masks. In fact, Trump made fun of some who showed up wearing masks, and he complained that local pandemic restrictions were holding down the size of the crowd.

Because both sides were telling their voters that it was the most important election of their lifetimes, the number who voted broke records everywhere.

When the Democrats began encouraging their voters to stay safe and use mail-in ballots, Trump began to rant against them. **He** suggested that mail-in voting could be used to "steal" the election from him. For that reason, he said Republican voters shouldn't be afraid to go in and vote in person. As a result, some began to suggest it might meant the outcome of the election might not be known until all the mail-in ballots had been counted.

Not liking what the polls were indicating, Trump said the only way he could lose reelection was if it was "rigged" against him. He said the **surge of mail-in ballots would be used to "steal" the election from him**. He repeated over and over again that the Democrats would somehow use mail-in ballots to "rig" the election. Anticipating a Democratic surge in mail-in voting, Trump began to argue that they were somehow illegal.

By election day, Trump was still saying the only way he could lose was if the election was stolen from him. He indicated that no matter what happened, he was not going to leave the White House. That led to concerns about post-election violence, and many stores began boarding up their front windows in anticipation of trouble should Trump lose.

There had been the constant threat of violence from Trump's supporters even before the election. In Texas, a pro-Trump contingent, many of them armed, surrounded the Biden campaign bus and tried to force it off the interstate highway. The Biden team, fearful of what might happen next, canceled the Texas campaign event they were heading to. Trump applauded their actions, calling them "patriots."

Biden chastised Trump for siding with the drivers who had swarmed his campaign bus, saying, "We've never had a president who thinks **voter intimidation and harassment is a good thing.**"

The 2020 Election Outcome

On **the day before election day**, the polls were still showing Biden in the lead nationally by ten points. But as we learned from prior presidential elections, because of the Electoral College system, **you can win the general election by millions of votes and still not get to be the president**. In 2020, the media had finally fully recognized that the election day voting doesn't count; to be president, **you have to win 270 votes in the Electoral College**. And as we have seen, the Republican-leaning smaller-population states have such an advantage in the Electoral College, a Democratic candidate has to win enough votes in the so-called swing states to overcome that advantage. That explains why both candidates spent the final weeks in those swing states.

The day of the election started with worry that the expected Biden victory might trigger violence in the streets. Businesses were boarding up their windows, and the White House erected an "unscalable fence all the way around.

However, if people were hoping for a quick Biden victory, they were in for a disappointment. The first state to report, Florida, was close, but it was clear Trump was holding a steady lead.

Despite how close the race seemed, early in the counting, **Trump went on TV to declare victory**. He was widely criticized for doing such an outrageous thing while the voting was still going on, and even many Republicans said it was not an appropriate thing to do. But that didn't bother Trump. He said even if he lost, he was going to take it to the Supreme Court. Nobody was sure what good that would do, but he continued to say it.

With all the TV networks and internet sites closely following the vote counting moment by moment, state by state, it was easy to see what was happening: it was becoming clear that the Republican voters had done as Trump wished and voted in person, while many Democratic voters had mailed their votes in. Nevertheless, both candidates seemed to be were winning the states the opinion polls had indicated they were likely to win. However, the votes from the Midwestern tier of states that Trump had flipped from Democrat to Republican in 2016—Wisconsin, Michigan, and Pennsylvania—were showing Trump with big leads. It looked as though he might hold them again in 2020. But then, they started counting those mail-in ballots Trump had dreaded, and Biden slowly, but surely, began to catch up.

That spurred Trump into action: he began to file lawsuit after lawsuit trying to stop the vote counting He said if they only counted the "legal" votes (the in-person votes), he would win.

However, in a Democracy, you can't stop the vote counting, and one by one, his lawsuits were being thrown out of court.

At the same time, a number of prominent Republicans turned against Trump and began telling him to stop making such outrageous statements and wait for the count to be concluded. That did not stop Trump; he held a televised press conference from the White House to say the election was being stolen from him. Unfortunately for him, most of the TV networks cut him off in mid-sentence. It soon became obvious that a rare event was about to happen: an incumbent president was going down to defeat.

When it was finally all over, Biden had won the states he was expected to win, plus two more, Arizona and Georgia, both traditionally Republican states that had gone for Trump in 2016.

In the largest turnout in history, Biden won the popular vote overwhelmingly by more than seven million votes, and he also easily won the Electoral College vote, 306 to 232, the same margin of victory that Trump had called his "landslide win" in 2016.

On the day Congress was to go through the supposed formality of certifying the Electoral College votes, Trump called for a huge rally of his supporters to protest it. He held the rally close to the Capitol Building, and at the rally, Trump said, "Our country has had enough. We will not take it anymore." He said they should "fight" to stop this illegal election, and he said he would lead them to the Capitol to put a stop to it.

Although Trump did not actually lead them, thousands of his most loyal and most extremist supporters did march straight to the Capitol where they overpowered the unprepared and outmatched police. They stormed through the building, and they broke into the chamber where the vote to confirm Biden's election had been taking place. Television viewers were shocked to see live coverage of hoards of Trump supporters inside the Capitol Building, some of them beating policemen with Trump flags and American flags.

The rioters did manage to interrupt the confirmation vote, forcing the lawmakers to retreat to a safer place, but after police and national guard troops finally chased the rioters out of the building, they returned to resume the vote. Despite some Republicans still continuing to vote against accepting the Electoral College vote, Biden was finally officially confirmed as the next U.S. president.

After it was all over, it clearly showed Biden's first task in office would be to try to bring a polarized country back together.

INDEX

Adams, John 13, 20
Adams, John Quincy 13, 50. 56
Alien and Sedition Acts 24
al-Qaeda 196
American Party 93, 145
American system 243
Anthony, Susan B 96
Apprentice TV show 210
Barkley, Alben 121
Barr, William 261
Barrett, Amy Coney 284
Benghazi 196, 222
Bentsen, Lloyd 167
Bernstein, Carl 156
Biden, Hunter 269
Biden, Jill 276
Biden, Joe 189, 270, 277
Blaine, James G. 94
Bleeding Kansas 74
Bloomberg, Michael 232
Bolton, John 262
Booth, John Wilkes 80
Bradshaw, Sally 235
Breckenridge, John 90
Breyer, Stephen 205
Bryan, William Jennings 113, 128
Buchanan, James 73
Buchanan, Pat 204
Burr, Aaron 21, 31
Bush, Barbara 235
Bush, George W. 174
Bush, George H. W. 160, 163,167
Bush, Jeb 176, 202
Buttigieg, Pete 277
Byrd, Harry 130, 150
Byrd, Robert 130
Calhoun, John 53
Calley, William 144
Carson, Ben 202
Carter, Jimmy 155
Case-Church Amendment 143
Casey, William 164
casino bankruptcies 190, 202
Chafee, Lincoln 201

Cheney, Dick 169 174, 186
Christie, Chris 203
citizens united 283
Civil War 34, 68, 74
Clay, Henry 42, 53, 64
Cleveland, Grover 91
Clinton ,George 20, 33, 147
Clinton, Bill 167, 175, 188, 214, 246
Clinton, DeWitt 36
Cohen, Michael 262
Collins, Susan 235
Comey, James 231, 252
Compromise of 1850 40, 70
constitutional convention (1787) 9
Contras 165
Coolidge, Calvin 111
coronavirus crisis 256, 264, 272, 292
corrupt bargain 55
Crawford, William Harris 44
Cruz, Ted 202, 206
Curiel, Gonzalo 236
Daniels, Stormy 263
Dean, John 154
deep throat 155
deplorables 221
Dewey, Thomas E. 119
Dole, Bob 171, 235
Douglas, Stephen 78
Dred Scott decision 76
Dukakis, Michael 151, 167
dust bowl 116
economic panic of 1835 77
Edwards, John 185
Eisenhower, Dwight D. 124, 134
Epstein, Jeffery 260
faithless electors 145
Federalists 167 25, 35, 46
Ferraro, Geraldine 162
Ford, Gerald 150
First Gulf War 168
Fourteenth Amendment 81
free soil party 68
Fremont, John C. 74
Gallatin, Albert 44
Garfield, James A. 88
Garner, John Nance 113
Gerry, Elbridge 35
Ginsburg, Ruth Bader 284
global warming 188, 227

gold standard 98
Goldwater, Barry 133
Gore, Al 169, 174
Graham, Lindsey 236
Grant, U.S. 80, 83
Green Party 175, 197, 216
Guthrie, Woody 209
Hamilton, Alexander 20, 27, 32
Hamlin, Hannibal 79
Hanna, Richard 236
Hancock, Winfield Scott 89
Harding, Warren G. 111
Harris, Katherine 178
Harris, Kamala 279, 290
Harrison, William Henry 14
Hart, Gary 162
Hayes, Rutherford 84, 149
Hemings, Sally 13, 43
Hendricks, Thomas A. 84
Hollywood Access audio tape 230
Hoover, Herbert 113
Hospers, John 146
Huckabee, Mike 202
Humphrey, Gordon 236
Humphrey, Hubert 133, 157
Indian Removal Act 69
Iran Hostage Crisis 159, 199
ISIS 2267 234, 244
Jackson, Andrew 14, 38, 46, 54
Jay Treaty 21
Jefferson, Thomas 13, 23, 33
John Birch Society 145
Johnson, Andrew 80
Johnson, Lyndon B. 132, 232
Johnson, Richard Mentor 61
Khan, Humayun 212
Kaine, Tim 211, 232
Kansas Nebraska Act 73
Kasich, John 202, 280
Kemp, Jack 171
Kennedy, Edward M. (Ted) 162
Kennedy, John 127
Kent State University shootings 144
Kerry, John 151, 184
King Caucus 144
Korean War 124
Kuwait 168
laissez-faire approach 57
lamestream media 257

Landon, Alf 113
LeMay, Curtis 139
Lewinsky, Monica 171
Libertarian Party 145, 150, 167, 215
Lieberman, Joseph 173
Lincoln, Abraham 66, 75
Madison. James 12, 33
manifest destiny 66
manumission 41
Marshall, Thomas R. 105
Marshall, Humphrey 47
McCain, John 173, 188, 210, 226, 266
McCarthy, Joe 123
McCarthy, Eugene 139, 157
McClellan, George 79
McDougal, Karen 262
McFarlane, Robert 163
McKinley, William 97
Mexican-American War 64
Missouri Compromise 39, 69
Mitchell, John 153
Mondale, Walter 157
Monroe, James 12, 34
Mormon Polygamy 95
Mueller , Robert 259
Muskie, Edmund 139
My Lai massacre 143
Nader, Ralph 174
NAFTA 242
Napoleon 32
National Rifle Association 230
New Deal 113
Nineteenth Amendment 96, 108
Nixon, Richard 123, 128, 138
North, Oliver 164
Obama, Barack 187, 193, 199, 215
October surprise 198
Osama bin Laden 182, 192
Palin, Sarah 188
pandemic 255
Paul, Rand 201
Paul, Ron 191
Paulson, Henry 235
Pearl Harbor 117
Pence, Mike 204, 232, 273
Perot, Ross 159
Pierce, Franklin 68
Pinckney. Charles Cotesworth 32
Poindexter, John 164

Polk, James K.   14, 65
Powell, Colin   235
Pressler, Larry   236
Putin, Vladimir   221
Quayle, Dan   167
Reagan, Ronald   139, 160
Reaganomics   163
Racicot, Marc   236
Rockefeller, John D.   115
Romney, Mitt   188, 197, 251, 271
Rosenstein, Ron   261
Roosevelt, Franklin D. (FDR)   111
Roosevelt, Theodore   100
Rousseau, Jean-Jacques   45
Rubio, Marco   202
Saddam Hussein   183
Sanders, Bernie   201, 240, 277
Sanford, Mark   277
Santa Ana   67
Scalia, Antonin   237, 285
Scott, Winfield   67, 89
Seymour, Horatio   82
Shah of Iran   59
Shultz, George   164
Smith, Al   112
Soleimani, Qasem   267
Sparkman, John Jackson   133
spoils system   57, 90
Stein, Jill   197
Starr, Kenneth   172
Stevenson, Adlai E.   124, 150
Sumner, Charles   74
Taft, William H.   104
Taylor, Zachary   14, 67
Three-Fifths Compromise   10
Tilden, Samuel J.   85
Tompkins, Daniel D.   147
Tonkin Gulf Resolution   137
Trail of Tears   72
Treaty of Cahuenga   68
Treaty of Guadalupe Hidalgo   67
Tripp, Linda   172
Truman, Harry S.   119, 149
Trump family business   259
Trump Hotel   259
Trump impeachment   269
Trump, Mary   263
Trump Casinos   210
Tweed, William (Boss)   84

Twenty-Third Amendment   18
Twitter   256
Tyler, John   14, 63
Ukraine   232, 261, 295
unpledged electors   127, 150
Van Buren, Martin   14
Vietnam   133
voodoo economics   163
Walker Report   140
Walker, Scott   202
Wallace, George   132
Wallace, Henry A.   117
Warren, Elizabeth   280
Washington, George   13, 20, 29, 40
Watergate   153, 189, 199
waving the bloody shirt   86
Webb, Jim   201
Weber, Vin   236
Weinberger, Caspar   164
Wheeler, William   84
Whigs   58, 70
Weld, Bill   277
whistleblower   269
White House plumbers   155
White League   86
Wilkins, William   148
Will, George   191
Willkie, Wendell   117, 121
Wilson, Woodrow   106, 111
winner-take-all system   25
Women's suffrage   96
Woodward, Bob   154, 264

About the Author

Dr. Everett E. Murdock is an Emeritus Professor at California State University, Long Beach.

www.ingramcontent.com/pod-product-compliance
Lightning Source LLC
LaVergne TN
LVHW051622080426
835511LV00016B/2120